Praise for *Precious Precarity*

When (or perhaps, *if*) future theologians and ministers survive the crises of our day to look back on life in the 2020s, I am convinced that they will define our times in terms of a complex intersection of contributions and challenges: the needed corrective of contextual, diverse, non-Eurocentric voices in the church and academy, a rise in awareness of the impact of human-made climate change, ongoing attempts to overcome a problematic bifurcation between pastoral and systematic theology, and—likely above all—our response as a human race to the staggering numbers of people on the move. In *Precious Precarity*, Helen Boursier offers a gritty and textured account of a spirituality of the borderlands which weaves together many of these themes that define Christian witness in our day, one which highlights the enduring goodness to be encountered in the "badlands."

—Michael M. Canaris, PhD, associate professor of ecclesiology and systematic theology, and co-director, Miguel Pro, S.J. Iniciativa de Protagonismo Pastoral, Loyola University Chicago

Helen Boursier's book *Precious Precarity* will break your heart and lift you toward a new appreciation for life, love, and the possibility of a future worth living. Using Ecclesiastes to ground and frame what she calls the "spirituality of dissent" at the border, she interprets what it means to live a hope-against-hope life in an unjust environment. Boursier uses migrants' own words to communicate their experiences of death and relentless suffering as they seek a new life on the other side of the border. Their words show how tenaciously they cling to their trust in a God who is with them and protecting them; a faith that sustains their quest for sanctuary and transforms those who meet and support them. The book is a clarion call to religious leaders and other practitioners of the Global North to leave our functional patterns of indifference and apathy to what is happening at the border since, in truth, our lives and futures are deeply intertwined with these asylum seekers. This is a timely work that can speak persuasively to our shared time of precarious living. Practical theologians, pastors, and secular volunteers will find the stories and insights compelling and inspiring. The visual illustrations are remarkable and help bring the text to life, while the incredible number of quotes and references invite the reader to explore more deeply the themes and questions raised in the text. The bibliography is a treasure in itself.

—Rev. Dr. Sharon G. Thornton, PhD, professor emerita, Andover Newton Theological School, and author of *Broken Yet Beloved: A Pastoral Theology of the Cross*

This book is a must-read: a brilliant, compelling, and timely exploration of one of the greatest ethical, theological, and political challenges of our time. How do we counter the political denial of the humanity of those families migrating to the United States in search of safety, and instead honor their integrity and profound courage? Boursier provides an evocative resource for this vital work, honoring the spiritual resilience and deep faith of those families seeking safety and the life-changing solidarity of those volunteers and advocates who support them with compassion and creativity in this painful and precarious endeavor—the search for a safe place that can become home, where justice is embodied and all can thrive.

—Sharon D. Welch, author of *After the Protests Are Heard: Enacting Civic Engagement and Social Transformation*

Precious Precarity is a gift for all of us who want to live with humanity but don't always have access to human stories, especially when they pertain to the most vulnerable among us. This book is a wake-up call, both for our dehumanizing politics and for our ignorant hearts, and it creates space for compassion at a time when we need it most.

—Simran Jeet Singh, author of *The Light We Give: How Sikh Wisdom Can Transform Your Life*

We may remember weary Jeremiah saying, "You have seduced me, and I have let myself be seduced." We may use contemporary jargon about "compassion fatigue." Whatever our language, we are recognizing that prophets get exhausted. Depths of spirituality are needed so that one does not internally or externally flee the harsh and ambiguous realities of the borderlands. Boursier opens up to us the paths of deep spirituality by juxtaposing words and images from immigrants, volunteers, and those around, with the words of wisdom from Ecclesiastes. She does not deny the struggle. She does not deny the hope and joy. By getting close to "the other," one can move away from controlling fear into a peaceful sense of deep purpose.

Recently we were able to offer overnight hospitality in our convent to a ninth grader and his father from Venezuela, who had gone through months of dangerous and exhausting travel to reach the US border and ask for asylum. A thoughtful judge affirmed they could be in the US for now and be considered. Before the student and his father left to join a relative, I shared a vocabulary-building workbook that our mother, a high school English teacher, had used with her students. As I touched Momma's handwriting for the last time, I realized that twenty years after her death, this gift book was her life and love continuing. The student lit up with joy and wanted me to inscribe the book. We, like Sarah and Abraham, were blessed by the strangers who came. Boursier writes with boundless compassion and creative skill. She opens our eyes, that we may let the strangers in.

—Sister Martha Ann Kirk, ThD, professor emerita, University of the Incarnate Word, San Antonio, Texas

In her best and most thought-provoking book yet, Rev. Dr. Boursier takes a unique look at migrants seeking refuge in the US, this time through the lens of the special kind of spirituality that develops when the line between life and death is thin and the reality of the fragility of existence is pervasive. Trapped between the homes they fled and a new life where they don't and likely may never belong—the reality of placelessness—migrants cope by relying on a deep and ever-present faith in God. *Precious Precarity* beautifully expresses what I have witnessed, particularly the strength and resilience arising from the spirituality that is in the very nature of these strong and determined people—the constant sense of the presence of God that guides and protects. I have seen this profound spirituality in children detained for months with no idea when they might be reunited with their loved ones. Some fill notebooks with prayers, smiling and trusting in God. *Precious Precarity* captures the sustaining hope that is necessary for survival when the world is precarious and the future uncertain. *Precious Precarity* is the antidote to the divisive narrative raging around immigration. This thoughtful and comprehensive work will change attitudes about migrants and hence the choices we make regarding what we need to do and how we should do it. The insights in this book remind me that I am one of the lucky ones.

—Hope M. Frye, executive director, Project Lifeline

Helen T. Boursier's passion for employing art as embodied pastoral action and her deep knowledge of scriptures and feminist scholarship are masterfully woven in this volume, guiding us in understanding and appreciating the lives and persistent issues of displaced migrant women and children, as well as the volunteers she has encountered in the borderlands.

—Yudit Kornberg Greenberg, PhD, George D. and Harriet W. Cornell Endowed Chair of Religion, Rollins College, Winter Park, Florida

Precious Precarity by Helen Boursier is a refreshing approach to the book of Ecclesiastes for the modern day, as it impinges on the lives of migrant families on the southern border. Dr. Boursier does this by engaging several major themes from Ecclesiastes ("striving," "time and chance," "gain," "joy," etc.) and applying them to the experience of migrants and those who work with them. *Precious Precarity* both recovers a neglected, and often misunderstood, biblical book and shows us a way forward in the faithful application of its teaching. Heartily recommended!

—R. Mark Shipp, professor of Old Testament, Austin Graduate School of Theology (retired)

Precious Precarity

Precious Precarity
A Spirituality of Borders

Rev. Dr. Helen T. Boursier, PhD

FORTRESS PRESS
MINNEAPOLIS

PRECIOUS PRECARITY
A Spirituality of Borders

Text copyright © 2024 by Fortress Press, an imprint of 1517 Media. Illustrations copyright © 2024 Helen T. Boursier. All rights reserved. Except for brief quotations in critical articles or reviews, no part of this book may be reproduced in any manner without prior written permission from the publisher. Email copyright@1517.media or write to Permissions, Fortress Press, PO Box 1209, Minneapolis, MN 55440-1209.

Library of Congress Control Number: 2023945649 (print)

Cover images: collage of art by Helen T. Boursier

Print ISBN: 978-1-5064-8957-5
eBook ISBN: 978-1-5064-8958-2

Dedicated to the displaced migrant families, and to the compassionate and dedicated volunteers and advocates who graciously share their love, passion, and witness for justice and peacemaking in the borderlands, always respecting and honoring the precious precarity of and for life

Contents

	List of Illustrations	ix
	Acronyms	xi
	Preface	xiii
	Acknowledgments	xv
	Introduction: Where Differences Intersect	xvii
1.	Cynicism	1
2.	Dissent	21
3.	Paradox	45
4.	Striving	65
5.	Chance	85
6.	Time	103
7.	Choice	123
8.	Risk	145
9.	Gain	167
10.	Joy	189
11.	Legacy	207
	Conclusion: Holy and Whole	225
	Bibliography	237
	Index	245

List of Illustrations

Precious Precarity Collection digital montage with no fixed dimensions of the enlarged details of nine interior illustrations representing a cross-section of precious precarity in the borderlands. Art © Helen T. Boursier.

Illustration I.1 *Clinging to Life* 9" × 12" colored pencils on a black-and-white image transfer from the author's photograph of the western edge of the border wall at the San Ysidro Port of Entry, San Ysidro, California. Art © Helen T. Boursier.

Illustration 1.1 *Precious Precarity* 11" × 14" graphite pencil portrait on Toned Tan against the pink floral paper of a little girl who was waiting with her mother at the Greyhound bus station in San Antonio after they were released from family detention, April 4, 2017. Art © Helen T. Boursier.

Illustration 2.1 *#NIUNAMENOS* 12" × 12" mixed-media portrait of a mother and her two daughters shortly after they were released from GEO Karnes on December 19, 2014, where they were detained for three months before being granted government permission to pursue their claim for asylum in the United States.

Illustration 3.1 *My Case for Asylum* 9" × 12" immigrant artwork watercolor with collage over a handwritten testimony from Art Inside Karnes, July 13, 2016, where a mother wrote about the violence in her homeland and her quest for asylum in the United States so that she and her children can live in peace. Art © Art Inside Karnes.

Illustration 4.1 *Shipping Container Border Blockade* 12" × 8" cut paper collage of the border wall outgoing Arizona governor Doug Ducey hired contractors to build in late 2022 along portions of public land at the Arizona-Mexico border. Art © Helen T. Boursier. Based on a photo by Melissa del Bosque; shared by permission.

Illustration 5.1 *Rugged Terrain* 7" × 7" black-and-white acrylic painting of the Sonoran Desert with ocotillo cactus and a distant mountain range in

LIST OF ILLUSTRATIONS

the southern Arizona desert, where migrants often lose their way, become disabled, and die alone. Art © Helen T. Boursier.

Illustration 6.1 *Disengaged* 11" × 15" blue charcoal portrait against patterned paper of a migrant child living with his family in a migrant encampment in Matamoros, Mexico, December 15, 2019, during MPP. Traumatized by all that had happened to him, this child remained off by himself and disengaged from the education activities that Team Brownsville was facilitating with the children in the borderlands. Art © Helen T. Boursier.

Illustration 7.1 *Stuck in Mexico* 15" × 11" mixed-media collage portrait of a four-year-old whose family was stuck at a migrant encampment in Matamoros, Mexico, December 15, 2019, during MPP. The collage includes elements of the art/reflections created by mothers and children while they were detained at GEO Karnes, including their testimonies for asylum.

Illustration 8.1 *Camping Alongside the Rio Grande* 9" × 12" black-and-white acrylic painting based on a photograph by Kay Geurin of the Rio Grande River in Piedras Negras, Mexico, April 9, 2022, where migrants sleep in the shadow areas underneath the bushes along the riverbank. Art © Helen T. Boursier.

Illustration 9.1 *Vulnerability* 11" × 14" colored pencil portrait on yellow and green patterned paper of a migrant girl in Matamoros, Mexico, December 15, 2019, during MPP. Art © Helen T. Boursier.

Illustration 10.1 *Hug of Joy* 11" × 15" graphite pencil with watercolor portrait of two little girls hugging a volunteer after she gave them Barbie dolls, April 9, 2022. The children were living with their parents along the riverbank of the Rio Grande River near Piedras Negras, Mexico (see illustration 8.1). This illustration is based on a photograph by Kay Geurin; shared by permission. Art © Helen T. Boursier.

Illustration 11.1 *Biding Our Time* 11" × 14" cut paper collage portrait of a father holding his baby daughter on his lap in a hammock, December 15, 2019, while his family languished at a migrant encampment in Matamoros, Mexico, during MPP. Art © Helen T. Boursier.

Illustration 12.1 *Holy and Whole* 11" × 9" graphite pencil sketch against a poured watercolor background of *Pastora Helena* and a migrant child at the Greyhound bus station in San Antonio, April 4, 2017. The child was traveling with her mother after they were released from family detention. Art © Helen T. Boursier.

Acronyms

CBP   US Customs and Border Protection (formerly Customs Border Patrol)
GEO Karnes GEO Group Karnes County [Immigrant Family] Residential [Detention] Center
GVS   Green Valley-Sahuarita, Arizona Samaritans
ICE   US Immigration and Customs Enforcement
IWC   Interfaith Welcome Coalition of San Antonio
MPP   Migrant Protection Protocols
NAFTA   North American Free Trade Agreement
TBD   To Be Determined
UCC   United Church of Christ

Preface

This book emerged from my work as a volunteer chaplain with refugee families seeking asylum, including while they were detained at the GEO Karnes Country (Immigrant) Family Residential Center in Karnes City, Texas. I've also volunteered with the families in various contexts on both sides of the US-Mexico border. In every case, I've been deeply and profoundly moved by the spirituality of the families and also by the dedication and commitment of the volunteers and advocates who work for justice and peace in the borderlands. In addition, from my first volunteer experience with the families onward, the testimonies, experiences, and shared stories of the families, volunteers, and advocates in the borderlands resonated with the key themes in Ecclesiastes. I'd taken a research and writing intensive course on this ancient wisdom literature in the Hebrew Bible and Christian Old Testament during my preparation for ministry, and it immediately struck me how much the experiences in the borderlands parallel the main themes in this sacred text.

The families never mentioned Ecclesiastes, though they often quoted from Psalms, Isaiah, and Jeremiah in the Hebrew Bible, as well as numerous books in the Christian New Testament. Nevertheless, their lives embody the quest for the meaning of life with a spirituality that resolutely trusts in God, despite the awful current circumstances they're struggling through. *Precious Precarity* came into being because the words and witnesses of these displaced families, together with the words and actions of volunteers, advocates, and environmentalists in the borderlands, stand in striking contrast to the silence of the Christian church in responding to the humanitarian crisis in the borderlands. In particular, when I completed a research project that documented the excuses my clergy peers readily gave regarding why they didn't preach, teach, lead, and/or participate in any compassionate ministries in the borderlands, I couldn't help but reflect on how much these colleagues are missing from the unique spirituality in the borderlands. By uplifting the beautiful spirituality

PREFACE

that emerges among the displaced migrants, volunteers, and advocates there, *Precious Precarity* is a rebuttal to my earlier work, which documented the rationales of my ministry colleagues regarding their silence and inaction around immigration.[1] Spirituality in the borderlands also offers an antidote to the negative public and political rhetoric that consistently defames and villainizes these vulnerable families.

Rev. Dr. Helen T. Boursier, PhD
Texas, October 2023

NOTE

1 See Helen T. Boursier, *Willful Ignorance: Overcoming the Limitations of (Christian) Love for Refugees Seeking Asylum* (Lanham, MD: Lexington Books), 2022.

Acknowledgments

I'm grateful to the families in the borderlands who've so graciously shared their testimonies of courage, commitment, and love. I'm also grateful to the volunteers, advocates, and environmentalists who shared why they do what they do in the borderlands and how this creates meaning in their lives. Foremost, I appreciate their dedicated presence for justice and peacemaking in the borderlands.

The influence of Professor R. Mark Shipp is evident throughout *Precious Precarity* because it was his enthusiasm for Ecclesiastes that has remained in my spirit ever since the spring semester in 2004 when I took an exegetical course on this biblical text with Dr. Shipp at Austin Graduate School of Theology in Austin, Texas. Each class was packed with his insights, passion, and zeal for the wisdom of Ecclesiastes and its relevance for contemporary culture, particularly its contribution to what makes life meaningful. Special thanks to Fordham University students Madeline Hilf and Afrah Bandagi for graciously sharing access to the interviews they conducted with several volunteers and activists in Arizona. I extend my gratitude to Green Valley-Sahuarita Samaritan volunteer Rowland VanEss for his feedback on an early draft of *Precious Precarity*. I also extend my gratitude to my students in Introduction to Spirituality at the College of Saint Scholastica. Their passion for justice and peacemaking continually impresses and encourages me for a hopeful future of a more just, kind, and equitable world.

I also appreciate the helpful feedback from artist Roxana Tuff on my arts-based research illustrations, most of which are visual representations of my digital field documentation. I offer a special thanks to Melissa del Bosque and Kay Geurin, who graciously gave me permission to create illustrations based on their original photographs in the borderlands. Thank you both.

ACKNOWLEDGMENTS

Finally, this project could not and would not have been possible without the extremely gracious, patient, and supportive encouragement from my beloved husband. Thank you, Mike, for being who you are while also always encouraging me to be who I am. You bring out my best, and I am grateful.

Rev. Dr. Helen T. Boursier, PhD
Texas, October 2023

Introduction

Where Differences Intersect

Life is *precious* because life is *precarious*, bounded between the finite physical limitations of birth and death. *Precious Precarity* examines the particular spirituality that emerges at the intersections between life and death as these are exacerbated through forced displacement of vulnerable raced migrants who must leave their homelands, traversing through harsh environments to seek safety in an often very unwelcoming foreign land. The spirituality of these displaced people mingles with the volunteers, advocates, and environmentalists at the southwestern US-Mexico border, creating a unique and distinct spirituality in the borderlands. It's a spirituality that's shaped by the reality of death and the passionate quest for safety and for *life*. Death is what makes life precious. Everyone's going to die; it's just a matter of the time, chance, and circumstances of the actual Big Event: The "Big C" Chance—Death. The struggle to remain alive shapes spirituality in the borderlands. In *Gravity and Grace*, Simone Weil proposes, "Death is the most precious thing which has been given to [humanity]."[1] Weil connects this inevitability of death to a pervasive sense of vulnerability, which makes life "precious" and "beautiful because vulnerability is a mark of existence."[2] Respect and appreciation for this precious and precarious vulnerability flow through spirituality in the borderlands.

The context for *Precious Precarity* moves back and forth along the southwestern border, but the insights also apply more broadly to the places and spaces of transitions and interactions where differences intersect. Whether a border is an international line drawn in the sand demarcating two countries;

Illustration I.1 *Clinging to Life* 9" × 12" colored pencils on a black-and-white image transfer from the author's photograph of the western edge of the border wall at the San Ysidro Port of Entry, San Ysidro, California. Art © Helen T. Boursier.

tense relations between an estranged sibling, parent, ex, or in-law; or a major vocational or health-related life change, navigating a spirituality of borders is part of the ongoing ebb and flow of individual and communal life together on Planet Earth. In whatever form or context borders occur, they are transitional points of entry or conversion where there exists the possibility for a spirituality that embraces, rather than rejects, the difference mingling together in this borderland space. It's at the intersections of these various points of difference, transition, or overlapping where a unique spirituality emerges. *Precious Precarity* focuses on the spiritual border in the liminal space of transition among displaced migrants fleeing their homelands, and the volunteers who assist them, on their journey to survival. The conversation also includes advocates and environmentalists whose work and witness embrace justice and peacemaking in the borderlands. It's a spirituality of borders that navigates, and even embraces, the challenges, differences, contrasts, unpredictability, vulnerability, and difficult choices that exist where the Global South meets the Global North, where East meets West, and where compassion and action meet the basic needs that have been exacerbated due to forced displacement and/or environmental abuse in the borderlands.

DEFINING SPIRITUALITY

Spirituality isn't the same as being religious. Spiritual people aren't necessarily religious, and religious people aren't necessarily spiritual. When I invite my college students to include their definition of *spirituality* as part of their self-introduction to peers during an Introduction to Spirituality course, no two definitions are exactly alike, but there are a few overlapping themes. For some, spirituality is intensely personal, individual, and private, about finding the meaning in one's own life. It's also typically defined as believing in a higher power that then calls one to a personal and public ethic of integrity as the guidon for moral actions that contribute to the greater good. In *A Spirituality of Resistance: Finding a Peaceful Heart and Protecting the Earth*, Roger S. Gottlieb explains, "In this everyday sense of the spiritual, we are not called by an external authority, but by an increased attention to our own inner truth. As that truth is ours alone, it cannot be imposed on another, nor will we be critical of those who find their relation to truth differently." He adds, "In this sense of the word, 'spirituality' is a way to be fully at home in our lives and on this earth."³ For those who profess to be religious, Gottlieb specifies, "doing the will of God necessarily includes a response to what is going on around us." He emphasizes, "That we comply with religious rules is not enough."⁴ It's a holistic spirituality that isn't inward and personal, "all about me." Rather, an ethically informed spirituality attempts to make a transformative difference for the better with whatever injustice is happening in our midst.

Spirituality necessarily encompasses the entire person, including who and what's happened to shape someone's internal and external expressions of spirituality. Life experiences, past and present, remain part of each person's spirituality, contributing to shaping its understanding and expression into the future. Whenever anyone relocates to a new location, forced or voluntary, their past remains part of the lifelong shaping, forming, and informing of their spirituality, which necessarily encompasses the fullness of who each person is. Spirituality encompasses each person's past, present, and future. Similar to John Steinbeck's beautiful explanation in his American classic *The Grapes of Wrath*, where he describes the forced migration during the Dust Bowl migration in the 1930s of thousands of midwestern families, whom he terms "people in flight," spirituality encompasses past experiences and present contexts, as well as future hopes, dreams, fears, and anxieties.⁵ Spirituality cannot be cut and pasted or separated from the lived context of any given person. For example, in describing the parting scene of sharecropper families who were forced off the land they had worked for generations, people who were packing up a handful of their belongings for their migration toward California, Steinbeck makes the important point that adults cannot "start over" in their new location because what's past will always be a part of the essence of their reflective thought and internalization about feelings, beliefs, emotions, regrets, longings, bitterness, and more, which will continue to form and inform their spirituality.

While it's possible for spirituality to be personal, such as taking an internal focus on meditation, deep breathing, contemplative silence, and/or prayer without ever engaging any connection with the wider community, internal personal focus alone too easily becomes self-absorbed, skewed, and distorted from reality. As Roger Haight explains in *Spiritual and Religious: Explorations for Seekers*, "Private spirituality is not necessarily irresponsible, but statistically it tends in that direction."⁶ Instead of a self-centered *internal* focus, spirituality in the borderlands embraces an *external* connection to the greater community, joining spirituality to the fullness of life with Planet Earth.

AUTHOR'S (BIASED) PERSPECTIVE

I bring a very biased perspective to this project on two points. First, I've had the privilege of interacting with countless migrants, including several thousand mothers and children while they were detained inside the GEO for-profit immigrant family detention center located in Karnes City, Texas, where I served as a volunteer chaplain and facilitated art as spiritual care (2015 and 2016), what I refer to as Art Inside Karnes. After Immigration and Customs Enforcement (ICE) rescinded my security clearance on December 15, 2016, and that of two volunteer chaplains who assisted, I volunteered with displaced migrant families in various contexts on both sides of the US-Mexico border. My work and witness with the families look through a theological-pastoral lens that prioritizes spirituality through justice and peacemaking in the borderlands.

Second, I'm unabashedly a feminist theologian who seeks to foster gender and racial equity. As Jewish scholar Anita Diamant highlights in her foreword to *New Jewish Feminism: Probing the Past, Forging the Future*, "Women hold up half of the sky—Jewish women among them."[7] My perspective prioritizes displaced raced migrant women who also are among those holding up half the sky yet whose voices are consistently ignored, silenced, or snuffed out behind locked detention center walls/cells or, worse, deportation and ultimately early death. Following the exemplary lead of Jewish feminists, *Precious Precarity* also engages midrash to further share the witness of the borderlands. Jewish feminists have embraced midrash as their methodology to challenge the silencing, dismissal, and oppression of women in the Hebrew Scriptures. Midrash is an important feminist tool to challenge silenced voices, misogynistic misinterpretations of sacred texts, and reappropriate these texts as a powerful witness for contemporary social concerns of gender and racial in/equity. Midrash doesn't seek to "change" a sacred text. Rather, it moves forth from the holy words, using interpretive imagination to bring in female voices that had been excluded.

The midrash in *Precious Precarity* engages the voices of migrant women and children and includes visual midrash through arts-based images. This midrash connects scriptural themes from Ecclesiastes about the meaning of life with the spirituality that weaves together in the borderlands to generate what Hans-Georg Gadamer famously explains in his *Truth and Method* as "coming to an understanding" to interpret and apply language, written or spoken, that transmits ideas and knowledge from one being to another.[8] *Precious Precarity* seeks to foster an understanding of what makes this short, precarious life meaningful.

CONVERSATION PARTNERS

Precious Precarity engages three primary conversation partners: (1) scriptural reflections on Ecclesiastes with its examination of the key question: in light of the fact that we're all going to die, how ought we to live?; (2) the volunteers, advocates, and environmentalists in various contexts on both sides of the US-Mexico border who work for justice and peacemaking there; (3) the written, verbal, and art-documented experiences of displaced migrants seeking asylum, primarily mothers and children who are fleeing their homelands to seek protection in the United States.[9]

Ecclesiastes

Precious Precarity juxtaposes the themes of Ecclesiastes, included in the Hebrew Scriptures and also the Christian Old Testament, with the words and witness of migrants and the volunteers and advocates in the borderlands. Ecclesiastes shapes its spirituality by beginning with the end in view (death), which isn't meant to engender negativity, pessimism, hopelessness, or gloom and doom. Rather, it's through this finiteness, what theologians and philosophers term *finitude*, that it becomes possible to experience life to the fullest in the here and now.

Categorized in the wisdom literature genre of sacred scriptures, Ecclesiastes seeks to discern the possibilities of what knowledge or wisdom humans are able to learn, gain, know, understand, appreciate, and follow. Traditional, conventional, or "retributive" wisdom in the ancient world idealized a neat and tidy view of ethics and justice. Similar to the *rule of law* in the contemporary world, conventional biblical wisdom extols that the honest, good, and hardworking people ultimately will prosper, while evil people will receive appropriate retribution and punishment. It's an ideology (mythology) of "you reap what you sow." Good sowers net positive results, and bad sowers suffer the consequences of their poor choices. These idealized views are helpful to a point because they provide overarching parameters of what should be productive, equitable, and just, helping to guide us through life. But, of course, life doesn't always work out this way. Sometimes bad things happen to good people. Shit happens; now what? Ecclesiastes offers its wisdom of dissent in the sense of a dissenting or alternative position, which questions, challenges, and disagrees with a normative, mainline, or traditional view. *Precious Precarity* engages the wisdom of Ecclesiastes, bringing it into conversation with stories of the displaced migrants. Because migrants, whether traveling individually or as a family, are mothers and fathers, sons and daughters, brothers and sisters, aunts and uncles, cousins and grandchildren, and grandmothers and grandfathers, hereafter I will refer to displaced migrants as *the families*.

Displaced Migrants: The Families

From the very beginning of my interactions with the detained migrant mothers and children while they were locked up inside the GEO Karnes immigrant family detention center, I was struck by the reality that these families are a living embodiment of the themes of Ecclesiastes. The mothers and children never spoke or wrote any of the words from this sacred scripture, as they frequently did with the Psalms, but their lives embodied the themes of Ecclesiastes, contextualized through the words and actions of these detained mothers and children. In particular, absolute belief in God is consistent among many of these families, not all, but it's a notable commonality in their written and verbal testimonies. Similarly, Ecclesiastes also never questions or doubts the existence of God. *God is*. Period. It isn't any more complicated than that one hardcore fact. It's this profound confidence and belief in God that shape the spirituality of the families, intersecting at the border with those who assist them.

Precious Precarity isn't about the families or migration per se. Rather, it's about the spirituality that emerges as it intersects with migration in the borderlands amid their precious and precarious lives and their zealous pursuit of life, for themselves and for their children. The families at our southern border have experienced suffering beyond suffering. They know that life is precious, which is why they're fleeing early death and pleading for a little bit longer life. Their pasts come with them, shaping their spirituality that informs their difficult decisions and shapes their uncertain futures. Paralleling Steinbeck's point he makes in *The Grapes of Wrath*, these families can't forget the pasts, good or bad, and magically jump into a fresh new life like children calling a do-over in a game. The past, present, and future are inseparably integrated in their present spirituality, which mingles in the borderlands with volunteers, advocates, and environmentalists.

Volunteers, Advocates, and Environmentalists in the Borderlands

The vast majority of the volunteers and advocates whom I interviewed are retired, many with the various limitations that come during the waning side of life. They volunteer through Team Brownsville in Brownsville, Texas; the Interfaith Welcome Coalition (IWC) of San Antonio; Green Valley-Sahuarita (GVS), Arizona Samaritans; and various nonprofit agencies located near the southwestern border in Texas, Arizona, and northern Mexico. By mutual agreement, their testimonies are anonymous with a few exceptions whose conversations were on the record. Some work directly with the families, and others do support work or activism and environmental witness. A few are professionally religious clergy or Catholic sisters. Many of the others have staunch faith in God, but they're *nones*—none-of-the-above religiously disaffiliated—who've become disengaged from any formal religion because they've become disenfranchised with its integrity, lack of social action, and value to the community and world. They see religious institutions as being too self-serving, exclusionary, and negative, particularly regarding anti-LGBTQIA+, anti-immigrant, antiabortion, and antireligious diversity. Many of these volunteers and activists self-identified as being spiritual, but many also specified that they'd "stepped aside" from the religious formation of their earlier years. Most would affirm, with Ecclesiastes and with the families, that *God is*, but many of these same volunteers are intentionally disconnected from any religious institution. Instead, they seek to make meaning in their lives through their response of compassion to the suffering of their displaced migrant neighbors and/or the abused environment in the borderlands.

STRUCTURE AND CONTENT OVERVIEW

The chapter titles reflect the main themes of Ecclesiastes, which resonate with the leitmotifs of the families at our southern border and also the volunteers and activists there. The themes don't always neatly fit within the confines of a particular chapter. Because each of these main ideas is reiterated throughout Ecclesiastes, and also with what occurs in the borderlands, there's a bit of inevitable overlap, particularly around cynicism, striving, chance, choice, death, and legacy as these themes resurface as this conversation unfolds.

Chapter 1, "Cynicism," discusses the postmodern a/religious western context as it relates to the thesis statement of Ecclesiastes 1:2, whereby life is meaningless with its treadmill-like futility and seeming senselessness. It suggests shifting from the stereotypical cynicism of Ecclesiastes and also that of the postmodern ethos to a broader interpretive perspective that embraces the meaning of life.

Chapter 2, "Dissent," explains how the wisdom of dissent offers a balm for the polarized judgmental dichotomy of the West with its either/or mandates of extremism that don't have a place for a mediating middle. This chapter brings in the feminist perspective to extrapolate on the benefits of the wisdom of dissent and its logical, valid, and encouraging alternative options for understanding what, when, and why bad things happen to good people.

Chapter 3, "Paradox," covers the harsh reality of this precarious life, which often challenges, questions, and even makes a mockery of conventional wisdom that posits that hard work pays off, honesty is the best policy, and the Horatio Alger–styled accounts whereby anyone can pull themselves up by their bootstraps and become an American success story. This chapter highlights the conundrum of suffering and injustice amid otherwise doing the "right thing." It reflects on how this disparity intersects with spirituality, particularly in the borderlands.

Chapter 4, "Striving," addresses striving for the "good life," a perennial goal that's embedded in the DNA of this nation that's been designed around life, liberty, and the pursuit of happiness. This perpetual striving might produce surface success, but it's often counterproductive to peace, centeredness, and true happiness. Striving also contributes to blindness about the environment and the basic human physical needs of fellow sojourners. Striving negates spiritual peace. This chapter contrasts the striving of affluent America and the problems of wealth attainment with the spiritual peace of displaced and impoverished migrants who are striving for safety and a peaceful place to live but who forever after end up in a sense of placelessness with a deep longing for home.

Chapter 5, "Chance," highlights the theme that life is filled with unpredictable events, actions, encounters, and people, some good and some bad. Whether these chances are little-c small encounters (chance), the "Big C" (Chance) death (9:11–12), or the miserable raw deal lamented in Ecclesiastes (4:8, 5:14, 10:5), these unpredictable large and small events and encounters are the inevitable aspect of the precariousness of this fragile life on Planet Earth. Navigating these chance/Chance experiences interfaces with a spirituality of borders amid the *finitude of life*, literally the *finiteness* of this short life. It's the response to precarious encounters that contributes to—or not—finding calm within the storm.

Chapter 6, "Time," is set in conversation with there being a "time for everything" (Ecc. 3:1–8) as this chapter reflects on time from the perspective of migrants and the religiously disaffiliated, a/religious, or nones who serve as volunteers and advocates. It considers how time/timing intersects with the families leaving their homelands to seek refuge in a foreign land.

Chapter 7, "Choice," is about learning how to navigate the liminal differences between two apparently equal evils, which requires identifying and affirming those nuanced variables. Against the backdrop of the better-than statements of Ecclesiastes (7:1–10), "Choice" considers what's better than something else, even if only minuscule, and how this reality intersects with spiritual well-being. It ultimately shows the international blending of spirituality in the borderlands as theirs and mine become ours.

Chapter 8, "Risk," weaves the words of Ecclesiastes with the words and witness of displaced migrants who take calculated risks and seize the day. It also includes narrative reflections of volunteers and advocates who witness, and are inspired by, the courageous spirituality of the families.

Chapter 9, "Gain," with the Ecclesiastes theme of *yitron* in view ("benefit" or "gain"), engages the witness of a/religious volunteers and what they *gain* from their interactions with the families. It includes an analysis of spirituality and its role as a vehicle for justice.

Chapter 10, "Joy," engages the experiential witness of the volunteers and advocates with narratives by the families as this chapter reflects on how to recognize and celebrate joy within the muck of life.

Chapter 11, "Legacy," examines, given the cynicism of the postmodern condition and Ecclesiastes, what could be the antidote to finding or making meaning amid this seemingly meaningless life where you can't take any worldly gains with you into death, the ultimate and inevitable great leveler for us all. What's a worthwhile legacy to leave behind, and how does this intersect with spirituality regarding the unknown life after physical death? Against a reflective reading of the five summary statements of Ecclesiastes, this chapter offers an antidote to the futility factor through the words and witness of the families and the meaning-making of the volunteers and advocates in the borderlands.

The conclusion, "Holy and Whole," integrates the lessons of *Precious Precarity* into a spirituality for sacredness amid secularity that fosters peace and inspires an antidote for futility, despair, or feelings of pointlessness. Accepting the times or seasons of life, living into them as blessings, and acknowledging joy in the good times and also in the bad all culminate with creating a place and space for *holy ground*, which fosters a spirituality for a precarious *precious* life.

NOTES

1 Simone Weil, *Gravity and Grace* (London: Routledge, 1947, 1999), 85.
2 Weil, *Gravity and Grace*, 108.
3 Roger S. Gottlieb, *A Spirituality of Resistance: Finding a Peaceful Heart and Protecting the Earth* (Lanham, MD: Rowman and Littlefield, 2003), 9.
4 Gottlieb, *A Spirituality of Resistance*, 27.
5 John Steinbeck, *The Grapes of Wrath* (New York: Penguin Books, 1939), 122.
6 Roger Haight, *Spiritual and Religious: Explorations for Seekers* (Maryknoll, NY: Orbis Books, 2016), 9.
7 Anita Diamant, Foreword to *New Jewish Feminism: Probing the Past, Forging the Future*, ed. Rabbi Elyse Goldstein (Nashville: Jewish Lights Publishing, 2009), xi.
8 Hans-Georg Gadamer, *Truth and Method*, 2nd ed., trans. revised by Joel Weinsheimer and Donald G. Marshall (New York: Continuum, 1975, 1989), 443.
9 For an explanation of why stories matter for gender equity and women's studies in religion, see Clare Hemmings, *Why Stories Matter: The Political Grammar of Feminist Theory* (Durham, NC: Duke University Press, 2011).

CHAPTER ONE

Cynicism

"Meaningless! Meaningless!" says the Teacher. "Utterly meaningless! Everything is meaningless!"
—Ecclesiastes 1:2 (NIV)

Ecclesiastes seeks to discover what, if anything, is meaningful, worthwhile, fair, and equitable in life. The opening remark in Ecclesiastes 1:2 in this Jewish wisdom literature, "everything is meaningless" (NIV), or the traditional "vanities of vanities" (KJV), sets the tone and focus throughout the musings of its author, a cynical old man who proffers a reality check on the conditions of life in the ancient world. Throughout this short scriptural narrative, Ecclesiastes laments the futility, vanity, or senselessness of life for humans and also the natural world. There's a repetitive nature of reality. Humans are transient and ephemeral, and the cycle of seasons also has a sense of endless or vain repetition, as the sun rises and sets, and rises and sets again and again (Ecc. 1:5). The entire created order appears to be nothing but tedious redundancy and pointlessness. Amid the weary repetition of life, Ecclesiastes asks, what advantage is there?

The cynicism in Ecclesiastes consistently emphasizes that human beings are limited by their finitude, which comes from their finite time on earth and also from the inadequate view or perspective each person has that limits their ability to fully see or understand due to their short lifetime and their limited contextual frame of reference. Each person can only see/know so much in their limited worldview, and then they die, and the next generation has to take it from there, sometimes benefiting from earlier knowledge but sometimes ignoring or disregarding it and starting all over from scratch.

This understanding of a limited or finite worldview, what could be termed a *spirituality of finitude*, resonates with the postmodern perspective, the ethos of the Global North, which inevitably intersects and interacts with contemporary spirituality, including in the borderlands. Not unlike the cynicism in Ecclesiastes, the postmodern condition in the Global North maintains an outlook that evokes a pessimistic view about the value, benefit, or meaning of this life, not only for human beings but also for the future of Planet Earth.

To make it more manageable to understand the differences in the historical timeline, history has been divided into smaller chunks, with each era having somewhat similar characteristics but differing from what went before and what comes after. Familiar names marking the past include the Stone Age, Bronze Age, Iron Age, Ancient Egypt, Ancient Rome, Middle Ages, Islamic Golden Age, Renaissance, Enlightenment, Modern Era, Roaring Twenties, Great Depression, and the Cold War. Despite these conveniently labeled time frames, Rabbi Abraham Joshua Heschel explains that "the uniqueness of history is something which is hard to comprehend."[1] Sometimes God hears and responds differently than at other times.[2] Nevertheless, the Jewish tradition maintains that God continues to speak through the prophetic word in the biblical text. These voices that have been canonized as the authority of God, even though written long ago, still bear witness to answer or respond to what's happening in the present, including the wisdom of Ecclesiastes for the cynical present with its postmodern condition.

THE POSTMODERN CONDITION

Postmodernity began to emerge in the 1930s as a transitional era between what had gone before (modernity) and whatever something new will be coming next. It's termed *post*modernity because it comes after modernity, and in fact, it seeks to challenge and change much of the ideology of the previous modern time frame in global history.[3] Postmoderns disagree with modernity's view that there's one single correct method or view and that everything else is incorrect. Postmodernity affirms diversity, something that's particularly evident in the myriad of theologies that emerged during the twentieth century to give voice to those who are marginalized, beginning with liberation theology from Central and South America and continuing through the intersectionality of diverse voices that currently endorse engagement in social justice concerns across a broad socioeconomic-political-racial span, including feminists and womanists who work to challenge and change the patriarchal domination of males over females.[4] Some view diversity as pluralism in a negative sense as an "anything goes" approach, but the postmodern point is to recognize that there are many different truths. The idealized universal or grand narrative view embraced during the earlier modern era is invalid. One truth can't and doesn't apply unilaterally to everyone everywhere. When it comes to making a sweeping truth claim, a common fallacy of modernity, postmodernity says there's no such thing as one size fits all. The key is to acknowledge each person's or community's particular limited view while also respecting the differing perspectives of others, including agreeing to disagree. Instead of feeling threatened by difference, postmoderns, at least in theory, embrace diversity as the reality of what it means to be fully human.

Postmodernity also disagrees with modernity's idealism that knowledge is objective. Instead, it affirms each person is born in a particular context that includes its own set of assumptions, traditions, and presuppositions, which are passed along to the newborn offspring, who grow up taking on the same ideologies and traditions without necessarily being aware of the blind spots, biases, skewed perspectives, or limited views these traditions encompass. It requires a lifetime of intentional experiential education to move out of what postmodernist Merold Westphal, in *Whose Community? Which Interpretation?: Philosophical Hermeneutics for the Church*, would call the "cave of tradition."[5] Tradition is important, necessary, and inevitable. It gives each person a starting point, but it can also become a chokehold of prejudice that prevents intellectual, emotional, and spiritual maturity. People are physical, spiritual, and cultural beings who are influenced by their surroundings. As Westphal quips, "It remains undeniably the case that even the most mindless couch potato does not live by instinct alone. Our lives are embedded in ideas (and thus texts) and practices (and thus institutions) that are handed down to us and that we make our own, thus giving form and content to our existence, by (re)interpreting them."[6] Spirituality in the borderlands shares the postmodern perspective regarding the importance of reflective rethinking about current (mis)interpretations, (mis)understandings, (dis)beliefs, and (harsh) practices. The idea is to revise any outdated ideals and practices to reflect the updated reality generated by experiential insights, paralleling what Westphal highlights Gadamer advising: "Listen carefully. You might learn something. The voice you hear is not your own, but one that from a different perspective makes a truth claim on you."⁷ The role, goal, and purpose of this careful listening are to learn something new, not to reinforce what we think we already "know." This listening and learning inform individual spirituality, which shows up in community through each person's lived response during their journey to spiritual maturity, expressed at the in-between borders in life, moving into these messy places and spaces with expanded insight, compassion, and acts of tangible care.

Cynicism in Postmodernity

Postmodernity includes a large measure of cynicism about there being such a thing as objective, dispassionate knowledge, an idealistic but misguided core theme of modernity. Since objective knowledge is questionable to nonexistent, it isn't possible to solve, resolve, or mediate the massive world problems that make the daily headline news, generating a cynicism that resonates with Ecclesiastes. Postmoderns are also more likely than moderns to have greater respect for the fragility of Planet Earth, disputing the elitist attitude of modernity that humans were created to have "dominion" over the earth (Gen. 1:28). Such patriarchal colonialism led to a callous disregard of the interconnectedness of all living organisms for the sustainability of the entire earth, which is pushing the world closer to extinction, exacerbating the cynical postmodern ethos, vanity of vanities, senselessness, and meaninglessness.

This same cynicism never seems to be far from the personal or public consciousness in the global community as the tragedies, dramas, and evils occurring in a nation halfway around the world become headline news. The latest worst issues rise to the surface again and again. The topics vary, spanning the globe with crisis coverage on the never-ending coronavirus pandemic and the newer monkeypox to the Russian missile strikes and war crimes in Ukraine. There's also always political drama, such as accountability for the January 6 siege on the US Capitol; the political stunt of flying migrants from Texas to the island of Martha's Vineyard off the coast of Cape Cod, Massachusetts; and the US Supreme Court leaving in place the Trump-era Title 42 border policy, thereby exacerbating the humanitarian crisis in the borderlands.⁸ Headline news around civic unrest also includes widespread racial injustice, response to the US Supreme Court repealing *Roe v. Wade*, the rapidly worsening environmental crisis, and school shootings like the senseless massacre at Robb Elementary School in Uvalde, Texas, on May 24,

2022. Any of these dramatic challenges easily generates cynicism about the present and future. In short, it's easy to feel cynical in this postmodern world.

Cynicism in postmodernity also spills over to an increasing disconnect with community, what Robert Putnam documented twenty years ago in *Bowling Alone: The Collapse and Revival of American Community*, with his social analysis of the declining participation in community-based group activities. Instead of joining any of the civic, community, and religious organizations common in earlier generations, cynicism generates distrust of organizations in general and organized religion in particular. Rabbi Heschel argues, "*Religion is an answer to [humanity's] ultimate questions. The moment we become oblivious to ultimate questions, religion becomes irrelevant, and its crisis sets in.*"[9] Cynicism in a postmodern context in general inevitably overflows into religion and/or spirituality, but the response to this differs from one person to another. Christian theologian Paul Tillich suggests this "mysterious character of the holy produces an ambiguity in [each person's] way of experiencing it."[10] While the concept of God remains absolute, the response to what that looks like dramatically differs. Cynicism does, however, contribute to religious disaffiliation and the increase of the *nones*.

Cynicism, Declining Religious Affiliation, and the Nones

Cynicism is pervasive in contributing to the declining religious affiliation in the postmodern West, and it's particularly notable with Christianity in America. For example, a student in my Introduction to Spirituality course at a Catholic (Christian) college bluntly said, "In my personal experience church has been used as an obscure invention to heaven versus a pathway to god and righteous life. Although communities can be helped by these [Christian] communities when disaster strikes, the action seems to be selfishly driven by a golden ticket to the pearly gates."[11] This sentiment is reiterated consistently by multiple students each time I teach this theology and religious studies course for nursing students.

In *The Nones: Where They Came From, Who They Are, and Where They Are Going*, Ryan Burge links the increase of those who self-identify as being religiously disaffiliated and who mark the category "none of the above" in a survey on religious participation, with the increase in Evangelical right-wingers who've hijacked their religion and church, aligning them too tightly to the political rather than to the gospel of Jesus Christ as proclaimed in the biblical text (i.e., Matt. 25:31–46). Burge argues that the overly vocal and overzealous political aspect of these Evangelical churchgoers pushes the more liberal ones into a silent corner without voice or vote, contributing to the exodus of Protestant Christians of all ages from mainline churches across America. It's not that those exiting their former religious tradition aren't spiritual or even that they don't believe in God. Rather, they disaffiliate because they no longer "want to label themselves as a Christian, Mormon, or Buddhist."[12] For instance, during a recent visit back home to Wichita, Kansas, where there are a bazillion churches throughout this conservative midwestern city, my best friend there who'd regularly attended church during her childhood and continued into her early years of parenting innocuously remarked, "I wonder how they support all the churches here. I don't know anyone who attends church anymore." Church is no longer part of the weekly or even monthly spirituality for more and more Americans.

Explaining her disassociation with her childhood religious upbringing, a physician who organizes medical professionals to volunteer with migrants in the borderlands, and who also leads public witness events in solidarity with the displaced families said she was raised and confirmed as a Roman Catholic but discontinued participation around high school. She said, "I stopped going to church because there was just a lot of church doctrine that I felt was out of alignment with my personal values. I didn't feel very connected to the Catholic Church for sure. I very much resisted. My mom is still very, very Catholic. And very devout. She gets up at five a.m. every morning and prays. I respect people who have those practices, particularly if those practices and those beliefs actually motivate them to do the right thing." She clarified, "And 'by the right thing,' I mean equity and justice in the world so that it's inclusive. That, to me, is the right thing. I don't find that in any particular organized religion." Instead, the physician said she "feels more spiritually connected in nature and with belief in the reality of our interconnectedness," what she describes as "truly remarkable." This interconnection of all humanity is an important aspect of her disaffiliation from religion because of religion's lack of engagement for equity and justice. Interconnectedness is also the very strong spiritual moral compass for this physician's work in the borderlands. She emphasized, "I think that it's something that if we all collectively realized our interconnection, then we would move a lot differently in the world." At a minimum, there'd be a lot more compassion for other human beings and also more respect for the environment.

The decline of religion in the United States is more noticeable than ever, following after what began a generation or two earlier in Europe. For example, while Lutheran pastor and theologian Dietrich Bonhoeffer was detained for sedition against Hitler shortly before the end of World War II, he wrote a letter to his dear friend Eberhard Bethge saying, "We are moving towards a completely religionless time; people as they are now simply cannot be religious any more. Even those who honestly describe themselves as 'religious' do not in the least act up to it, and so they presumably mean something quite different by 'religious.'"[13] On a parallel note, I've long argued that the Christian church's lack of participation in matters of contemporary social concerns has made and is making the church increasingly irrelevant in the globalized community of the postmodern ethos.[14] Benedictine sister and proponent for justice and peace Joan Chittister eloquently writes, "The truth is that faith requires the awareness that God is, and that God is holding all of us responsible for the other. Being a card-carrying member of a religious tradition does not give us the right to consume the world for our own ends and in the name of God. We do not have the right to loose havoc on the rest of the world in the name of the God we have made in our image."[15] What Chittister describes as a lack of connection between the profession of faith and action for justice is a popular reason for the increasing disaffiliation from organized religion.

In theological language, even the more socially minded denominations like Presbyterians and Methodists can become too internally concerned about orthodoxy (correct belief) over external involvement in orthopraxis (correct action).[16] Younger *and* older generations notice this disconnect, and they express their dissent through their cynical disaffiliation from formal religion.

Volunteers with migrants in the borderlands often connected their exodus from organized religion with their cynicism about the Christian church, a cynicism they made a point to explain doesn't include God or the biblical teachings of love, justice, and compassion for those who are marginalized and oppressed. Some called it "stepping aside." Others said their church's silence and inattention to the immigration crisis was so disheartening that they could no longer respect it for any ethical, moral, religious, or spiritual leadership. For instance, a longtime volunteer said, "I no longer identify as a religious person . . . though I do believe deeply in God. I believe in the Divine. It is simply The God." Where Black theologian James H. Cone asks, "If God is righteous and is in control of history, why is God not setting things right?"[17] the volunteers in the borderlands who've exited from organized religion are more likely to ask, "If the Christian Church is supposed to be about love and compassion in response to believing in the Creator God, why isn't it more active in setting things right?" Although there's increasing disaffiliation among volunteers and advocates from organized religion, confidence in the definitive presence of the Ultimate Divine remains steadfast.

Nevertheless, *God Is*

In all of the philosophical conversations circling around the theme "God is dead," Merold Westphal's argument for who God still is particularly resonates with spirituality in the borderlands in a postmodern context. His colleague Edith Wyschogrod explains that Westphal offers three postmodern correctives to philosophy of religion and theology that are formal yet faithful indications of the terms on which biblical God *can* appear: "God is a mystery exceeding the terms of human wisdom. God is irreducible to our vision or comprehension. God is the gift of love exceeding all our ways of imagining, thinking, or seeking God."[18] Despite cynicism about religion or religious people, spirituality in the borderlands affirms, nevertheless, *God is*. Similarly, amid its preponderance for pessimism, Ecclesiastes also maintains a definitive affirmation of the existence of God (Ecc. 8:12, 12:13–14). God is. Period.

Ecclesiastes is a helpful conversation partner for this journey to understand spirituality in the borderlands because this sacred text, despite its cynicism, doesn't doubt or challenge the existence of God. Ecclesiastes questions what human beings can know given each person's limited perspective and finite existence, but God definitely still is God.

This belief in God shapes response in the borderlands. An immigration attorney, who also works pro bono with the families, remembered an experience early in her career when she was getting ready to do an asylum case for girls from Colombia. She said, "I was stressing and stressing, and so I called this venerable Buddhist whom I was very close with and expressed how worried I was about this case. The venerable said, 'Who do you think you are? Do you think you're that important? This isn't what this is about.' She said, 'You get prepared, you do the best you can, and the rest of its karma. Do you think you're in charge? Who are you that you are so important?'" The pro bono attorney reflected, "That experience was very enlightening to me. She pointed out that I was taking on a burden that was presumptuous and also not real. I need to be prepared, but at the end of the day, I'm not responsible for what my client did or didn't do. There are so many things out of my control that will affect the outcome. From this venerable Buddhist's point of view, it was the karma of all the people who were involved, and especially of this client." She further explained, "In the bigger context, the Divine is there, and there's power in that. We think we have power. We have nothing, but there *is* strength in belief in the Divine, which can be a powerful force within us. We have to show up. Do I think that's how we become important? No, I think we just need to do it, to show up and be present despite any vulnerabilities or inadequacies we may feel. We are in this life for each other, at this time, in this space, where we are." The pro bono attorney added, "Yet, at the same time, we need to maintain a sense of humility so we don't get too carried away." Even when everything seems senseless, crazy, out of control, and in vain, despite all of the effort a volunteer expends in the borderlands, the call remains to press on through the muck, maintaining the inner calling to do that thing that has been placed before them, all while trusting in the greater Divine, the Holy One, the Power of Being, The God. It's about centering and recentering through perspective while also finding meaning-making amid the seeming meaninglessness and out-of-control mess.

A Helpful Perspective

Not knowing exactly who or what God is contributes to what Heschel insists is the very essence of God: mystery. Heschel observes that one of the critical insights from Ecclesiastes is "the existence of the world is a mysterious fact... the world of the known is a world of unknown; hiddenness, mystery."[19] Heschel's emphasis on mystery, rather than cynicism, suggests there are different options for how to view or respond to the "cynicism" in Ecclesiastes that's also part of the postmodern perspective, which contributes to shaping spirituality in the borderlands. Although cynicism is the most noted and quoted description for both Ecclesiastes and the postmodern context, is it really cynicism, or is it about embracing a particular tweaked cynicism perspective?

In *Old Testament Wisdom: An Introduction*, biblical scholar James Crenshaw differentiates among skepticism, pessimism, and cynicism. He suggests skeptics hopefully want to believe in something, but they harbor a smidge of doubt that prevents them from fully accepting it. When they lose hope in the possibility that something's valid or true, they slide down to pessimism, which emotes indifference. Pessimists stop caring about what they once wanted to believe in while they were skeptics. They throw in the towel and give in to pessimism. For Crenshaw, "*Cynics* go a step further; by their disdain for creaturely comforts and sensual pleasure they show contempt for everything life has to offer."[20] He suggests skeptics are somewhat common in the Hebrew Scriptures, with rare bursts of cynicism. Scholars and general readers typically describe Ecclesiastes as being one of these rare bursts of cynicism. These variations miss an important option that intersects with the postmodern condition and spirituality in the borderlands: Ecclesiastes is a *realist*. Bad stuff happens in life, including the grievous evils (chapter 3) that force innocent people to flee their homelands as displaced migrants who must seek safety somewhere else.

SPIRITUALITY AND CYNICISM IN THE BORDERLANDS

The limited view of any given person, including finitude and the finite nature of human life, doesn't have to leave anyone feeling powerless. Spirituality offers another option. The intersection of cynicism and the staunch belief in the presence of God despite suffering empowers volunteers to do what post–World War II German theologian Dorothee Soelle is well known for saying: "Changing sides in favor of life, ceasing to be complicit with death. It means letting go of the drive to kill and the apathy that comes so close to that drive. It means letting go of the fear of dying and the fear of coming up short," what she describes as "two fears that look so alike they are easily confused."[21] Changing sides from death to life is spiritually informing and life-changing, pushing aside cynicism and moving into difference-making.

Volunteers and Cynicism

The cynicism of Ecclesiastes intersects with the spirituality in the borderlands in several ways. Cynicism isn't from or about the migrants themselves. Rather, cynicism gathers steam and moves forth from the bigger picture of this nation's lack of acknowledgment or respect for its interconnectedness with the global community. In particular, cynicism surfaces in the borderlands because volunteers and advocates realize that America and Americans are complicit in why these families are displaced, most notably because of the harsh side effects of global warming and also the devastating economic policies like the North American Free Trade Agreement (NAFTA). Cynicism also gains traction from the US public and the negative political discourse lobbed against the "illegals" in the borderlands, many of whom are vulnerable families seeking protection in this country. As a Team Brownsville volunteer who assists migrants on both sides of the Texas-Mexico border explained, "Cynicism comes in, not with anything the migrants have done, but it's with us, in the United States." She added that her cynicism comes into play because once the families pass through the border area, where the volunteers offer practical assistance through compassionate response, they move throughout the country to be with their families who are already here. This volunteer lamented, "All of a sudden, they discover that all of America isn't treating them with the same kindness and respect that we do."

Cynicism among volunteers also intersects with the lack of response from spiritual and religious leaders who turn aside from the suffering at the border. A volunteer shared when he'd been part of a Christian church that went on mission trips to Costa Rica to help build a church there. Each participant paid their own way, and they also brought three thousand dollars as a donation to help with materials. After he and his spouse relocated closer to the southern border and began volunteering with displaced migrants in the borderlands, they invited this pastor, who'd organized and led the Costa Rica mission trip, to visit and experience the volunteer assistance with migrants in Matamoros, Mexico, during Migrant Protection Protocols (MPP) that forced asylum seekers to remain in Mexico while awaiting the much-delayed legal process to enter the United States. The volunteer thought of it as a "global mission" done locally at the Texas-Mexico border. He remembered, "We were taking food across the border and feeding people in the plaza in Matamoros when the border was first closed to asylum seekers and before the camp opened. There were only about two hundred people camped in the plaza, and we brought meals over." The volunteer said, "I thought this pastor probably would enjoy seeing exactly what was going on, so I invited him, and he came down and went across the border with us." The volunteer added, "From the comments this pastor made, you could see that he was basically indoctrinated in anti-immigrant sentiments beyond the point of return." This volunteer said it was disappointing and disillusioning to hear such negative comments about people in need from their former spiritual leader.

The volunteer remembered, "The pastor made comments like 'I wonder how many of these kids are really here with their parents.'" The volunteer explained that the caustic remark aligned with the pervasive public rhetoric at that time regarding a misguided theory that "people kidnap or borrow kids in order to get across the border." The volunteer added, "When we were explaining how many people we were feeding each evening, our former pastor responded with basically 'Well, of course! Look at all the free food you give them.'" This volunteer's spouse interjected that their former pastor left early from the ministry experience with the impromptu excuse "'I think I have to go.'" The spouse added, "We told our pastor how to get back to the port of entry and leave Mexico, and we haven't talked to him since." The volunteer added, "The pastor's response to the dire condition of the families really surprised me. He was all for going to their country, and oh, 'Let's help them there, but welcoming them into our country? Oh, no, that's different,' and that really upset me a lot."

Similar deliberate disconnect of religious leaders with their inattention to immigration and the suffering exacerbated during forced displacement is an increasingly common lament from volunteers with migrants, contributing to lifetime/former church members opting out of formal religion. For example, a Texan who leads small groups to volunteer with displaced families on both side of the Texas-Mexico border said, "I don't sit in the pews anymore. I think I'll always consider myself a Mormon. It's just such a part of my life." Instead of sitting in the pews, she started a nonprofit organization to support migrants at the border, and she organizes friends and family to take service trips to provide tangible assistance. She said those who join her on these border mission trips give a "similar vibe" about why they are disconnected from formal religion. She explained:

> There was a hunger there for me that wasn't getting filled sitting in the pew. Now don't take me wrong. I learned a lot about service through my church. I was raised in the Mormon Church, and I will always give credit to their example and encouragement to serve people. They're very good at that. But there was something blocking a real freedom for me. I wanted to step outside of the church. I was hungry for something else. For me, when I go to the border, that's where I see the face of God. [See illustrations 1.1, 2.1, 6.1, 7.1, 9.1, and 11.1.] I wasn't seeing it so much in my congregation sitting in the pew on a Sunday. I wasn't seeing it anymore in the lessons. Something was pushing me to get out of my seat, even more than the service they'd always encouraged. There was something else saying, "There's more here; there's more here."

When I responded that this volunteer didn't sound cynical about disaffiliating with her forty-year religious connection, she explained, "I think I went through stages of grief, like you would for any other thing. So I think I've kind of been through an anger stage. But I don't know that that really serves

Illustration 1.1 *Precious Precarity* 11" × 14" graphite pencil portrait on Toned Tan against the pink floral paper of a little girl who was waiting with her mother at the Greyhound bus station in San Antonio after they were released from family detention, April 4, 2017. Art © Helen T. Boursier.

me anymore. So I kind of let some things go and just move on from that." She emphasized that her spirituality is most fulfilled through being present in solidarity with the families.

POLITICAL CYNICISM INFLUENCES SPIRITUALITY

Spirituality directly intersects and interacts with the political. It can't not. Of course, the intersection between the political and spirituality isn't limited to immigration. Clearly, these categories overlap and overflow into other public or political concerns. For instance, I'm living in a state (Texas) that was the catalyst for the US Supreme Court's repeal of *Roe v. Wade* and where racism, gun violence, and anti-immigrant sentiments are the norm. All this state-pushed negativity is pervasive in the spiritual well-being of the people who live here, including friends, neighbors, clergy colleagues, and strangers. Those who are pushing the angry agenda often do so with anti-everything spirits. While those who don't support this expansive negativity say they're spiritually drained, embarrassed to live here, and just plain tired of the anger. Several close friends have opted to flee in search of a more peaceful place, ironically, not dissimilar to what the displaced families are experiencing in their journey to a peaceful, safe new place. Spiritual well-being cannot thrive or be at peace when the political climate is so overwhelmingly negative, nasty, and angry.

Some disaffiliated cynics take more drastic measures than others to protect their spiritual well-being. For example, a longtime immigration volunteer and advocate for unaccompanied immigrant minors who are detained in US custody said, "I just couldn't take this country anymore." She did a parachute drop-style relocation to a small city in Mexico where many other expats live. She explained she needed to distance herself from the angry anti-immigrant policies and practices, particularly the mistreatment of unaccompanied immigrant children seeking protection in this country. This retired pro bono attorney continues doing education and advocacy for migrants via the internet, but she said it's a relief to her spirit to no longer have to endure the constant onslaught of anti-immigrant public rhetoric that precipitated her relocation to Mexico.

Volunteering as Antidote to Cynicism

The negative anti-immigrant rhetoric in America also becomes a catalyst for the strong at heart to renew their spirits through compassionate response with the families, combined with public action to challenge the misinformation about this vulnerable population at our southern border. Spirituality in the borderlands embraces a passionate concern to work for transformative justice and doing so with what theologian Paul Tillich terms "infinite passion." It's a passion that responds in love and with love through action, for, as Tillich argues, "the immediate expression of love is action."[22] Instead of running away, shifting to a position of "head down; mouth shut," French philosopher and political activist Simone Weil proposes "the contemplation of human misery wrenches us in the direction of God, and it is only in others whom we love as ourselves that we can contemplate it. We can neither contemplate it in ourselves as such nor in others as such."[23] For instance, a rabbi who was filling an interim position in a synagogue in southern Arizona described how impressed he was on arrival to this area because there are so many "religious people" who are deeply involved in immigration assistance at the Arizona-Mexico border. The rabbi explained that while these volunteers in the borderlands don't wear their religious attire or necessarily still participate in a religious institution, they're on the front lines providing compassionate response to displaced migrants. The rabbi pointed out, "These people have strong spiritual grounding in general," He mused, "Maybe that's true in all the different organizations in town, whether it's the food bank or whether it's a homeless shelter or whatever it happens to be." He said it's the spiritually grounded people who serve as volunteers. They're the people who are looking for opportunities to offer assistance. While many volunteers aren't connected with a church, the rabbi highlighted they do compassionate response because they have an internal compass, a spiritual motivation to do it.[24]

Volunteering with migrants becomes an excellent antidote to cynicism. A seventy-six-year-old practicing Episcopalian who said she has a very open view of an inclusive God and whose pastor regularly preached on the interconnectedness of all human beings who are "cousins" created by the same God said her spirituality is formed and informed around accepting the displaced migrants at the Texas-Mexico border for who they are: human beings.[25] She explained, "I accept them, and they accept me, and that to me means God loves us both. And I don't care if they're Black, white, brown, whatever. They're people, and I have found that the majority of people are good. The families love each other; they love their children. When you are good and loving, as a parent, you want to make your children's lives better." She added, "And there's something else that I've discovered too. It's not that people don't love their country. They do. The people coming to this country are just like you and I. They love their country. They just can't live there because the governments there are so bad." She sees these families as part of the same beloved community, created by the same God. Her antidote to cynicism is to offer a compassionate response to these displaced families experiencing grievous evils at the Texas-Mexico border.

Working for justice and peacemaking in the borderlands also becomes a gateway for others to step in and participate. The former Mormon who organizes and leads small groups of volunteers, traveling eight hours to the southern border to offer direct assistance to displaced families and children, remembered when she took a thirteen- and a fifteen-year-old on one of the trips. She said, "When we got back to the Airbnb after a long stretch at the migrant respite center in McAllen, Texas, they both just said, 'We don't know that we can lay down in these nice beds. We don't know that we can do that.'" The leader added, "This topic is huge. There are so many people who are disaffiliating from their religions in droves. They are hungering for something else. And I find that many of them find what they're looking for in service at the border with the families. People are people, and they're starving for something else." What the church currently is/does doesn't fill the spiritual hunger.

Spirituality of the Families Counters Volunteer Cynicism

Many of the volunteers connected their spirituality of response to the spirituality and enfettered faith that's indicative of so many of the migrants at the southwest border. In other words, the spirituality of the families uplifts the spirituality of the volunteers. For example, the prayer a mother wrote while she was detained inside GEO Karnes is typical of the confidence the families have that God is present in their lives:

God Is Our Compass
God is my refuge.
    You know my concerns.
Prepare me for the future
    for my children.
You are all I desire.
You are our compass
    along our walk.

> Nothing disturbs me.
> Nothing troubles me
>   because
> I have faith in you.
> Everything is on the wings of you.
>   O my God.[26]

Mara, a migrant stranded at the US-Mexico border, simply explained, "The migrant's life is very hard. I came because the lack of work and the failure of our traditions and culture scare me. The goodness and honest way of life no longer exist. I trust that God has a plan and a purpose for me, so I continue on my journey in the will of God."[27] Similarly, after quickly summarizing the litany of injustices her family had experienced in their attempt to seek protection in the United States, including "hunger, cold, suffering of every sort, and sadness in our souls to leave our family," a thirteen-year-old migrant shared, "US Immigration sent us [back] to Nuevo Laredo. We were not given the chance for a better life. But everything is for a cause. God has a plan for us. We thank God we are alive. We thank God for keeping us healthy. We thank God for the kindness of people who help us. We thank God."[28] Always, the families give thanks to God.

Trust in God is such an important part of the migrant's journey because, as a volunteer observed, "In the context that many of these women live, it's a very real faith for them. It's also the place that they can count on. The rules don't change, like everywhere they go. They're on shifting sand." For the displaced migrants, as with Ecclesiastes and many of the volunteers and advocates, cynicism is dispelled and displaced by their firm and certain belief: God *is*. When everything else is uncertain, their trust in the existence of God is the one reality they can count on. When bad stuff happens, God still is. In fact, the perspective that guides their decisions is their unquestioned belief in God, "even though they walk through the valley of the shadow of death" (Ps. 23:4), which undergirds their difficult choice to migrate. Essentially, migration becomes their enacted spirituality of dissent *from* suffering *for* life.

NOTES

1 Abraham Joshua Heschel, *God in Search of Man: A Philosophy of Judaism* (New York: Farrar, Straus and Giroux, 1955), 204.

2. Heschel, *God in Search of Man*, 205.
3. See Boursier, *Willful Ignorance*, 229–230.
4. See Boursier, *Willful Ignorance*, 207–237.
5. See Merold Westphal, *Whose Community? Which Interpretation?: Philosophical Hermeneutics for the Church* (Grand Rapids, MI: Baker Academic, 2009).
6. Merold Westphal, *Overcoming Onto-Theology: Toward a Postmodern Christian Faith* (New York: Fordham University Press, 2001), 128.
7. Westphal, *Whose Community? Which Interpretation*, 73. See Gadamer, *Truth and Method*; and James Risser, *Hermeneutics and the Voice of the Other* (Albany, NY: SUNY Press, 1997).
8. Robert Barnes and Ann E. Marimow, "Supreme Court Leaves in Place Title 42 Border Policy for Now," *Washington Post*, December 27, 2022, https://www.washingtonpost.com/politics/2022/12/27/title-42-supreme-court-decision/.
9. Heschel, *God in Search of Man*, 3, italics his.
10. Paul Tillich, *Dynamics of Faith* (New York: Harper, 1957; First Perennial Classics 2001), 16.
11. Student, Introduction to Spirituality, College of St. Scholastica, 2022; shared by permission.
12. Ryan P. Burge, *The Nones: Where They Came From, Who They Are, and Where They Are Going* (Minneapolis: Fortress Press, 2021), 129.
13. Dietrich Bonhoeffer, "Holding Out until the Overthrow April to July 1944: To Eberhard Bethge [Tegel] 30 April 1944," in *Letters and Papers from Prison*, enlarged ed., ed. Eberhard Bethge (New York: Simon and Schuster, 1953, 1997), 279. Editor's note: "Dietrich Bonhoeffer was executed in the concentration camp at Flossenbürg on 9 April [1945]," 411.
14. See Helen T. Boursier, "The Necessity of Social Just-Ness as Ecclesial Praxis in a Postmodern Context," *Theology Today* 72, no. 1 (April 2015): 84–99.
15. Joan Chittister and Rowan Williams, *Uncommon Gratitude: Alleluia for All That Is* (Collegeville, MN: Liturgical Press, 2010), 6–9.
16. For example, see Peter Weber, "439 Texas Churches Split from United Methodist Church as Slow-motion Schism Continues," MSN News, December 5, 2022, https://www.msn.com/en-us/news/us/439-texas-churches-split-from-united-methodist-church-as-slow-motion-schism-continues/ar-AA14Vqws.
17. Cone is connecting the similarities and differences between the spirituals sung by enslaved Africans and later lyrics in the blues. James H. Cone, *The Spirituals and the Blues* (Maryknoll, NY: Orbis Books, 1972, 1991), 55.
18. Edith Wyschogrod, "Remaining Faithful: Postmodern Claims, Christian Messages," in *Gazing through a Prism Darkly: Reflections on Merold Westphal's Hermeneutical Epistemology*, Perspectives in Continental Philosophy, ed. B. Keith Putt (New York: Fordham University Press, 2009), 92.
19. Heschel, *God in Search of Man*, 56.
20. James L. Crenshaw, *Old Testament Wisdom: An Introduction* (Atlanta: John Knox Press, 1981), 192.
21. Dorothee Soelle, *The Mystery of Death* (Minneapolis: Fortress Press, 2007), 125.
22. Tillich, *Dynamics of Faith*, 133–134.
23. Weil, *Gravity and Grace*, 78.

24 Madeline Hilf conducted this interview as part of her academic project with Fordham University; shared by permission.
25 See Boursier, *Willful Ignorance*, 315–316.
26 A detained mother, "*Oramos*—We Pray," Art Inside Karnes, September 23, 2016.
27 Mara, stranded at the US-Mexico border while waiting for a court appointment to decide her case, December 4, 2019.
28 Jazmin, age thirteen, while staying with her family at a migrant shelter in Nuevo Laredo, Mexico, November 5, 2019.

CHAPTER TWO

Dissent

I found more bitter than death the woman who is a trap, whose heart is nets, whose hands are fetters; one who pleases God escapes her, but the sinner is taken by her.

—Ecclesiastes 7:26 (NRSVUE)

Ecclesiastes might seem like an unlikely conversation partner for a gender-justice-focused spirituality because, while it offers profound insights on the meaning of life, it also contains misogynistic elements, most notably its harsh indictment in Ecclesiastes 7:26–29 about a woman being "more bitter than death." In addition, written through the perspective of an affluent male in a dominant and patristic context that would equate today to a rich and powerful white male in the Global North, it's a notable absence that Ecclesiastes doesn't address the fourfold mandate so common elsewhere in the Hebrew Scriptures. The command "Do not oppress the widow or the orphan, the stranger or the poor" (Zech. 7:10 NASB) is reiterated in various forms throughout the Hebrew Bible and also in the Christian New Testament, but this focus is absent from Ecclesiastes. Instead, its content primarily addresses fancy first-world priorities about maintaining wealth and power. Despite these negative attributes, Ecclesiastes *is* an appropriate conversation partner because it's a canonized holy text that affirms absolute belief in God while also questioning and challenging the standard or stereotypical principles of its day, particularly surrounding fairness, equity, and justice. Though its focus is on an affluent context, this sacred text models a methodology that engenders the possibility to redeem even its own misogynistic and exclusionary fallacies as Ecclesiastes pushes its readers off center to think more *third-dimensionally*, to use a phrase from the *Back to the Future* science-fiction movie trilogy, about what's fair, equitable, and just.[1] This consistent push to dissent with current norms or standards is its *hermeneutical* or interpretive strength for a *spirituality of dissent* in the borderlands.

THE NATURE OF WISDOM

Wisdom in all its forms is a reflective genre that weighs the pros and cons, carefully considering the various elements before making a thoughtful and carefully formulated response. It's the extreme opposite of contemporary social media platforms like Facebook, YouTube, Instagram, TikTok, and Twitter, where it's more normative to crank something out for the public without doing any background reading, independent research, or reflective thought. Social media adherents too often spontaneously upload pictures, videos, online links, and quick commentary, as these quickly move forth unchecked into the World Wide Web of cyberspace. I am guilty of doing likewise.

The wisdom genre functions exactly the opposite of this social media spontaneity. Wisdom carefully, thoughtfully, and responsibly searches for meaning. It assumes that there's an order in the apparent (dis)order because, if God laid down a natural order, then there also must be a moral order that God established during creation. Wisdom deals with the world as humans observe it, from the ground up. Wisdom has a much broader meaning in the biblical text than how the contemporary world understands it. Biblical wisdom is earthy and practical. It deals with concrete phenomena in everyday life. It makes distinctions between something that's a philosophical ideal compared with an actual fact of life as it really is. It also lets nature give witness to the realities of life, with examples in the natural world often holding equal value to observations of or about humans.

Spirituality of Dissent

Using the radicalized interpretation style of Ecclesiastes that questions hierarchical norms, a spirituality of dissent examines life through a *hermeneutic of suspicion*, a term feminists adopted from liberation theologians as a method of interpretation to examine sacred scriptures through a lens or perspective of suspicion to probe, question, and render a gender-inclusive alternative regarding how a sacred text has been received, interpreted, and applied. This new interpretation disagrees, destabilizes, or *dissents* from a received or inherited perspective, just as the wisdom of dissent in Ecclesiastes subverts the conventional wisdom of its day. What professor of Bible and religious studies Douglas Miller describes as *destabilization* in *Symbol and Rhetoric in Ecclesiastes*, which then seeks to offer *restabilization* that serves as a reality check for what actually is occurring.[2] In particular for this conversation, feminists use this process to deconstruct and challenge antiquated views enmeshed in colonialism and patriarchy.

Despite its elements of misogyny and inattention to the marginalized of its day, Ecclesiastes models this wisdom of dissent, which means it gives a dissenting opinion or differing perspective to explain injustice at the edges, calling out exceptions to the standard or normative rule. While conventional wisdom says you *can know*, a wisdom of dissent says this is *not necessarily so*. Wisdom of dissent challenges an inherited norm, including a dominant perspective about the rule of law in the borderlands, as it considers the exceptions to a rule, norm, or prevailing worldview. Dissent also examines the details, including the silenced voices of marginalized people who suffer when bad things happen due to intentional or unintentional evil from the natural or human world.

Wisdom of dissent is directly relevant to spirituality in the borderlands, where it challenges conventional wisdom, the rule of law, and societal norms. Displaced migrant families are living and breathing exceptions to the normative rules-based wisdom of this day, and their voices often are externally silenced so their witness remains unacknowledged and unheard. Throughout this dissenting perspective, Ecclesiastes, and many of the families, steadfastly affirms that God is in control, even though it's impossible to know who, what, when, where, or how God will ultimately dispense justice, paralleling a spirituality of borders that also trusts the ultimate *justness of God*.[3] Similarly, many of the volunteers and advocates affirm belief in God, not necessarily a churchy or religious god but a Supreme Something that imbues a moral calling to justice. Conventional wisdom affirms it's possible to learn and discern best practices, right action, and what's good and true and just. Wisdom of dissent insists each person has to be ready, willing, and open to wanting to learn or wanting to gain true wisdom.

"Softmindedness"

Lazily going with the flow and not seeking to become personally educated or enlightened about injustice is a common malady, what Martin Luther King

Jr. terms *softmindedness* because, King says, "nothing pains some people more than having to think."[4] Softmindedness applies to spirituality in the borderlands because it requires intentionality, effort, and what MLK calls "the toughness of mind to judge critically and to discern the true from the false, the fact from the fiction."[5] Paralleling dissent in the borderlands, King's connection to racism specifies, "Softmindedness is one of the basic causes of race prejudice. The toughminded person always examines the facts [first, before reaching any] conclusions," waiting to judge afterward. King continues, "The tenderminded person reaches a conclusion before [examining] the first fact." They *prejudge*, which makes them *prejudice*, what MLK applies to race, where "prejudice is based on groundless fears, suspicions, and misunderstandings."[6] King believes "there is little hope for us until we become toughminded enough to break loose from the shackles of prejudice, half-truths, and downright ignorance."[7] Embracing a wisdom of dissent to challenge and change injustice in the borderlands isn't automatic. It isn't a given. It requires interest, openness, effort, and desire. It's challenging this unjust status quo, which contributes to spirituality in the borderlands.

Challenging the Shoulds

Wisdom literature acknowledges tension exists between what someone thinks *should* happen in life compared with what actually occurs. Idealism about what *should be* is not necessarily incorrect or invalid, but it presupposes that my view *should be* God's view, our timing *should be* God's timing, and the humanmade rule of law is also God's, which is something the evangelical right consistently claims when imposing its political position based on its often misplaced and erroneous *biblical view*. A wisdom of dissent questions, examines challenges, and offers an alternative narrative to these *shoulds*. Ecclesiastes is comfortable acknowledging that the human view from below the dome of heaven has significant limitations compared with what God's view would be from outside the dome of heaven looking down toward the created order. Humans are *down here*, and God's view is much more expansive and inclusive *up there*. Explaining the significance of Ecclesiastes for contemporary readers, J. A. Loader notes this book "demonstrates how dangerous such self-sufficient [religious] systems are. From this point theology has much to learn. When all the answers can be so easily given, when all is cut-and-dried and people think they have enclosed God within a foolproof system, reaction is inevitable."[8] The same concept applies to the humanmade rule of law in the borderlands.

Instead of holding God "prisoner" to "fixed patterns, however pious they may be," Ecclesiastes dissents from the norm and offers an alternative view. Theologian James Loder argues, "When theology [or the contemporary rule of law] presents itself to the world with too much self-confidence, and the church has lost the ability to listen to others and just listens to itself, then an unsparing reaction of rejection is bound to come."[9] Loder's warning intersects with the increasing number of those who choose to disaffiliate from religion. Wisdom literature in general, and Ecclesiastes in particular, challenges this notion of shoving God into a neat and tidy box, preferably with the lid tightly closed, so human ideologies prevail over the much larger wisdom and vision of The God. Instead, Ecclesiastes, along with a spirituality of borders, dissents from a picture-perfect idealized view, offering an important reality check that bad things do happen to good people and vice versa.

A key difference between a wisdom of dissent and conventional wisdom includes the ability to have certain knowledge that's definitively absolute and broadly applicable to everyone everywhere—a modern view. Instead, a wisdom of dissent, like the postmodern perspective explained earlier, says it's impossible to know for certain, partly because it's impossible to know the timing or the exact judgment of something because these belong to God alone. It's not that justice fails to occur; it's that each human being has a very limited and often biased viewpoint. No human being can possibly know or understand God's timing or God's methods. Meanwhile, the wisdom of dissent offers a dissenting perspective on what could and should be an ethical and just response. It's not so much an impatient insertion for action while interminably waiting for God's ultimate justice to prevail. Rather, dissenting observations engender a reflective and pragmatic response during the unknown in-between time before God's justice ultimately prevails. Wisdom of dissent affirms bad stuff does happen to good people, but it also follows with "Now what is mine to do?"

RACIAL AND GENDER INJUSTICE EXACERBATES PARADOX IN THE BORDERLANDS

Ecclesiastes only seems interested in those who are poor as a comparative analysis with those who are not poor (4:1–3). So, while this wisdom literature dissents with the conventional norms of its day, it silences or skips how these insights impact the marginalized and oppressed groups in the same contexts.

Highlighting the paradox of such an omission in her essay "The Personal Is Political," Sheila Collins proposes, "Racism, sexism, class exploitation, and ecological destruction are four interlocking pillars upon which the structure of the patriarchy rests. The structures of oppression are everywhere the same, although the particular forms in which oppression is manifested may at first glance look different."[10] These patristic categories of oppression are preeminently relevant in the paradoxes around injustice, particularly for spirituality in the borderlands. Most of the displaced migrants who are seeking admittance through the US-Mexico border are Black and brown, many of them females traveling with young children. These families are often forced to migrate due to "natural disasters" related to environmental or patristic policies that harm the marginalized. Many of these displaced families have been oppressed, pushed into the margins of their homelands for the duration of their lifetime through systemic domination due to their gender, race, and/or religion.

With its focus on those who are powerful and affluent, Ecclesiastes laments that when "eaters" come to eat off of the affluent, the more likely there will be a feeding frenzy (Ecc. 2:18, 5:11). Ecclesiastes doesn't question or challenge what this might look like for oppressed groups. Ecclesiastes simply presumes injustice against those who are poor is a given fact of life (4:1–3). In this ancient scripture, oppressed groups just *are*. Dissent begins with *de*stabilization of the existing/inherited scriptural interpretation and/or rule of law with their preconditioned and predetermined perspective. A wisdom of dissent is forthright in its witness in solidarity with the displaced families, acknowledging and objecting to the oppressive strangers—gang members or government officials who take all the families have, leaving them desperate, homeless, and broke (Ecc. 6:2). The families frequently lament that the money they earn to provide a safe life for their children in their homelands makes them become prey for the gangs who extort money from them in exchange for not forcing a son to join a gang or for not raping a daughter. Once their funds have been extorted down to nothing, the families feel their only recourse is to leave their country to seek safety elsewhere.

Just as Ecclesiastes dismisses gender in/justice connections, in *See No Stranger*, founder of the Revolutionary Love Project, activist, attorney, educator, and faith leader Valarie Kaur points out, "Dr. King named three evils—racism, poverty, and militarism. But he left out a fourth—sexism. The assumption that women and girls are less than equal and therefore deserve less dignity and freedom is perhaps the most ancient, pervasive, and insidious evil of them all."[11] Dissent adds the gender-based marginalization and racial injustice that exacerbate suffering as this wisdom genre provides the missed contexts to destabilize and then restabilize to foster a spirituality for justice and peacemaking in the borderlands. Raced persons bear the brunt of the wealth-related disparities that generate injustice, but gender also factors in to exacerbate inequity.

GENDER IN/EQUITY AND IN/JUSTICE

American mythology presupposes that everyone is equal in this country, even though that's never been even remotely the reality since 1492, when Columbus sailed the ocean blue and supposedly "discovered" a new land, and this nation's sordid legacy of racism began. Nor has equality ever been true for any person of color. Women in America also have never ever had equal rights, including the basic human right to make choices about their own bodies, self-evident when the Supreme Court reversed *Roe v. Wade* on June 24, 2022. In *Down Girl: The Logic of Misogyny*, Kate Manne aptly notes that it's not so much that things are "*not* equal; indeed, it may be as unequal as can be."[12] The players move around a bit on the playing field / game board as one moves higher up the food chain toward affluence and a *better life*, but gender and race remain the dominant anti-equality factors.

While raced women are the recipients of the worst gender inequity in the hierarchy of wealth paradox, Rosemary Radford Ruether, in *Sexism and God-Talk: Toward a Feminist Theology*, cynically summarizes how male dominance turns affluent women into shallow bobblehead trophy wives while trapping working women in a lifetime of servitude. Ruether is well respected for her first-wave feminist argument on the connections between male domination that begins with controlling the womb, which "means the subjugation of her person," and then moves to exploiting her labor. Ruether specifies:

> Her labor belongs to him. To labor from dawn to after dusk in his household is her purpose for existence. She has no need to read and write, no need to learn, to travel, to dream. Her sphere is defined, confined; she must not stray from it. Each generation of daughters must have its wings clipped early to be fed back into the treadmill.... He is known at the gates. She is not to be known in public. She is to remain invisible. When he returns in the evening, his food shall be ready, his clothes in order, his couch prepared. In this way her history is stolen

PRECIOUS PRECARITY

Illustration 2.1 *#NIUNAMENOS* 12" × 12" mixed-media portrait of a mother and her two daughters shortly after they were released from GEO Karnes on December 19, 2014, where they were detained for three months before being granted government permission to pursue their claim for asylum in the United States.

from her. It is said that she did nothing. It is his achievements that we read about in books; his laws, his wars, his power, his mayhem. He is the achiever, carried about on the backs of the laborers. The laborers who carry him have done nothing; they are invisible, silent. No scrolls testify to their experience. No monuments mark the places of their sufferings and deaths. Their laboring hands and backs hold him to the light of history, and they sink down into the dark earth again.[13]

It's all about *him*, and she and the children are to remain silent, forever in the man's subservient shadow and at the man's mercy until the male children grow to manhood and repeat the insidious cycle.

Clearly, there's a strong intersection with gender injustice and the females who are fleeing their homelands where patriarchy is alive and well and machismo is the masculinity rule of law.[14] Paradox and wealth also impact women of means. Ruether specifies:

> Woman, the nonachiever, becomes woman the nonworker, the ornament of conspicuous consumption, the object of pride of ownership and economic prowess. Her furs testify to her husband's success. She adorns his household, displaying dainty feet that cannot walk, polished nails that cannot work. The pinnacle of his success is to no longer need to work, to possess her only as a toy and a plaything. Black women, brown women, immigrant women toil silently in the background, supporting the display, polishing the cage of the songbird. The wife herself must conceal the signs of her own toil, ease the lines of suffering from her face, the marks of labor from her hands, keep up appearances. Women are set at enmity with each other while collaborating in his service.[15]

Ruether's *Pretty Woman* image of the subjugated affluent trophy wife intersects with spirituality at the border because this cynical shallowness about American life is what volunteers and advocates, male and female, refute through their words and deeds.[16] They want something more meaningful in life than the silly shallowness and superficiality of Ruether's description.

DESTABILIZATION: FEMINIST MIDRASH CHALLENGES MISOGYNY IN ECCLESIASTES

Jewish feminists adapted midrash as their methodology to bring in the witness of female voices that were silent or altogether absent, destabilizing sacred texts from their patristic view and women's marginality by imagining the silenced voices and missing witness of women, and then restabilizing these same texts so they have relevance for present generations.[17] One of the earliest proponents of midrash, Jewish feminist Judith Plaskow, explains:

> The open-ended process of writing midrash—simultaneously serious and playful, imaginative, metaphoric—has easily lent itself to feminist use. Feminist midrash shares the uncomfortable self-consciousness of modern religious experimentation: elaborating on the stories of Eve [Gen. 4:1–2] or Dina [Gen. 30:21], we know the text is partly an occasion for our own projections, that our imaginative reconstructions are a reflection of our own beliefs and experiences. But if its self-consciousness is modern, the root conviction of feminist midrash is utterly traditional. It stands on the rabbinic insistence that the Bible can be made to

speak to the present day. If it is our text, it can and must answer our questions and share our values; if we wrestle with it, we wait for the words of women "to rise out of the white spaces between the letters in the Torah" as we remember and transmit the past through "the experience of our own lives."[18]

Explaining why she engages midrash, Rabbi Sandy Eisenberg Sasso notes, "We are responsible for the stories we tell and for those we choose not to tell. Our silences speak volumes about whom and what we value."[19] She emphasizes the importance of asking, "What of the stories we have chosen not to tell? What of those struggles that take place at the foot of the mountain, by the well, on the side of the river with Rachel and Leah?"[20] She uplifts these two classic examples from the Hebrew Bible (Gen. 29:16–20), which easily compare with migrant women and children who are traveling through the mountains in Mexico during the arduous overland journey to reach the Rio Grande River and the US-Mexico borderlands. Plaskow points out "the great silence that has shrouded women's history testifies not to women's lack of historical agency but to the androcentric bias that has shaped historical writing. . . . They have made gender a central category of historical analysis, seeing it not just as a biological given, but as itself subject to historical development and change."[21] The work behind reclaiming the words and witness of women in the sacred texts parallels a similar need to hear the voices of the families. Uplifting these displaced migrant families, particularly women and children who flee for their lives, is a vehicle to dissent to the injustice and silence surrounding their circumstances. It also contributes to giving a place and space for the voices, actions, and witness of women in the present and future.

Whose are the missing voices, and what would they say if they could join us in conversation, witness, and action today? It's urgently necessary to ask what the silences are saying, or not saying, but also, as Maria Harris asks in *Dance of the Spirit*, "What are those who are silent *doing*, and what has caused their lives to be shaped in this way?"[22] One of the earliest and most valued tenets of feminist theory has been to identify missing voices and then listen into that void. The more normative voices loudly speaking from the patristic past in the present are the white male voices of privilege, which makes their "objective" perspective significantly warped and one-sided from a tiny peephole-sized and very skewed view that can't and doesn't represent reality for the rest of the world, particularly for the missing and silent females and marginalized minorities.[23]

Midrash and Ecclesiastes

In her article "'And I Find a Wife More Bitter Than Death' (Eccl. 7:26): Feminist Hermeneutics, Women Midrashim, and the Boundaries of Acceptance in Modern Orthodox Judaism" in the *Journal of Feminist Studies in Religion*, Ronit Irshai considers how midrash creates a behind-the-scenes feminist perspective to dissent the patriarchally rendered "bitchiness" of the woman who Ecclesiastes laments is "more bitter than death" (Ecc. 7:26), offering an alternative view of why a wife might act uncharitably toward her husband. A midrashic storytelling includes examples of when the husband said he was going to do one thing, like come home early for supper, only to do the exact opposite and come home late. Or when he asks his wife to prepare a huge meal for a large group of cohorts that he said he'd bring home for dinner, which she does, but then he shows up by himself. Other times, he doesn't warn her that he'll be bringing colleagues home for dinner and then unexpectedly shows up with a houseful of people, but of course there isn't enough food prepared since the wife had no advance notice. The midrash continues that when the husband "knows that his wife has cooked peas, he [purposely] asks for lentils and when she has cooked lentils, he [intentionally] asks for peas. So, she remains silent and says nothing to him, but she gives him [not what he requested], but what she has already prepared in her pot."[24] Of course, the husband in the midrash then complains, as in Ecclesiastes, that a woman "is more bitter than death," a biased perspective that fails to include the reality behind the criticism. The midrash intentionally dissents with the sacred scripture by shifting the emphasis from the "woe is me" husband toward the lack of appreciation and respect for his wife. Through midrash, the wife's response is exonerated and justified, shifting the negative gaze from the wife to the husband.

Midrash and Migrant Mothers

Similarly, through words and actions, the families and the volunteers and advocates who assist them offer their dissent to the conventional rule-of-law wisdom that says what a woman should or shouldn't be or do, including how this conventional view denigrates her role and responsibility for protecting herself and her children. Midrash is an excellent newer tool for education and advocacy in response to what feminists have long lamented: the lifelong patriarchal abuse, misuse, and dismissal of women as being secondary to males, what Simone de Beauvoir famously argues in *The Second Sex*.[25] In the context of the displaced migrant mothers, once a woman reaches a strong enough cognitive dissonance between the harsh reality of her life and that which her faith-based spirituality propels her to see as the possible actualized reality, she says, "Done! I'm outta here." Her spirituality of dissent informs, compels, and then propels her from *un*safety and oppression toward, hopefully, a *better life* for herself and her children. In the context of the displaced families, *better life* is a technical term for a *safe life*.

The witness of the migrant mothers resonates exactly with Irshai's midrash of Ecclesiastes, giving voice to the abuse women experience who've been mistreated and/or silenced until the wife says she's endured enough suffering. For instance, Maria, fifty-nine, from Honduras exclaimed, "I did not care for my husband. He insulted me. He pushed me. He hit me. He threw plates of food at me. He got angry when I went to church on Sundays. He mocked me in front of the pastor. I had enough!"[26] Through her gutsy and faith-based actions of fleeing immanent death in her homeland to seek life with her children in a safe country, each migrant mother challenges what Judith Butler terms the "regulatory norm" of gender. The abused wife and/or mother doesn't have to remain stuck, oppressed, and fearing life for herself and her children. Through her dissenting actions and flight for life, she joins, consciously or unconsciously, the feminist movement for what Butler calls "the social transformation of gender relations."[27] Their dissent to injustice becomes a prayer, a plea, and a demand for justice in the receiving nation. Although Ruether notes that "much of the strongest feminist consciousness arises not in teenagers or young adults but in older women who have already played out these roles and learned their hollowness," in the case of the women in flight from violence who are seeking asylum in this country, many of these families traveling to the borderlands are young mothers toting young children.[28] The violence in their homes and homeland forces the issue.[29] They can't stay, so they follow their faith vision and deep spiritual conviction that there's a possibility for life if they physically dissent and make their pilgrimage to the promised land.

DESTABILIZATION: DISSENT OF THE FAMILIES AT THE BORDER

The mothers fleeing violence and seeking protection for their children enact their dissent *from* suffering *for* life. Their radical break from oppression becomes their *de*stabilization of conventional wisdom, which forms and informs their spirituality of dissent. For example, a migrant mother shared:

> I am a twenty-four-year-old woman who is tired of being beaten and mistreated by my husband. We are no longer friends. I am very, very afraid to go back to his house because one day he threatened me that if I reported him to the police then he would kill me. I wanted to file a complaint, so I prayed and prayed that one day God was going to let me leave my country, Honduras. Then I would be safe to file my complaint. Then I would be far, far away so he could never bully or mistreat me again.
>
> I asked my God to get me to the United States so that I could be happy for the remaining years of my life. I never want to be mistreated again. I also want my son to be able to study. I want my neighbors to be happy. I want God to be happy.
>
> I could not pass immigration, so we are stranded here in this shelter in Nuevo Laredo. I continue to suffer. I am a suffering woman.[30]

Gender-based violence is a very common theme that the mothers, in particular, are dissenting against. They could remain in their home and homelands and "put up with it" until they come to an early death, or they can be proactive and seek protection elsewhere. These mothers enact their physical and spiritual flight of dissent to protest the lethal misogynistic abuse in their homeland. It's their human right and gender-based necessity for survival, whether or not others agree with or support their decision. Black lesbian feminist Audre Lorde insists, "No woman is responsible for altering the psyche of her oppressor, even when that psyche is embodied in another woman."[31] It's not any woman's job to suck it up and tough it out until she (quickly) comes to an untimely early death. Each woman has the right and the responsibility to say, "*Ya!* [Enough!] It's time to go." It's her physical dissent that moves each woman forth, relying on her internal spiritual strength. A mother from El Salvador explained:

> For many years, I suffered domestic violence from my husband. I could not cope with all the mistreatment, the physical, emotional, and spiritual abuse. He also stole the money I had for food for our children. He used it to buy drugs and get high. I finally left him—but even after three

years of being separated, he continued to stalk me. When I returned from work one day, at four o'clock in the afternoon, he was waiting for me. He had broken into the house. He threatened to kill me if I did not come back to him. The police took him away, and he went to jail, but already he has been released, and he is again looking for me.

I prayed to God to give me someone to help me leave the neighborhood. I thought I did not have a friend in the world who would risk their life for me, but God sent me a protector to help me and my son. We stayed with this person for three months while I raised the funds to leave my country. I had to sell everything I owned.

I am afraid. My ex is out of jail and looking for me. I managed to get to the US-Mexico border, but they said they will not let us enter. We have to wait for the court appointment they gave us. It is months away.

Please help me. I give thanks to God for sending me to this shelter and for the people who are helping me to keep my son safe. This is the short story of my life. I give God thanks. May God bless you greatly. God bless me. God keep us safe.[32]

Their enacted spirituality of dissent is intricately interwoven with their steadfast faith that God is present in, around, and through every aspect of their lives. They are dissenting the human-inflicted suffering while also maintaining their absolute faith in the presence and providence of God. A mother from Honduras explained:

My father started sexually abusing me when I was fifteen. One day I said, "Enough!" I left. But it became worse because my partner abused me. When I became pregnant, he immediately started hitting me and saying that the child was not his. [Her wounded expression and the shrug of her shoulders said, "Of course it's his!"] I endured his abuse for six months. He threatened to kill me if I reported him. I took my son, Don, and left. I walk without documents because everything was stolen from me: clothes, papers, everything. But I thank God that my son and I are fine.[33]

Yes, the perception of the world, particularly those living comfortable "normal" lives in affluent countries who've never experienced anything even remotely as horrific as the injustices meted against the families, is that these foreigners are coming to the United States for that so-called *better life*. However, the catalyst and spiritual motivation guiding their actions are a spirituality of dissent against the violence in their homelands. God is their compass and constant companion along their journey. Their dissent through exodus, grounded in their steadfast trust in the care and compassion of the God they love, intersects in the borderlands with *restabilization* through the dissent of the volunteers who assist them.

RESTABILIZATION: DISSENT OF THE VOLUNTEERS

Then I looked again at all the acts of oppression which were being done under the sun. And behold, I saw the tears of the oppressed and that they had no one to comfort them; and power was on the side of their oppressors, but they had no one to comfort them.

—Ecclesiastes 4:1 (NASB)

Whereas the fleeing families enact their dissent through leaving their homelands and seeking protection in another country, the volunteers and advocates express their dissent through welcoming these displaced migrants with practical assistance. There are various rationales behind their spirituality of dissent, which intersect with timing (chapter 6), chance (chapter 5), willingness to embrace risk (chapter 8), and the sense of joy (chapter 11), that contribute to their spirituality being holy and whole (conclusion). Their individual and collective *restabilization* through dissent to anti-immigrant nationalism often is faith-based and spiritually grounded, though many have stepped aside from any formal religious participation. Their spirituality can be implicit or explicit, but the commonality among volunteers and advocates, including the few who are still actively engaged in a local religious institution and the majority who self-identify as "spiritual but not religious," "stepped aside and disengaged," or "nones" is their insistence that their volunteer work with displaced migrants is their moral, ethical, and faithful global citizenship response to offer compassion to the displaced migrants who pass through their communities in the borderlands.

The volunteers' and advocates' experientially based observations about the reality of the suffering and injustice that oozes through the borderlands also serve as a paradox (chapter 3) to the conventional wisdom surrounding current rule of law that fosters exclusionary policies, practices, and bad attitudes against the families. In the spirit of Ecclesiastes, spirituality in the borderlands embraces what biblical scholar Lisa Michele Wolfe describes as "rigorous questioning of traditional views."³⁴ Through doing and being present in solidarity, volunteers and advocates discover spirituality outside of the confinements of this nation's dominant anti-immigrant view, embracing an informed perception through experiential solidarity with the families. It's a spirituality that sees the paradoxes between idealized America and the truths that the advocates for peace and justice witness in the borderlands.

As a volunteer who regularly visits Piedras Negras, Mexico, said when she was questioned/challenged by fellow Texans for helping migrants:

> I told them, "I believe there's some screening that needs to be done. We don't need to let murderers coming in. We don't need to let in pedophiles, that kind of thing. There's some screening that needs to be done [which there is]. But I want to tell you," this group I was talking to I said, "if I was a mother down there, and I thought I could provide a better life for my children, I'd be up over my ears in water [Rio Grande River]. I'd come across that river," and that's the way I still feel today.

She said she wants to help people have a better life, and it "just warms my heart to do that." She also believes helping in the borderlands is a mission God gave her.

Dissenting from Religious Silence

Intersecting with cynicism and the postmodern condition explained in the previous chapter, some of the volunteers and advocates are dissenting to religion's lack of presence and compassionate response. A clergy colleague spoke about a journalist who conducted some random Q&A "people on the street" interviews with people who self-identified as attending a Christian church. The reporter asked what these churchgoers thought the Bible would say about welcoming neighbors. The pastor explained, "A little old church lady said, 'Jesus said to welcome the legal neighbor.'" This pastor, who led her congregation at the time to becoming a Sanctuary Church that hosted migrant families when they were attempting to be reunited with their families following the family separation fiasco of 2018, observed, "Pastors have failed to proclaim the gospel, and this woman, a lifetime Christian who literally could have been a member at multiple churches, is the 'fruit' of that failure to preach the gospel."³⁵ In particular, the *non*response of Christians and the Christian church informs and shapes a spirituality of dissent in the borderlands that expects eventual accountability.³⁶

A volunteer who, after a lifetime of active church membership but who recently had stepped aside and stopped participating in a congregation, said that although her family is no longer active in a church, they firmly believe there will be accountability for the mistreatment of migrants. The volunteer said it won't likely be in this lifetime, but the same certainty the families have that God has a plan for their lives overflows to the people who assist them with their firm and certain belief that, eventually, there will be accountability for any mistreatment of these displaced migrants. Meanwhile, volunteers and advocates dissent to the present injustice that's been formed and informed by the prevailing rule of law in America as they show up with compassion, love, solidarity, and practical assistance in the borderlands.

Their dissent also stands against anti-immigrant public rhetoric. Volunteers and advocates don't feel threatened by difference. They also acknowledge the connection between the injustices and mistreatment of all people of color and the exclusionary policies and practices at the border. By choosing to be present in solidarity with displaced migrants, dissent in the borderlands challenges the longtime historical connection between racism and exclusion from asylum, embodying Lorde's argument that "by ignoring the past, we are encouraged to repeat its mistakes."[37] Spirituality in the borderlands chooses not to ignore the differences generated by race and social context, affirming Lorde's point that "refusing to recognize difference makes it impossible to see the different problems and pitfalls facing us as women."[38] As womanist Diana L. Hayes insists in *No Crystal Stair: Womanist Spirituality*, "Difference is not dangerous; it is of God. Difference has been divinely sanctioned in the act of creation. It is our responsibility, as sharers in that creation, to turn away from divisiveness and move toward community."[39] Difference is an elemental aspect of being human. Difference is also part of the sacred signature of God, who rested on the seventh day after declaring that what God had created was *very good* (Gen. 1:31). God said *all* of creation is very good. Difference isn't scary. Difference is holy, sacred, and blessed by God (Gen. 1:28).

Voice of Conscience

Many of these people responding with compassion are living, working, and sharing the same overlapping spaces where the borderlands merge in the ebb and flow of what once was a much more fluid space. A volunteer who lives in southern Arizona and helps with searches in remote sections of the Sonoran Desert said, "What do you do when somebody dies in your neighborhood?

For us, we have decided we want to be present."[40] Their dissent moves forth from what Martin Heidegger would call the "voice of conscience."[41] In his well-known *Being and Time*, he argues that the essence of being is to be present with care and concern for the others around us. He believes the conscience is the essence of each person's core sense of self and being and that this then *discloses* the real essence or importance of what it means to be alive. Conscience informs dissent through words and deeds.

When conscience intersects with the vulnerability and suffering of those around us, then it becomes possible to truly be in this world through actions of care and concern. Heidegger would say it's this essence of being true that calls someone to dissent as conscience discloses the possibilities for "Being-in-the-world."[42] The reality of dissent cannot be understood merely through words or theoretical ideals but also through actions. As Rabbi Heschel explains regarding Jewish spirituality, which is the scriptural context for Ecclesiastes, "The world needs more than the secret holiness of individual inwardness. It needs more than sacred sentiments and good intentions. God asks for the heart because [God] needs the lives. It is by the lives that the world will be redeemed, by lives that beat in concordance with God, by deeds that outbeat the finite charity of the human heart."[43] Rabbi Heschel adds, "God asks for the heart, and we must spell our answer in terms of deeds."[44] Dissenting to the injustice of anti-immigrant rhetoric, the spirituality in the borderlands affirms that doing shows the reality of who and what each person believes. It's enacted spirituality with or without any sense of religion, whether or not it's named as such. Dissenting against a misplaced current rule of law in the borderlands, volunteers would affirm with Rabbi Heschel, "The worth of religion is the worth of the individuals living it."[45] In other words, for someone who professes faith in God, in whatever religious context that may take, they need to "put up or shut up." True faith requires each person to put up their profession of faith through embodied actions of compassion, love, and justice.[46] Silence and adherence to injustice equate to reinforcing the rule of law status quo. Instead, a spirituality of dissent looks at the particularities of injustice, literally face to face with displaced migrants in the borderlands.

Differing Forms of Dissent in the Borderlands

Dissent takes many forms in the borderlands, ranging from low-key entry-level types of response that people with a marginal interest of mild curiosity could easily and comfortably engage, to ones that require more time, energy, resources, and spiritually intense activities that press more rigorously against hostile anti-immigrant views. For some, dissent is physically showing up to be present with the families in the borderlands, at a migrant shelter in Mexico, at a bus station in an interior gateway city like San Antonio or Tucson, as part of a search party to locate lost or stranded migrants in the Sonoran Desert, or by participating in a Sanctuary community in cities across the United States.[47] For other volunteers, their spirituality of dissent is enacted through writing, public speaking, music, art, or generating historical records to document the suffering and injustice of migrants. As an advocate in southern Arizona said, "The oppressors must be held accountable to remind them of the injustice. It's about bearing witness so the world hears the cries and the oppressors can be held accountable. Power and privilege have always been used to harm the families, not just today, but through the centuries."[48] The written, spoken, and visual dissents are the enactment of spirituality in the borderlands to hold the oppressors accountable and to set the families free from injustice (Isa. 61:1).

In whatever form the practical actions take, volunteers and advocates give tangible expression through their spirituality of dissent. The interactions among volunteers and migrants in borderland spaces reinforce a spirituality of dissent because being in close proximity to people who have suffered, are suffering, and will continue to suffer exemplifies the point Lorde makes in her essay "Age, Race, Class, and Sex: Women Redefining Difference," in *Sister Outsider*, what she calls a truism that "unless one lives and loves in the trenches it is difficult to remember that the war against dehumanization is ceaseless."[49] A core member of Team Brownsville said, "Hopefully when people come here to volunteer with us, they get more than just learning the facts, which of course are horrible, in terms of the hardships of the people who come here to request asylum. I hope they also get a sense of their own capacity to be compassionate and to help, and not just see the suffering of migrants as some factually based thing, but as a larger call to treat people in a decent way. If you just look at the facts and stop there, people get discouraged. They won't do anything." The volunteer added that it takes some spiritual growth to connect a short-term border volunteer experience to the bigger realities that propel the families to leave their homelands and seek protection elsewhere.

Whether one-time, part-time, or a regular presence with the families, dissent looks beyond the "facts" of immigration and sees the humanity of the people, which provides a window for the particularities of each migrant's experience to begin to be taken into consideration with the larger issues at stake and the interconnectedness of the global human family, a point Martin Luther King Jr. consistently emphasized in his preaching and speaking. As one of my spirituality students noted, MLK spoke about the role of seeing humanity in others, and he saw the lack of seeing this humanity as a reason people fail to be good neighbors and instead allow injustice to occur. It's through disregarding or *not seeing* the true humanity in others that self-centered individuals disregard the reality that all human beings are interconnected and related as one human family.[50] This sense of shared humanity reminds each person to reflect on their interrelatedness as one species.

Though not necessarily named as such by every volunteer or advocate, their decision to consistently make time to be present with the families is a spiritual choice that informs their way of life. Volunteering with the families isn't merely what they do; it's who they are. It's a spirituality that embraces three essential components that comprise a sacred holiness, including what the volunteers and advocates see and feel, and then making choices based on their seeing and feeling.[51] Their actions embrace the sacred humanity in the borderlands.

Loder sees this holiness as occurring in transforming moments at the intersections of what's empty or missing, a "void."[52] With spirituality in the borderlands, this sacredness occurs at the tangible intersections of experience together with the various people who move through the borderlands. It's never just *my* personal experience; it is always *ours*. In the *Spirituality of Imperfection: Storytelling and the Search for Meaning*, Ernest Kurtz and Katherine Ketcham explain, "Spirituality points, always beyond: *beyond* the ordinary, *beyond* possession, *beyond* the narrow confines of the self, and—above all—*beyond* expectation. Because 'the spiritual' is beyond our control, it is never exactly what we expect."[53] A spirituality that imbues discontent with paradoxical injustice moves beyond selfish self-centeredness to informed actions of compassion with the families.

STEPPING ASIDE FROM SELF

In *Love in the Void: Where God Finds Us*, French philosopher and mystic Simone Weil insists that part of stepping aside from the self, an important component of a spirituality of dissent, requires letting go of "our imaginary position as the center, to renounce it, not only intellectually but in the imaginative part of our soul, that means to awake to what is real and eternal, to see the true light and hear the true silence."[54] Weil adds, "The face of this love, which is turned toward thinking persons, is the love of our neighbor; the face turned toward matter is love of the order of the world, or love of the beauty of the world, which is the same thing."[55] It's only by letting go of an arrogant sense of self-importance, which cannot be defined or described using any complimentary language, that it becomes possible to recognize the paradoxical vain foolishness and vanity of the happily-ever-after affluent host nation and the struggling-for-bare-life migrant other. *A spirituality of dissent* embraces letting go of this unrealistic and imaginary self-importance to see, feel, and experience love. *A spirituality of borders* also notices, acknowledges, and is shaped by paradox in the borderlands.

NOTES

1. See Robert Zemeckis, director, *Back to the Future* (Universal City, CA: MCA Home Video, 1985).
2. Douglas B. Miller, *Symbol and Rhetoric in Ecclesiastes: The Place of Hebel in Qohelet's Work* (Atlanta: The Society of Biblical Literature, 2002), 164–166.
3. See Helen T. Boursier, "Faithful Doxology: The Church's Allyship with Immigrants Seeking Asylum," *International Bulletin of Mission Journal* 41, no. 2 (April 2017): 170–177. https://doi.org/10.1177/2396939317693716.
4. Martin Luther King Jr., *Strength to Love* (Philadelphia: Fortress Press, 1963), 14.
5. King Jr. *Strength to Love*, 14.
6. King Jr. *Strength to Love*, 16.
7. King Jr. *Strength to Love*, 17.
8. J. A. Loader, *Ecclesiastes: A Practical Commentary*, trans. John Vriend (Grand Rapids, MI: William B. Eerdmans Publishing Company, 1986), 15.
9. Loader, *Ecclesiastes*, 15.
10. Sheila D. Collins, "The Personal Is Political," in *The Politics of Women's Spirituality: Essays on the Rise of Spiritual Power within the Feminist Movement*, ed. Charlene Spretnak (Garden City, NY: Anchor Books, 1982), 362–367, 363.
11. Valarie Kaur, *See No Stranger: A Memoir and Manifesto of Revolutionary Love* (New York: Random House, 2020), 95.
12. Kate Manne, *Down Girl: The Logic of Misogyny* (Oxford, UK: Oxford University Press, 2018), 158.
13. Rosemary Radford Ruether, *Sexism and God-Talk: Toward a Feminist Theology* (Boston: Beacon Press, 1983, 1993), 261–262.
14. See Helen T. Boursier, *The Ethics of Hospitality: An Interfaith Response to US Immigration Policies* (Lanham, MD: Lexington Books, 2019), 117–120, 124, 138.
15. Ruether, *Sexism and God-Talk*, 262.

16 See *Pretty Woman*, directed by Garry Marshall (Burbank, CA: Buena Vista Home Video, 1990).
17 One of the best-known examples of Jewish feminist midrash is "The Coming of Lilith" by Judith Plaskow, what she wrote in response to the midrash in *Alphabet of Ben Sira*, a much earlier male-authored midrash based on the creation story in Genesis 1–3, see "Alphabet of Ben Sira 78: Lilith," Jewish Women's Archive, 2022, https://jwa.org/node/23210. Plaskow categorizes her version as a midrash on midrash more so than a midrash on scripture. See Judith Plaskow, *The Coming of Lilith: Essays on Feminism, Judaism, and Sexual Ethics*, 1972–2003, ed. with Donna Berman (Boston: Beacon Press, 2005), 81–86.
18 Lynn Gottlieb, "The Sacred Jew: An Oral Tradition of Women," in *On Being a Jewish Feminist: A Reader*, ed. Susannah Heschel (New York: Schocken Books, 1983), 273; cited in Judith Plaskow, *Standing Again at Sinai: Judaism from a Feminist Perspective* (San Francisco: Harper Collins, 1990), 54.
19 Rabbi Sandy Eisenberg Sasso, "Vayetze: Wrestling on the Other Side of the River," in *The Women's Torah Commentary: New Insights from Women Rabbis on the 54 Weekly Torah Portions*, ed. Elyse Goldstein (Nashville: Jewish Lights Publishing, 2000), 79–84.
20 Sasso, "Vayetze," 80.
21 Plaskow, *Standing Again at Sinai*, 37.
22 Maria Harris, *Dance of the Spirit: The Seven Steps of Women's Spirituality* (New York: Bantam Books, 1989, 1991), 186.
23 See Sally Haslanger, *Resisting Reality: Social Construction and Social Critique* (Oxford, UK: Oxford University Press, 2012), 100.
24 Nehama Weingarten-Mintz and Tamar Biala, eds., *Dirshuni: Israeli Women Writing Midrash* [in Hebrew] (Tel Aviv, Israel: Yedioth Ahronoth, 2009), 156–157; cited in Ronit Irshai, "'And I Find a Wife More Bitter Than Death' (Eccl. 7:26): Feminist Hermeneutics, Women Midrashim, and the Boundaries of Acceptance in Modern Orthodox Judaism," *Journal of Feminist Studies in Religion* 33, no. 1 (Spring 2017): 69–86.
25 See Simone de Beauvoir, *The Second Sex*, introduction by Judith Thurman, trans. Constance Borde and Sheila Malovany-Chevallier (New York: Vintage Books, Random House, 1949, 2009).
26 Maria, fifty-nine, from Honduras while in a migrant shelter in Nuevo Laredo, Mexico, during MPP, November 27, 2019.
27 Judith Butler, *Undoing Gender* (New York: Routledge, 2004), 204.
28 Ruether, *Sexism and God-Talk*, 185.
29 See Helen T. Boursier, "Femicide in Global Perspective: A Feminist Critique," in *The Rowman and Littlefield Handbook of Women's Studies in Religion*, ed. Helen T. Boursier (Lanham, MD: Rowman and Littlefield, 2021), 231–246; Boursier, "Call to Accountability: Women's Studies in Religion Critiques State Culpability to Feminicide through Border Controls and Exclusion from Asylum," in Boursier, *The Rowman and Littlefield Handbook of Women's Studies in Religion*, 247–262.
30 Migrant from Honduras while stranded in Nuevo Laredo, Mexico, during MPP, November 27, 2019.
31 Audre Lorde in her keynote presentation at the National Women's Studies Association Conference in Storrs, Connecticut, June 1981, "The Uses of Anger: Women

Responding to Racism," in *Sister Outsider: Essays and Speeches by Audre Lorde*, ed. Audre Lorde (Berkley: Crossing Press, 1984, 2007), 133.
32 Migrant from El Salvador while stranded in Nuevo Laredo, Mexico, during MPP November 5, 2019.
33 Migrant mother from Honduras while stranded in Nuevo Laredo, Mexico, during MPP December 4, 2019.
34 Lisa Michele Wolfe, *Qoheleth (Ecclesiastes)*, Wisdom Commentary (Collegeville, MN: Order of Saint Benedict, 2020), 100.
35 Interview with a clergy colleague, July 24, 2018, Field Notes, vol. 6, 100–101. See also Boursier, *Willful Ignorance*, 267–273; and Helen T. Boursier, *Desperately Seeking Asylum: Testimonies of Trauma, Courage, and Love* (Lanham, MD: Rowman and Littlefield, 2019), 84–89.
36 See Boursier, *Willful Ignorance*, 162.
37 Audre Lorde, "Age, Race, Class, and Sex: Women Redefining Difference," in Lorde, *Sister Outsider*, 117. See also Boursier, *Willful Ignorance*, 23–53.
38 Lorde, "Age, Race, Class, and Sex," 118.
39 Diana L. Hayes, *No Crystal Stair: Womanist Spirituality* (Maryknoll, NY: Orbis Books, 2016), 78.
40 August 28, 2018, Field Notes, vol. 7, 71–72. See also Boursier, *Desperately Seeking Asylum*, 155.
41 Martin Heidegger, *Being and Time*, trans. John Macquarrie and Edward Robinson, foreword by Taylor Carman (New York: Harper and Row, 1962, 2008), 313.
42 Heidegger, *Being and Time*, 242.
43 Heschel, *God in Search of Man*, 296.
44 Heschel, *God in Search of Man*, 297.
45 Heschel, *God in Search of Man*, 310.
46 See Boursier, *Willful Ignorance*, 207–236.
47 See Boursier, *Desperately Seeking Asylum*, 155–157.
48 Boursier, Field Notes, vol. 6, August 26, 2018, 101–102.
49 Lorde, "Age, Race, Class, and Sex," 119.
50 See King Jr. *Strength to Love*; and Genesis 1:27.
51 See Ernest Kurtz and Katherine Ketcham, *The Spirituality of Imperfection: Storytelling and the Search for Meaning* (New York: Bantam Books, 1992), 68.
52 See James E. Loder, *The Transforming Moment*, 2nd ed. (Colorado Springs, CO: Helmers and Howard, 1989), 85.
53 Kurtz and Ketcham, *Spirituality of Imperfection*, 31; emphasis theirs.
54 Simone Weil, *Love in the Void: Where God Finds Us*, ed. Laurie Gagne (Walden, NY: Plough Publishing House, 2018), 34.
55 Weil, *Love in the Void*, 35.

CHAPTER THREE

Paradox

If you see in a province the oppression of the poor and the violation of justice and right, do not be amazed at the matter, for the high official is watched by a higher, and there are yet higher ones over them.

—Ecclesiastes 5:8 (NRSVUE)

The harsh reality of this precarious life often challenges, questions, and even makes a mockery of conventional wisdom, which posits honesty is the best policy and says that hard work always pays off to become an American success story. Examples in life abound of bad things happening to good people. In the *Ethics of Ambiguity*, Simone de Beauvoir points out that throughout time, wherever people have lived, "they have all felt this tragic ambiguity of their condition, but as long as there have been philosophers and they have thought, most of them have tried to mask it."[1] Instead of masking it, Ecclesiastes calls out the paradox of *in*justice. The conundrum of suffering and injustice amid otherwise doing the "right thing" is considered, in the terminology of Ecclesiastes, "bad business," "grievous evil," and a "heavy burden" (Ecc. 1:13, 5:14, 6:1), compelling the author to lament, "All is vanity and a chasing after wind" (Ecc. 1:14 NRSVUE), a reiteration of the meaninglessness of life whereby "everything is vanity." The grievous evils Ecclesiastes identifies contribute to paradox because they exacerbate injustice, so much so that even a small child would lament, "That's not fair!" The race is not always to the swift or the battle to the strong. It's not that Ecclesiastes, or other wisdom-genre scriptures like Job, doesn't believe in the principle of retribution theology, where the good prosper and the evil get punished, or even that this form of justice doesn't work. Ecclesiastes addresses the fact that God's retributive governing of justice can't be known by mere humans who exist "under the sun" (9:11–11:6). Nevertheless, Ecclesiastes still calls out these disparities. Evil is bad business that creates a justice/injustice paradox.

THE JUSTICE/INJUSTICE PARADOX

In her *Epistemic Injustice: Power and the Ethics of Knowing*, Miranda Fricker points out that "philosophy talks a lot about justice, and very little about injustice," arguing that this emphasis on "justice creates an impression that justice is the norm and injustice the unfortunate aberration," which clearly isn't accurate. Fricker adds, "It also creates the impression that we should always understand injustice negatively by way of a prior grasp of justice."[2] The observations Ecclesiastes calls out as grievous evils or bad business that intersect with spirituality in the borderlands would be categorized as a moral evil, bad business which often manifests through natural evil. Technically, natural evil includes evil that isn't deliberately produced by humans and doesn't occur as a result of human greed or negligence, but some so-called natural evils are the direct result of humans. The paradox of blaming God comes in because some so-called natural evils and diseases actually are the result of human or moral evil, most notably evident with the environment, global warming, and cancer.

Moral evil includes all of the evils intentionally caused by humans. It also encompasses evil generated by deliberate or accidental negligence. Moral evil has many layers of suffering, including ideas and social practices about gender, race, class, immigration, drugs, alcohol, children of divorce, family, sexuality, and working too many hours to pay off excessive consumer debt.[3] Because moral evil covers a wide range of interconnected issues, it's insufficient to address a particular obvious evil, such as chattel slavery, rape, domestic violence, femicide, and homicide, without looking at the interconnections among these grievous evils. The paradox of moral evil also includes economic forces, institutional structures, race, gender, customs, traditions, and ideologies of the particular setting where the moral evil occurs.[4] In its most basic sense, Paul Ricœur describes the intersection of action with evil because "evil is above all what ought not to be, but what must be fought against."[5] The point of acting to change any form of evil is to work toward a better, more just future. Hence, action for justice begins in the present context and moves toward something better, which is what propels humanitarian response in the borderlands. Ricœur does "readily concede that action alone is not enough. The arbitrary and indiscriminate way in which suffering is apportioned whether by violence or by the ultimate part of suffering that cannot be ascribed to human interaction—illness, old age, or death—keeps rekindling the old questions: not just Why? but Why me? Why my beloved child?"[6] These relentless questions may never garner an adequate response, but the asking pushes the response toward action informed by a spirituality of care and compassion.

Hiddenness of Evil

Whether moral or natural evil, the bad business Ecclesiastes laments isn't always self-evident. Evil is confusing because people tend not to identify evil within an immediate situation. People know evil exists but prefer to define it as being "over there" or located somewhere in the distant past, such as with the Shoah, gender injustice, or systemic racism. Evil always involves deception and lies that hide the truth.[7] Not all bad business is equal, nor is it distributed evenly. Some people have freedom of choice, which sometimes causes evils generated by their poor decisions. However, many others are the recipients of bad business through no fault or choice of their own. Similarly with natural evil, sometimes termed *acts of God* to offhandedly blame God, who has the power, authority, and freedom to cause or not to cause *natural disasters* such as typhoons, floods, and droughts. Ecclesiastes isn't interested in participating in the blame game or pointing a finger at God. Ecclesiastes trusts in the existence and supreme will of God. For Ecclesiastes, as with spirituality in the borderlands, the problem isn't with God but with human beings.

The Human Factor

The human factor that contributes to natural disasters frequently is quickly dismissed in the Global North, with the harsh consequences disproportionately falling on the Global South, creating a paradox with the postmodern and post-religious Global North passing off the blame to a god that many no longer affirm, follow, or worship through religious affiliation. Instead of blaming God for what's often termed natural evil, Shirley Guthrie argues that moral evil generated by human beings is far worse than all/any of the evil that is typically blamed on God. Guthrie explains, "Terrible as it can be, the worst form of evil is manifested not in natural misfortune that happens to us but in what we human beings do to each other. It appears not in pain, suffering, and death as such, but in the pain, suffering, and death we inflict on each other."[8] For Guthrie, a Reformed Christian theologian, the worst form of evil is moral evil that expresses itself as human wickedness.[9] This is the bad business Ecclesiastes calls out. Moral evil as human wrongdoing is compounded because "evil arises in the refusal to acknowledge our own sins."[10] Similarly, Ricœur argues the "cry of lamentation is most sharp" when humans generate harm to others, creating suffering either directly or indirectly that makes other humans suffer.[11] It's urgently important to look within ourselves to forthrightly discern our rationalizations for action and *in*action that contribute to the harm of others, as lines of the traditional prayer of confession notes, "for things said and left unsaid; done and left undone." Sometimes grievous evils are deliberate, but other times they're generated by happenstance and bad luck.

GRIEVOUS EVILS IN ECCLESIASTES

Ecclesiastes specifies three particular contexts of grievous evils that are bad business and the worst of all evil, generating paradoxical differences between what could and should be and what actually *is*. The first bad business that contributes to paradox is the never-ending struggle to be and do more, and more, and *more*, which prompts the observation in Ecclesiastes about the senselessness in trying "to straighten what is crooked" or "to fix what is broken" (Ecc. 1:13–15). More is never enough (see chapter 4). It's this greedy more in the Global North that nets the moral evil / bad business that disproportionately harms the Global South. Highlighting a disarming paradox of wealth that liberation, theologian Jon Sobrino argues, "The causes of the suffering in the Third World are, to a great extent, to be found in the First World."[12] Perhaps the greatest paradox of all for a spirituality of borders is the abuse and misuse of affluence in the Global North, which directly contributes to the suffering in the Global South, forcing the families to leave their homelands. This gross disjuncture paradox between justice and injustice falls on displaced migrants, thereby profoundly influencing and shaping spirituality in the borderlands.

The second grievous evil Ecclesiastes calls out is the injustice when someone works their fingers to the bone, becoming wealthy and rising to a place of honor in their community, only to lose everything in a bad venture. This travesty leaves them penniless and homeless, much like those fleeing their homes because of government corruption, gang violence, and environmental catastrophes the families didn't create or contribute to. Yet they lose their wealth and honor and become forced to migrate with literally nothing but a small backpack that contains the remainder of all their worldly goods. Ecclesiastes further points out that this injustice is so horrible "as they came from their mother's womb, so they shall go again, naked as they came; they shall take nothing for their toil that they carry away with their hands" (Ecc. 5:15), a scripture passage that's frequently offered during a funeral service with the intention to somehow offer comfort to the bereaved. Ecclesiastes also wants dignity in dying and in death, for the greatest indignity is to die alone, without respect, without burial, without appropriate homage for the deceased one's life. With this vision in view, the Samaritans in southern Arizona seek to restore dignity to displaced migrants as these volunteers diligently search the Sonoran Desert. Their proactive stance seeks to counter the grievous evil experienced by migrants who become stranded or disoriented in the harsh desert, which ultimately would lead to the indignity of death, with their bodies left to decay in the desert, suffering the ultimate grievous evil of becoming *desconocido* ("unknown"), the term used to designate the remains of an unidentified person.[13]

The third grievous evil Ecclesiastes decries is the person who's worked hard and achieved a measure of success in life, enough to ensure an easy life in the later years, only to have all this wealth stolen by a stranger (Ecc. 6:2). This grievous evil closely resonates with the migrants who've lost everything through no fault of their own. All their worldly goods were stolen or forcibly sold to cover travel costs to the United States due to a variety of complicit circumstances they didn't cause. Rather, they were, like the Ecclesiastes scenario, victims of the policies and practices of strangers who cheated them out of their livelihoods, homes, hopes, and dreams through disastrous foreign policy (e.g., NAFTA, Remain in Mexico, family separation, etc.), government corruption and gang violence (e.g., Guatemala, Honduras, and El Salvador), and environmental catastrophes generated by global warming, created by the Global North but felt most harshly in the Global South. The unacceptable disparity between what should be fair and just and the indisputable flourishing of evil that perpetrates *un*fairness and *in*justice affects affluent residents who are living in the land of happily ever after, but it's much more insidious on displaced families.

EXACERBATING PARADOX THROUGH AVOIDANCE, DENIAL, AND INDIFFERENCE

Wisdom isn't beneficial when cognition intentionally shuts down active listening and objective hearing, creating deliberate naivety about the existence of evil.[14] It exacerbates paradox to avoid, deny, or be indifferent about the grievous evils suffered by others, particularly when there's complicity through any remote or direct connection to what's causing the suffering. New Testament scholar and Anglican bishop in England N. T. Wright argues the Western world is in a state of denial regarding the problem of evil in the world, and this denial generates three characterizations: "First, we ignore evil when it doesn't hit us in the face. Second, we are surprised by evil when it does. Third, we react in immature and dangerous ways as a result."[15] He points out that the comfortable fool themselves into believing the world is basically a good place, and then they're shocked and unprepared when tragedy strikes. The affluent world isn't prepared to respond appropriately when bad business strikes close to home, contributing to why a root cause of grievous evil is centered on denial, human error, fallacy, and deliberate bad choices, which foster the Ecclesiastes sense of bad business as grievous evil through horrific injustice. Or, in the Christian lingo, human sin produces a disproportionate amount of bad business, including indifference to the suffering of others.

The Journey to Indifference

The journey to indifference to paradoxical injustice begins with avoidance, moves to denial, and then embraces indifference. When there's something someone doesn't want to really know about or deal with, they simply avoid coming into contact with the topic, person, or place. It becomes a matter of out of sight, out of mind. When avoidance becomes ineffective or insufficient, the next phase is denial. In *A Spirituality of Resistance: Finding a Peaceful Heart and Protecting the Earth*, Roger Gottlieb proposes "the difference between avoidance and denial is the difference between passivity and activity, or between the tacit and the overt. While avoidance takes those little hops and jumps away from what frightens us, in denial we look it right in the face and say it isn't there. And then that thought guides how we live."[16] Whether the focal point is global warming and the environment, racial or gender injustice, economic disparity, or inhumane policies and practices at the US-Mexico border, the denial mechanism offers rationalizations such as "It's not happening," or "It's really not as bad as the news says," or "It's not my problem anyway."

When the paradox disparities become too publicly obvious and difficult to deny, Gottlieb notes, "people attempt to hide it."[17] Denial is a spiritual concern because it contributes to a what W. E. B. Du Bois calls a "double consciousness" to juggle two distinctly different perspectives—the one that is the actual truth about present reality and the other version that the denier pretends is actually happening instead. Denial is a form of *spiritual schizophrenia*. Gottlieb points out this causes "pain, confusion, and sense of unreality" because deniers have to internally process what's an obvious disconnect between observed fact and internal dismissal of reality. Gottlieb elaborates, "As avoidance leads to the repression of energy, denial cuts us off from the truth, makes us doubt our own sense of how things are, keeps us from listening to others or the world and from changing the way things are."[18] By avoiding or denying the existence of paradox that nets injustice for the "other side" of the equation, it becomes a permission-giving rationale to leave it up to others to solve the problems while remaining *impassively* part of the problem through indifference.

Indifference

In his speech "The Perils of Indifference," which he delivered at the White House when Bill Clinton was president, Nazi concentration camp survivor and Nobel Laureate Elie Wiesel said, "The opposite of love is not hatred; it's indifference." He elaborated:

> Indifference is not a beginning; it is an end. And, therefore, indifference is always the friend of the enemy, for it benefits the aggressor—never his victim, whose pain is magnified when he or she feels forgotten. The political prisoner in his cell, the hungry children, the homeless refugees—not to respond to their plight, not to relieve their solitude by offering them a spark of hope is to exile them from human memory. And in denying their humanity we betray our own. Indifference, then, is not only a sin, it is a punishment. And this is one of the most important lessons of this outgoing century s wide-ranging experiments in good and evil.[19]

Illustration 3.1 *My Case for Asylum* 9" × 12" immigrant artwork watercolor with collage over a handwritten testimony from Art Inside Karnes, July 13, 2016, where a mother wrote about the violence in her homeland and her quest for asylum in the United States so that she and her children can live in peace. Art © Art Inside Karnes.

Volunteers and advocates in the borderlands refute indifference because, as Wiesel argued, "anyone who listens to a witness becomes a witness."[20] Volunteers and activists are forever formed and informed by their personal encounters in the borderlands. Moving forth from the entrapment of indifference requires intentionality as a core component for a spirituality that expresses its discontent with paradox and the injustice of the status quo.

The paradoxes between American affluence and the migrants who are struggling for existence and bare life intersects with spirituality in the borderlands, which creates placelessness (illustration 3.1).

PLACELESSNESS: THE ULTIMATE PARADOX IN THE MIGRANT'S LIFE

Placelessness is the ultimate paradox for the families because they're stuck between worlds. It's not safe to remain or to return to what once was home, but they also cannot and will not belong *here*. This is the conundrum John Steinbeck writes about in *The Grapes of Wrath* about the sharecroppers who were forced to leave during the Dust Bowl migration of the 1930s. They had to leave as the tractors were literally plowing over their homes to "keep the line straight" for the new fields, but these displaced American farmers also knew that they could never really "start over." Steinbeck eloquently describes the scene of a tenant farmer forced out of his home with his family, who watched the tractor cut a path closer and closer to this family's home:

> Across the dooryard the tractor cut, and the hard, foot-beaten ground was seeded field, and the tractor cut through again; the uncut space was ten feet wide. And back he came. The iron guard bit into the house-corner, crumbled the wall, and wrenched the little house from its foundation so that it fell sideways, crushed like a bug. And the driver was goggled and a rubber mask covered his notes and mouth. The tractor cut a straight line on, and the air and the ground vibrated with its thunder. The tenant man stared after it, his rifle in his hand. His wife beside him, and the quiet children behind. All of them stared after the tractor.[21]

Later in his bestselling novel, Steinbeck includes the musings of a tenant farmer who'd been forced off the land, slowly migrating west: "Maybe we can start again, in the rich land—in California, where the fruit grows. We'll start over." But, of course, starting over is impossible, as the musings continue: "But you can't start over. Only a baby can start. You and me—why, we're all that's been.... This land, this red land, is us; and the flood years and the dust years and the drought years are us. We can't start again."[22] The inability to really start again is a spiritual actuality with migrating families today, forced from their homes by various circumstances they didn't cause or choose and attempting to make some sort of new life in America. Although the families never can or will experience a total do-over, they still have to try to seek safety and attempt to recreate their lives. They can't remain in or return to what once was home.

Longing for Home

In his essay "Longing for Home," Elie Wiesel points out that after World War II ended and so many people were finally freed from the death camps, "a new species of human appeared in special camps for so-called Displaced Persons." Wiesel explains that after surviving the horrors of Nazi Germany, "yesterday's prisoners and survivors of un precedented tragedies, rejected by all civilized nations, with the sole exception of the State of Israel, dwelled in a state of utter humiliation." A survivor of these death camps himself, Wiesel's apt description parallels displaced people from the Global South who are awaiting reception today in the Global North as he adds, "Displaced persons: their official name suited them well. Orphans of hope and serenity, burdened with wounded memories, these homeless men and women were indeed displaced. Their spiritual beings were in exile. Their language itself, filled with pain and anguish, was displaced: it fell on deaf ears and indifferent hearts."[23] The seemingly simple question of where home is became a complicated unknown for the freed prisoners from the Nazi death camps, just as it is for those stuck in a quagmire of rules and regulations while waiting outside the international border of a possible receiving nation. Wiesel likens this to being in exile. It's not possible to return home, and yet there's no welcome in the next new place that a displaced person would like to call home.

The severity of such exile and the grievous evil of placelessness are evident in the well-known and ancient example of Socrates, who, given a choice between exile and death, chose death.[24] Wiesel explains, "Exile means breaking with family, friends, acquaintances, surroundings, culture, language, and work. Exile means beginning again—elsewhere—an existence filled with ambition, anxiety, and occasional reward, in the midst of new friends or adversaries."[25] He makes the point that this exile always includes separation from people and place, from all that is known. Hence, nostalgia enters in as those displaced fondly remember that place they once called home.

Describing life in the borderlands for the displaced migrants, a volunteer wrote in a blog about a recent trip to help in Matamoros:

> This is an odd sort of prison. There are no walls or bars but families here are stuck. They cannot move forward nor can they go back, though some do. If they stay, they find themselves in an uncomfortable, uncertain and untenable sort of limbo for an indeterminate length of time. They cannot build a life for themselves. They are not free to raise their children as their conscious dictates. With the unsanitary conditions and population density of this slum-like camp, many are ill. They cannot stay clean—their showers are makeshift privacy barriers of tarps and plastic garbage bags strung up between trees. They are not free to work for their families and must instead depend wholly on the generosity of volunteers and benevolent donors. They have little freedom to make any choice, really. They are truly a people being acted-upon. It's a soul-crushing problem with which to contend and it is no wonder desperation and depression are chronic problems in the camp.[26]

The volunteer explained that the families awaiting permission to pursue an asylum claim "know their chances are slim but they stay in the camp anyway." Describing their circumstances comparatively to Wiesel's description of post–World War II concentration camp survivors, the volunteer added, "They are displaced in the same way refugees in war-torn nations are displaced. Their war is not official, but it is, nonetheless, a war with violence and instability and stories of mind-boggling loss."[27] The volunteer's synthesis of her border trip experience also makes the connection to the placelessness of these families and the political game, noting, "The people at the heart of this issue are dehumanized in grand form the moment we turned them into pawns."[28] These families seem to be stuck in a no-win situation, unable to return home or press forward, and in all this, longing for new places to call home. The families aren't looking to replace "home" but to be in a safe place that can be*come* their home. While waiting in a migrant shelter in Nuevo Laredo, Mexico, for permission to enter the United States, Liliam from Honduras wrote:

> I regretted leaving my country.
>   But there is no work.
>   So there is no food.
> I thank God for my daughter.

I thank God we are in this shelter.
I thank God for the brothers and sisters in Christ who help us.[29]

For people in exile, there are so many impediments to finding a new place to call home. For example, a Catholic sister who volunteers regularly with IWC in San Antonio expressed her concern that it's increasingly common for the families arriving at the bus station in San Antonio, a gateway city located two to five hours inland from the diagonally cut Texas-Mexico border, to not have a family member or sponsor to receive them. They get as far as San Antonio, a portal for many other parts of the United States, East, West, and North, "but then there is nowhere definite they can then go to." She added, "The families keep coming. I'm so concerned about where they're going to end up. A couple of weeks ago there was a husband, wife and little child, maybe four years old, and they were going to Houston but they had no place to go." She said she called all of the shelters that she could think of, but each one passed her "to the next, to the next, and to the next." She bewailed, "They're all filled. I couldn't find a place for them. They were going to be on the street." The sister explained this happens regularly with the same result. She said there also are quite a few single men who have been stranded in San Antonio for a couple of weeks because they have nowhere to go, no family, and all the shelters are full. This finding no room at a shelter directly parallels the Christmas story of the holy family, who couldn't find room at an inn, so the Christ child was born in a stable (Luke 2:1–7), a point pro-immigrant pastors highlight but anti-immigrant clergy ignore, dismiss, or choose not to notice.[30]

Reflecting on the number of migrants who'd traveled through the Greyhound bus station in San Antonio the previous day, the sister said, "I'm going to say we saw maybe about three hundred people, and about half of those were housed in a hotel last night or at Travis Park Church overnight." She said, "This happens every day, every day, *every* day. So where are they going to go? Are they going to be on the street?" She said if someone doesn't step in with a solution, these vulnerable people will be stranded on the street and become at risk for trafficking, labor, drugs, and sexual abuse and exploitation. This Catholic sister wondered if the Christian communities across the United States could or would open their hearts, homes, and churches to receive these displaced families. Otherwise, they will be left to the mercy of the political will, which rounds them up in a plane that callously drops them off at Martha's Vineyard, an island located off the southern coast of Cape Cod, Massachusetts.

Being dumped off on an island located five miles offshore from the mainland or near the home of Vice President Kamala Harris in Washington, DC, on Christmas Eve to make a political point is one more grievous evil along the displaced migrant's journey to find a safe place to call home.[31]

In her memoir on what she terms "revolutionary love," Valarie Kaur reflects about the inner sense of what it means to be "home." She proposes that "home is the space within us and between us where we both feel safe—and brave. It is not a physical space as much as it is a field of being."[32] This ideal is a beautiful sentiment for people living in safety, but it remains out of reach for the families as long as they are in their exilic displacement, where they're stuck in a void between the home they had and the future place that calls to them. It's an unsafe displacement within displacement that fosters a terminal unsettledness and anxiousness amid ever-present new dangers and new threats to life. Even once they arrive to a quasi-safe place, there will forever remain a spiritual longing for home, for the familiar faces, sounds, foods, and memories they had to leave behind.

In their desperate need to leave home, the families also have an ever-present deep longing for home. Even as they're putting all their hopes into this myth, fleeing their homelands to seek safety and protection in America, they're longing for home every step of the way. It's a deeply painful longing that cannot be assuaged by anything but being home, and yet they cannot be home, or they wouldn't have left in the first place. Bonhoeffer wrote about this longing for loved ones while he was incarcerated prior to his execution:

> In my experience nothing tortures us more than longing.... When *we* are forcibly separated for any considerable time from those whom we love, we simply *cannot*, as most can, get some cheap substitute through other people—I don't mean because of moral considerations, but just because we are what we are. Substitutes repel us; we simply have to wait and wait; we have to suffer unspeakably from the separation, and feel that longing till it almost makes us ill. That is the only way, although it is a very painful one, in which we can preserve unimpaired our relationship with our loved ones. A few times in my life I've come to know what homesickness means. There is nothing more painful, and during these months in prison, I've sometimes been terribly homesick.[33]

The families regularly express similar longing for the loved ones they've left behind and also for their family members who'd fled home much earlier and were already living in their own sense of exile somewhere in the United States.

One of the spiritual care exercises I invited the mothers and children to participate in during Art Inside Karnes included writing symbolic letters home. I invited them to write a letter home, telling them whatever was in their hearts. Later that day, I wrote in my reflection journal:

> I am struck by how important it is for the women and children to write out how they are feeling, to put into words their expressions of care and concern and of love. I see how important it is to include the written word in their art pieces so the women and children have the opportunity to more fully express what's on their hearts. For instance, a mother wrote, "The heart is the organ that feels all the pain or sadness that there is; I prefer to feel much love and joy for this heart is very healthy (and strong)" and this heart "is able to be happy." One mother wrote three short letters on one page—to her mother, to her father, and to her love. She wrote how much she loves and misses each. To her love she closed her letter with saying how much she wanted to be together but that was not possible at this moment. However, "we are together because your love is in my heart." Another wrote her love about how much she longed to be by his side and instead she sends him her "love and kisses" and she closed saying, "I do not say 'goodbye' but 'see you soon.'"[34]

The families similarly express their abject loneliness amid their forced separation from loved ones, some who are on the departure side of their trip but others who are on the hopeful ultimate destination for reunion in the United States. Their spirituality wrestles with this longing for home amid the bitter experiences that forced their departure. While detained inside GEO Karnes, a mother from El Salvador wrote:

> *Forget the Bad * Remember the Good*
>
> I remember the bad.
> I remember when they took the lives
>   of three members of my son's family.
> I have lived with daily violence in El Salvador.
> I have so many painful memories
>   I do not want to record them.
> I want to forget all the bad.
>   I do not want to remember.
> We are here because my God is great.
>   God loves us.
> God gives us strength to continue
>   Fighting.
>   *

> I remember the good things we shared
>> together as a family.
> Faith also feels good.
> It is good to know God is with you.
>> Faith never despairs.
> It's also a good memory
>> being beside my son.
> Teaching him all
>> things that are good.
> It is a happy memory that
>>> I taught my son the good things
>>> the nice traditions of my country.
> Something only remains in the memory
>> when you have to leave.
> When it is necessary to travel
>> to another country.
> The good memories will always be present
>> in our minds.
> More, however, I feel happy because
>> my God is always with me.
> Like the praise songs
>> "God is peace in the storm."
>
> *
>
> Each day I ask God to bless me
>> and all who are around me.
> Thank God for one more day of life.[35]

The choice to leave behind their homeland, family, friends, and all of their worldly possessions except what they can carry in a backpack is not an easy decision or one that comes lightly. For the women, in particular, it's a bold affirmation of their faith, their belief that God will protect them. But it also moves them into the void of placelessness.

Terminal Placelessness

Asylum seekers can't remain in their homelands, where they once felt a strong place of belonging, despite the drudgery and endless repetition that goes with belonging in any given place. Much like the sense of futility Ecclesiastes laments in the opening chapter with the vain repetition of all life that contributes to the analysis that life is "utterly meaningless" (Ecc. 1:2), there's a monotonous repetition to anyone's place of home, their place of belonging. So many aspects of life require doing the same tasks again and again, such as washing clothing, preparing meals, and working at a job to get a paycheck that quickly gets spent. There's also repetition in nature, such as planting a garden in anticipation of abundant harvest, only to have the plants wither and die, with the planting/growing/harvest/dying cycle to then repeat itself the same time next year. There's tedium in the repetitiveness of home. Yet, oddly, home engenders a feeling of belonging because of this very sense of redundancy. You know exactly what to expect during the Monday through Friday work and school repetitiveness, as well as weekends with whatever extra chores or activities they entail. When friends, family, and familiarity with local customs, culture, and geography are factored in, home is simply where you feel that deep sense of belonging.

When a radical disjuncture enters in that puts life at risk, the balancing point of literally everything that once felt safe, predictable, normal, and mundane about home is thrown askew. When this longing for belonging at home with family and friends is radically challenged by threat to life, remaining in place is no longer an option. As Edward Relph explains in *Place and Placelessness*, "Balancing a need to stay with a desire to escape" is radically and irrevocably challenged by tangible threats to their lives.[36] No matter how much home pulls at their spirits, the displaced families can't remain there.

Though often made very quickly when threat to life unexpectedly invades one's physical and spiritual world, the decision to flee is never ever made thoughtlessly, carelessly, or without a deep appreciation for the extreme loss and displacement. The families know to a certain degree how much leaving will put their lives at risk along the journey to safety in the United States, but they never anticipate the depth of mourning and loss of home and family that they will ultimately experience, literally every step of their journey. A fifteen-year-old boy said the hardest part of his trip was saying goodbye to his family, including brothers and sisters who had remained in El Salvador. He added, "I also had to say goodbye to Maggy. She is a very special girl that God permitted me to know." He explained, "The most difficult part of the trip was feeling sad, lonely, and all the disappointment." He hoped they would be able to return to his homeland because he didn't want to live separated from his family or his special girl.[37] A mother from El Salvador said she knew her children "would suffer on the long journey, but it would only be for a few days." She explained that taking the risk and making the long journey would ultimately end their suffering, but if they remained in their homeland, "the suffering would never end."[38] Faithfulness in God's presence and protection remains steadfast amid the volatile journey and the uncertainty while waiting for the formalities and legalities of due process to gain temporary legal status in the United States. Delmi offered prayers for herself and her companions inside the detention center, saying, "I ask God for my companions here, that they have the strength to continue." She added, "I love God over everything. God is our refuge and salvation. I have faith in God that all goes well. Always, my confidence is in God. I love God."[39] The longing for home doesn't disappear when the families arrive at the borderlands. They long for what their home once was, but they also know that they cannot return.

Amid their sense of placelessness, faith in God continues to uplift and uphold their spiritual well-being. After going into great detail about the suffering that was the catalyst for her journey to the United States, including being denied access and being forced to return to Nuevo Laredo during MPP, a mother wrote, "We have to wait for the court appointment they gave us and it is months away. Please help me. May God bless you greatly. I give thanks to God for sending me to this shelter and for the people who are helping me to keep my son safe. God bless me. God keep us safe. This is my short story of my life. I give God thanks."[40] While detained inside GEO Karnes, a mother who was forcibly separated from her husband at the border by the border patrol shared her loves and longings. Beginning with her affirmation that God is always with her and that she feels God's presence and knows God loves her, she wrote, "I love my husband, although at this moment he is not beside us, my son and me. I have faith the day will come when we will be together again, as one family." She also wrote about her love for her mother, who always showed her unconditional love, and also siblings, aunts, and "two or three" nephews who were very dear to her. She added, "I can no longer see your faces here, or give you a strong hug. I cannot recover from our last time together; I will always miss you. I love you with all my heart. I miss you, and I have faith that one day we will come together." In her closing salutation, she offered a prayer to God that she'd be reunited with her husband "soon."[41]

Longing for Belonging

The longing for belonging is ongoing throughout their journey from placelessness to something, hopefully, much better, a longing that isn't guaranteed ever to be fulfilled. During an Art Inside Karnes session the afternoon before a mother was to be deported with her young daughter, she shared with me how much she missed her mother, whom she'd not seen in thirteen years. She also said how much she missed her husband, the father of her daughter, explaining, "They killed him. I really need to be with him." She added, "They gave me a negative on my asylum interview. I don't understand. The only one who knows is God, but I asked God for the opportunity to be with my mother. She lives in the United States. I miss her very much." This about-to-be-deported mother couldn't understand why she received a negative on her request to enter the United States. She said, "My mother is here. We belong together in the United States."[42] Her mother had been forced to migrate more than a decade earlier. When her daughter and granddaughter were in the same dire straits and attempted to reunite with her in America, the younger generations were about to be deported.

Displacement forces long-term misplacement and suffering that imbue in their spirituality, and this forced migration / ongoing displacement most often is directly related to the injustice meted out, intentionally and sometimes unintentionally, by the affluent nation where they come seeking protection from the harm we've done that's contributed to causing their forced migration.[43] Whereas the ultimate paradox of the families is the forced migration that ultimately leads to terminal placelessness, the definitive paradox for fancy first nations is *our* complicity in *their* pain. Spirituality in the borderlands expresses the sense of futility Ecclesiastes decries about staying on the perennial treadmill of striving for the good life in America in stark contrast to the prevalent inconsistencies and paradoxes of injustice along the southwest border, ultimately working to challenge and change bad business from suffering and death to abundant, safe life.

NOTES

1. Simone de Beauvoir, *The Ethics of Ambiguity* (New York: Open Road Integrated Media, 1947, 2018), 6.
2. Miranda Fricker, *Epistemic Injustice: Power and the Ethics of Knowing* (Oxford, UK: Oxford University Press, 2007), vi.

3 Frederick W. Schmidt Jr., *When Suffering Persists* (Harrisburg, PA: Moorehouse Publishing, 2001), 10.
4 James Newton Poling, *Deliver Us from Evil: Resisting Racial and Gender Oppression* (Minneapolis: Fortress Press, 1996), 126.
5 Paul Ricœur, *Figuring the Sacred: Religion, Narrative, and Imagination* (Minneapolis: Augsburg Fortress Press, 1995), 259.
6 Ricœur, *Figuring the Sacred*, 259.
7 Poling, *Deliver Us from Evil*, 113.
8 Shirley C. Guthrie, *Christian Doctrine*, rev. ed. (Louisville, KY: Westminster John Knox Press, 1994), 173.
9 Guthrie, *Christian Doctrine*, 173.
10 Scott M. Peck, *People of the Lie: The Hope for Healing Human Evil* (New York: Simon and Schuster, 1983), 233.
11 Ricœur, *Figuring the Sacred*, 250.
12 Jon Sobrino, *The Principle of Mercy: Taking the Crucified People from the Cross* (Maryknoll, NY: Orbis Books, 1994), 29.
13 The Migrant Quilt Project was designed to reclaim the dishonor of migrants who died unknown in the Sonora Desert. See Helen T. Boursier, *Arts as Witness: A Practical Theology of Arts-Based Research* (Lanham, MD: Lexington Books, 2021), 195–198.
14 See, e.g., Boursier, *Willful Ignorance*, 129–156.
15 N. T. Wright, *Evil and the Justice of God* (Downers Grove, IL: InterVarsity Press, 2006), 23–24.
16 Gottlieb, *A Spirituality of Resistance*, 43.
17 Gottlieb, *A Spirituality of Resistance*, 48.
18 Gottlieb, *A Spirituality of Resistance*, 49–50.
19 Elie Wiesel, "The Perils of Indifference," YouTube, April 12, 1999, https://www.youtube.com/watch?v=JpXmRiGst4k.
20 Wiesel, "Perils of Indifference."
21 Steinbeck, *Grapes of Wrath*, 38–39.
22 Steinbeck, *Grapes of Wrath*, 87.
23 Elie Wiesel, "Longing for Home," in *The Longing for Home*, ed. Leroy S. Rounder (Notre Dame, IN: University of Notre Dame Press, 1996), 17–29, 19.
24 Wiesel, "Longing for Home," 23.
25 Wiesel, "Longing for Home," 23.
26 Shared by permission; Rio Valley Relief Project, "The Resilience of the Human Spirit" (Blog), January 4, 2020, https://www.riovalleyreliefproject.org/post/the-resilience-of-the-human-spirit.
27 Rio Valley Relief Project, "Resilience of the Human Spirit."
28 Rio Valley Relief Project, "Resilience of the Human Spirit."
29 Liliam from Honduras while waiting in a migrant shelter in Nuevo Laredo, Mexico, during MPP, November 6, 2019.
30 For Pastor Natalie Webb's Christmas Eve sermon that centers around her experience with the families, see Boursier, *Ethics of Hospitality*, 211–213.
31 See Dan Rosenzweig-Ziff, Maria Sacchetti, Molly Hennessy-Fiske, Joanna Slater, Hannah Knowles, and Ellen Francis, "DeSantis Move to Fly Migrants to Massachusetts Stokes Confusion, Outrage from Critics," *Washington Post*, September 15, 2022, https://www.washingtonpost.com/nation/2022/09/15/marthas-vineyard-desantis

-migrants-venezuela/; Gillian Brockell and Jodie Tillman, "'Reverse Freedom Rides': An Echo of Martha's Vineyard Migrant Flights 60 Years Ago," *Washington Post*, September 16, 2022, https://www.washingtonpost.com/history/2022/09/16/reverse-freedom-rides-marthas-vineyard-desantis/; and Noah Gray, "More Migrants Dropped Off Outside Vice President's Home in Freezing Weather on Christmas Eve," *CNN*, December 26, 2022, https://www.cnn.com/2022/12/24/politics/migrants-dropped-off-vice-president-christmas-eve/index.html.

32 Kaur, *See No Stranger*, 127.
33 Bonhoeffer, "To Eberhard Bethge [Tegel] 18 December 1943," in Bonhoeffer, *Letters and Papers from Prison*, 167.
34 "Letters Home," Art Inside Karnes, July 29, 2015.
35 Mother from El Salvador, "Both/And: Naming the Bad and Celebrating the Good," Art Inside Karnes, August 10, 2016.
36 Edward Relph, *Place and Placelessness* (London: Pion Limited, 1976, 2008), 42.
37 Cited in Boursier, *Desperately Seeking Asylum*, 24.
38 Mother, Art Inside Karnes, "*Ya! Me Voy!*" (Enough! I Go!), January 20, 2016.
39 Mother, Art Inside Karnes, "*Quien Soy?*" (Who Am I?), July 23, 2015.
40 Mother at a shelter for migrants in Nuevo Laredo, Mexico, during MPP, November 5, 2009.
41 Mother, Art Inside Karnes, "My Love Story," February 10, 2016.
42 Mother, Art Inside Karnes, "Please Help My Country," November 11, 2015.
43 See Boursier, *Ethics of Hospitality*, 101–112.

CHAPTER FOUR

Striving

Yet when I surveyed all that my hands had done and what I had toiled to achieve, everything was meaningless, a chasing after the wind; nothing was gained under the sun.

—Ecclesiastes 2:11 (NIV)

Striving is another concern in Ecclesiastes that resonates in the borderlands for very different reasons and comes from very different contexts. Discontent with striving provides the motivation for dissent, which pursues proactive actions to engender life and to contribute to the greater good. The migrating families have exceeded their tolerance level for the grievous evils in their homelands and strive for a safe and peaceful life in the promised land. Volunteers, advocates, and environmentalists who've become dissatisfied with the meaninglessness of ceaseless striving for the good life in America shift their focus to striving for justice and peacemaking in the borderlands. Both aspects of striving—the families for life, safety, and peace and the Americans seeking a more meaningful life—exemplify what Ecclesiastes suggests contribute to ultimate gain (chapter 9). This repurposed striving shapes a spirituality that refutes grievous evils in the borderlands through justice and peacemaking.

STRIVING IN ECCLESIASTES

Ecclesiastes examines multiple problems with striving in the productive sense of attaining status, wealth, influence, and power, a theme that easily parallels the American dream. Ecclesiastes points out there's no relationship between how hard someone works and how successful or affluent they will become in this life. Despite continual striving, it never generates a guaranteed life of happily ever after. In addition, relentlessly working isn't healthy, nor is it sustainable. Incessant striving also doesn't guarantee happiness. The futility in striving is particularly evident in affluent nations where keeping up with the Joneses is a normative full-court press and push, push, push. Striving also contributes to blindness and/or willful ignorance about suffering and injustice. Excessive striving is also responsible for environmental misuse and abuse and the injustice propagated by affluent countries with the global influence, money, power, and might to initiate and enforce money- and power-driven ventures for financial gain. Fancy first countries reap the financial rewards from human labor and environmental abuse, while the rest of the world suffers the harshest consequences. Global warming may impact the entire world, but it harms minority people and nations disproportionately much more harshly. Ecclesiastes believes so much foolish or vain toil and striving are motivated by envying what someone else has—bigger, better, faster, more. Discontent is the inevitable result of senseless striving and the Americana manifesto for more.

Ecclesiastes highlights several dysfunctions and injustices around ceaseless striving to work toward wealth attainment. Foremost, there's never an end to striving (Ecc. 5:10). That ultimate dream job, house, bank account, litany of academic and/or professional degrees is never enough. Just as it's true with any sort of addiction, striving doesn't generate an end. There's no ultimate or definitive final goal, no finish line in view. Desire is insatiable. Enough is never enough. No matter how many hit records, Oscars, Emmys, Superbowl rings, or bestsellers, there's always someone coming along and pushing to earn or win this honor next time. Whatever wealth someone successfully gains is inevitably taken by the government via taxes, friends, and/or family, including the looming possibility that those who inherit after one's death will prove to be complete and utter fools (Ecc. 2:18). Sometimes, as is the case with the migrant families, strangers take all they have, leaving them desperate, homeless, and broke (Ecc. 6:2).

In addition, affluence also contributes to sleeplessness because of the anxiety property and asset ownership generates regarding how to hang on to the wealth (Ecc. 2:23). People pursue wealth even when it hurts them, something that's most evident in high-profile vocations, including celebrities, politicians, and sports figures (Ecc. 5:10). Lance Armstrong is a classic example. He had his record-setting seven wins in a row at the Tour de France stripped from him after being caught doping. In the business world, FTX crypto king Sam Bankman-Fried pleaded not guilty to fraud charges after he filed bankruptcy on November 11, 2022, leaving approximately thirty-two billion dollars in assets unaccounted for and lost to his investors.[1] The trial was scheduled to begin on October 1, 2023. In addition, the #MeToo social movement erupted when women had had enough gender abuse and sexual misconduct from the males in power over them. Perhaps among the most notorious examples are Hollywood producer Harvey Weinstein, who was found guilty of rape, and actor/comedian Bill Cosby, who was found guilty of three felony counts of aggravated indecent sexual assault, including against a minor.

Striving for more and more is foolishness because wealth itself, once attained, is uncertain and unstable. Anyone can still lose it, an ever-present risk that contributes to daytime anxiety and nighttime sleeplessness (Ecc. 2:21, 5:12, 14). Affluence also doesn't guarantee a happily ever after. It might attract friends on a surface level, but those who gather around the rich and famous are more likely to be false friends who want the benefits of someone's success more so than a genuine friendship (Ecc. 5:11). The rich and famous engender what Randy Newman made popular in his song "Lonely at the Top" (1972). Wealth also generates the Scrooge effect of hoarding everything for personal use, including eating alone and in darkness (Ecc. 5:17), what could also be called the Howard Hughes syndrome in honor of the business tycoon, aviator, and motion picture producer who became a total recluse in his later years. He continued the treadmill of ceaseless striving to his death, but Hughes did so "working for days without sleep in a black-curtained room, he became emaciated and deranged from the effects of a meagre diet and an excess of drugs."[2] This once-powerful and influential American dream striver became a miserable old codger with his claims to fame lost during his tragic later years.

The Great Equalizer: Death

The senselessness around striving exacerbates because no matter how long and hard anyone labors to reach the happily-ever-after sweet life, even the most affluent and worldly successful people are still going to die. It's the inevitable "Big C" Chance that happens to everyone (chapter 5). No matter how much money someone socks away, how many investments they make, or how many awards they receive, death is the inevitable end for everyone, including those who are rich and famous (Ecc. 4:4, 5:15–16). As Catholic priest Henri Nouwen beautifully expresses in *Our Greatest Gift*, "We all die poor. When we come to our final hours, nothing can help us survive. No amount of money, power or influence can keep us from dying."[3] For those who are rich or poor, citizen or displaced migrant, death is the ultimate equalizer. We're all going to die.

Length of life is another misnomer, particularly for those who are affluent, because if someone can't, doesn't, or won't appreciate and enjoy what they have while they're living, then there's no difference between life and death (Ecc. 2:16, 21–23). They might as well be dead if they're not going to enjoy the product of their hard work. Finally, earthly affluence doesn't guarantee postmortem success in the hereafter because whatever's in the life beyond is uncertain and to be determined (TBD). Life in the hereafter is a lovely thought and an idealized expectation in many religious traditions, but you still can't and won't know until you personally get there or not. In the Christian tradition, faith may be "the assurance of things hoped for, the conviction of things not seen" (Heb. 11:1), but it's still hope in the sense of a TBD religious belief. Despite what the Egyptian pharaohs attempted to do, they couldn't and didn't take it with them (Ecc. 3:9–11, 18–21; 6:12). Neither can you or I.

Ecclesiastes also affirms the inherent unfairness of life because wealth is fleeting and undependable. Even if someone has tons of money, there's no guarantee that they'll be happy or satisfied. Ecclesiastes calls this evil, not in the sense of moral corruption; rather, it's gross unfairness that's bad news. There's also unfairness in working hard for goods or benefits and then having it enjoyed by others, what Ecclesiastes describes about two heirs who disrespectfully and wastefully squandered what they'd inherited as if they were strangers who "eat" the wealth (Ecc. 2:18, 5:11). Even during someone's lifetime, wealth doesn't necessarily bring satisfaction, sometimes generating a life lived in discontent and without gratification.

Senseless striving also generates a shallowness and self-absorption that doesn't take the time, energy, or interest to respect or care about the world around us, including all living organisms. The environmentalists who dedicate their lives to tracking ecojustice in the borderlands, as well as the volunteers, most of whom are from the affluent American side of the international border, easily could fall prey to the fancy first focus on relentless striving for personal gain. They simply could remain complicit through avoidance, denial, or indifference, flatly not caring about the suffering of displaced migrants or the destruction of Mother Earth. Instead, their spiritual discontent with senseless striving at the expense of the paradoxical injustice disparities explained in the previous chapter forbids apathy or inaction. Their spiritual response is to join in the fight for justice. They recognize personal and national complicity, particularly that much of what the world calls *natural disasters*, which propel much of the forced migration, are actually the result of human gluttony, passion for power, and choice (chapter 7).

Discontent with Economic and Environmental Abuse

Contrary to the affirmation Ecclesiastes gives, "A generation goes and a generation comes, but the earth remains forever" (Ecc. 1:4), this earth is not remaining the same. Past and present economic and environmental abuse are pushing Planet Earth to an unknown place of fire and brimstone, drying up and burning away with the ever-shrinking ozone.[4] The previous chapter highlighted Rosemary Radford Ruether's argument on the suppression of females included in her *Sexism and God-Talk*. She also specifies the environmental subjugation, what she terms, "the rape of the Earth and its people," with the earth encompassing every living creature and natural elements of water, earth, and air. The connection of spirituality to discontent with environmental bad business in the borderlands is evident in Ruether's description of how patriarchy harms oppressed people and Mother Earth: "The labor of dominated bodies, dominated peoples—women, peasants, workers—mediate for those who rule the fruits of the earth. The toil of laboring bodies provides the tools through which the earth is despoiled and left desolate. Through the raped bodies the earth is raped. Those who enjoy the goods distance themselves from the destruction."[5] She explains how forced development pushed onto the Global South displaces the hardworking poor classes and enriches the rich conglomerates who gobble up land and callously cast aside the locals, whom they defame as being "lazy, backward, [and] that they are poor because they have few resources and no energy."[6] Ruether laments that while the rich countries build fancy factories, office buildings, and fruit companies in poorer nations where land and labor are cheap, they suck away the natural resources and cast the farmers off the land to fend for themselves, forcing them to relocate to the city to find any menial task so they can feed their families. Ruether summarizes, "They multiply like festering sores around the glittering steel and glass monuments to development."[7] Then, in all the prideful smugness ingrained in the overachiever strivers from the Global North, as Ruether explains, "On the backs, through the hands of vast toiling masses in Asia, Africa, Latin America, the affluent colonizers arise, congratulate themselves on their progress, and wonder at the poverty and ingratitude of those whose bananas, gold, oil they have consumed."[8] This economic injustice intersects with eco-injustice and spirituality in the borderlands because so many of the families are forced to flee their homelands due to economic injustice exacerbated by eco-*in*justice and the side effects of global warming.

ECO-*IN*JUSTICE INFLUENCES SPIRITUALITY IN THE BORDERLANDS

Eco-*in*justice is a rapidly growing cause for alarm for people in the borderlands who monitor the harm done to the environment when humanmade barriers are installed along an international border. While these walls go up under the guise of "national security" to keep out drugs and "illegal aliens," they also prevent all living creatures from fluidly migrating back and forth in the borderlands. In the *New Yorker* documentary *American Scar: The Environmental Tragedy of the Border Wall*, producer Daniel Lombroso shows the environmental devastation generated by the rapid expansion of the border wall along the Arizona-Mexico international boundary.[9] During the discussion following a film screening for this documentary, several environmental watchdogs explained how and why this documentary is urgently important to show the larger view of the land devastation and disruption of animal migration that previously had fluid access to move back and forth in the borderlands.[10] They also pointed out that this same environmental abuse in the name of national security along the southwest border could easily be pressed on the northern US-Canadian border.

John Kurc, the photographer and videographer who documented the footage included in *American Scar*, was shooting another assignment in Arizona when he decided to get a firsthand and up-close view of the southern border. He said, "I was horrified with the devastation of this incredible desert. And every day there will be three four more blasts and three to four more huge scars in the earth. Then my mission was to start documenting this ecocide. I wanted to show people how wrong it was and how senseless it was." He added, "This wall will never stop people. It will never stop drugs, but it will stop wildlife migration instantly." Myles Traphagen, borderlands program coordinator for

Wildlands Network, explained the particular part of Arizona where the wall was being rapidly expanded in 2016–2020 has tremendous biodiversity with vegetation, black bears, jaguars, and ocelots. He said, "There's really no other place like it on the continent." A rancher on the Mexico side of this border wall expansion location said, "Put cameras just before the construction of the wall you will see a lot of moving wildlife like bobcats or mountain lion or deer. Now when they build that wall in this construction, the animals could not walk through. You will not see any more wildlife because of the direct effect of the construction." Producer and reporter Stephania Taladrid added, "The animals that used to be able to roam between mountain ranges to find food, water, and shelter now have to make a U-turn and go back to where they came from, walking so many more miles in order to find the resources they need."[11] They may or likely may not access sufficient food and/or water.

The videographer elaborated on his shock at the escalation of environmental violence that quickly became evident from one visit and the next to this section of the Arizona-Mexico border. When he made his fourth trip to this section of the border after the coronavirus pandemic travel restrictions were lifted, he remembered, "Everything completely changed. I traveled all the way from Texas to San Diego on the border, any of it that was accessible. And when I got to Arizona, I was just horrified with what I saw in the destruction of these pristine places that I had seen prior." The blasting and reshaping of the land have forever scarred the natural environment, harmed the animals, and limited access to natural migration patterns and access to water. Kurc specified, "The violation of the international boundary and Water Commission treaties is so blatant. When I see these blasts going off, the boulders are not just falling into the US; they're falling into Mexico. This is a very severe violation."[12] In addition to the visual physical scarring of what once was magnificent beauty, animal migration in the borderlands comes to an abrupt standstill with the humanmade barrier to what could and should be a natural ebb and flow.

The environmental scarring continues to widen. A longtime reporter in the borderlands, Melissa del Bosque, posted a photo of a new section of the border wall winding along the Arizona-Mexico border that's made from two freight box cars stacked on top of each other with a roll of concertina wire on top, creating a solid line of metal (see illustration 4.1). The reporter tweeted: "In 20 years of reporting on the US-Mexico border this is one of the most destructive, truly damaging and wasteful things I've ever seen, which is really saying something. This will cost $100 million, keep nobody out &

Illustration 4.1 *Shipping Container Border Blockade* 12" × 8" cut paper collage of the border wall outgoing Arizona governor Doug Ducey hired contractors to build in late 2022 along portions of public land at the Arizona-Mexico border. Art © Helen T. Boursier. Based on a photo by Melissa del Bosque; shared by permission.

forever harm endangered ocelots, jaguars and other species."[13] Responses to Bosque's tweet showing the border barrier from shipping containers expressed the ridiculousness and environmental harm of this political stunt by outgoing Arizona governor Doug Ducey, who had the wall built on public lands without permission or permits. Environmentalists quickly protested because, as the Center for Biological Diversity posted, "This dangerous obstruction runs down the southwestern slopes of the Huachuca Mountains across the San Rafael Valley to the west in the Coronado National Forest. Construction crews have already placed 800 containers over more than three miles. This reckless and illegal construction on federal public land is causing great environmental harm, including blocking critical migratory paths for endangered jaguars and ocelots."[14] The junkyard blockade won't stop human migration, but it will stop the movement of animals, which need to move fluidly in the borderlands to find sufficient food and water.[15]

Spirituality in the borderlands acknowledges and respects the bigger picture, not only this nation's contributions that are part of the catalyst behind forced migration, but also taking into consideration migration in historical context. As ecojustice advocate Traphagen said, "People forget that in the 1930s, we had this happen in the US during the dust bowl. Nearly three million people migrated from the Great Plains to other places because of environmental conditions, because of drought, because of dust storms. So this is not the first rodeo we've all been in, and we need to really look at our history and say, 'Let's facilitate peaceful movement,' you know, constructive migration."[16] Focusing on the eco-*in*justice exacerbated by the humanmade wall at the southwest border, Traphagen added, "And what we've done with this archaic medieval steel structure is the most base, brutal way you could go about doing this. I would hope that we actually start managing by the data, managing by the numbers, and help move people and animals in a fair and humane fashion."[17] Migration has been a normal aspect of human and animal life for thousands of years. Putting a stop to it through an artificial humanmade barrier is physically harmful to humans and animals.

Striving for Ecojustice

The flagrant disregard for the well-being of the environment spurs spirituality for ecojustice in the borderlands. The spiritual and physical cannot help but intersect. Madeleine L'Engle explains in *And It Was Good: Reflections on Beginnings*, "In the Garden of Eden there was no separation of sacred and secular; separation is one of the triumphs of the devil. All of creation is God's, and therefore it is all sacred. And when everything is sacred, then we can understand something about freedom."[18] A humanmade border barrier harms the physical and the spiritual. Making a parallel argument in her letter to the editors of *Ms. Magazine*, Alice Walker writes, "Every affront to human dignity necessarily affects me as a human being on the planet, because I know every single thing on earth is connected."[19] It's common for guilty persons, nations, and governments to disregard this interconnectedness and remain intentionally ignorant of the suffering of others and the environmental harms that power perpetuates. It's even more common to deny any responsibility for causing their suffering.[20] In her essay "Sexism: An American Disease in Blackface," in *Sister Outsider*, Audre Lorde observes, "Oppressors always expect the oppressed to extend to them the understanding so lacking in themselves."²¹ Instead of denial, avoidance, or indifference, which harm spirituality, Lorde proposes it's "the quality of light by which we scrutinize our lives [that] has direct bearing upon the product which we live, and upon the changes which we hope to bring about through those lives. It is within this light that we form those ideas by which we pursue our magic and make it realized."²² It's a light that shines truth into darkness, brightening it enough to see a pathway for a spirituality of and for justice. It's a light that cares for the environment while also welcoming the otherwise unwelcome displaced families.

EMBRACING A SPIRITUALITY OF DISCONTENT TO TRANSFORM INJUSTICE IN THE BORDERLANDS

Spirituality in the borderlands embraces discontent to transform injustice, similar to what Simone Weil terms "contradictions." It's a spirituality that's discontent with multiple paradoxes or contractions to justice: North/South, rich/poor, citizen/alien, male/female, white / Black or brown dichotomies that exacerbate paradox to disproportionately dump injustice on the "lesser" side of the equation: South, poor, alien, female, Black or brown. In *Gravity and Grace,* Weil insists, "Contradiction alone is the proof that we are not everything. Contradiction is our wretchedness, and the sense of our wretchedness is the sense of reality. For we do not invent our wretchedness. It is true. That is why we have to value it. All the rest is imaginary."²³ A Jewish rabbi who volunteers with displaced families in southern Arizona names the contradiction permeating the definitive Americana paradox: "Strength is a weakness." Elaborating on a similar point, a GVS Samaritan said, "America is not number one in everything. People like to believe the lies because it's comfortable and it's easier, and it's also really, really sad."

Spirituality in the borderlands is an enactment of discontent with American indifference and its lackadaisical response to challenge and change injustice, including and especially the bad business this nation is responsible for generating. Rather than joining complicity through inaction and silence, this spirituality emits its discontent by opting to become part of the solution to grievous evils in the borderlands. It's a justice-focused spirituality that rejects the popular American ideal of circling the wagons to "keep America great" by protecting our wealth, our affluence, our jobs, our whiteness, our national identity, or whatever exclusionary vision lurks beneath the fear of losing American (white) identity, a supremely negative and counterproductive fear-based response that undergirds the harmful government policies and practices in the borderlands—what equates to *spirituality in reverse*.

Instead of this harmful and counterproductive approach, spirituality in the borderlands works for justice and peacemaking, which move forth from what de Beauvoir proposes comes from recognizing the moral essence of self.[24] This inner moral call refocuses internalized personal spirituality to the greater good through external interconnection to benefit the larger global community. It's this focus on what's honorable, moral, and just that motivates volunteers and environmentalists to work for justice and peacemaking to bless the greater good of all. Kurtz and Ketcham explain, "Spirituality is discovered in that space between paradox's extremes, for there we confront our helplessness and powerlessness, our *woundedness*.... Spirituality begins with the acceptance that our fractured being, our imperfection, simply is.... Spirituality helps us first to *see*, and then to *understand*, and eventually to *accept* the imperfection that lies at the very core of our human *be*-ing."[25] This focus shifts spirituality from overachieving (striving) self (-centeredness) to embracing the blessings and presence of others. Instead of generating cynicism, discontent with grievous evil, and perpetual striving, an ethical moral focus provides numerous places to enter in through practical response for those who choose to find meaning-making through a spirituality that works for justice and peacemaking in the borderlands or wherever else the moral muse pushes, pulls, or calls.

SPIRITUAL MATURITY: AN ALTERNATIVE TO PERPETUAL STRIVING

True spirituality is impossible amid the excessive striving and overproductivity that generate harsh human and eco-*in*justice fallout. Such striving inevitably perpetrates discontent (Ecc. 4:4). Danish philosopher-theologian Søren Kierkegaard is well known for arguing the priority *to will one thing*, and for Kierkegaard that *thing* is a right relationship with the Creator God. So instead of being so obsessed with striving to be somebody, Kierkegaard prioritizes the lifelong spiritual goal to constantly strive to become "a person worthy of relating to God."[26] Gottlieb explains that this is a lifelong process that levels the playing field. Instead of striving to become one of a handful of those who are rich and famous, genuine success becomes an option for anyone and everyone when that success is measured by being worthy to be called "a friend of God" (James 2:23). Gottlieb explains, following the Kierkegaardian priority of striving, "To devote oneself to being worthy of a relation with God, then each person's life is of infinite importance." This Kierkegaardian perspective is particularly important as an antidote to traditional monetary/success striving because "no one's success comes at the price of anyone else's insignificance, no one can do the job for another, and the task itself carries on for a lifetime."[27] Living into this spiritual aim, though not necessarily specified as being directed toward right relationship with God so much as right relationship with the entire created world—human, animal, and the natural environment—informs the outlets for response that volunteers and environmentalists choose as antidotes to their proactive dissent to US injustice. Sometimes they express this as righteous anger through the work they do to challenge and change injustice at the border but also through their compassion, generosity, gentleness, and joy in their interactions with displaced migrants. These experiential interactions diffuse cynicism, meaninglessness, and futility through the blessedness of personal connections with the families and difference-making for the environment.

A Spirituality of Resistance

Instead of the American drive with its ceaseless striving for more, Gottlieb proposes an alternate spiritual viewpoint that "offers gratitude instead of grasping, simple joy instead of compulsive consumption, openness to life instead of a driven (and fruitless) attempt to control everything."[28] It's a perspective that moves someone to engage in what he terms a "spirituality of resistance." Instead of being part of the problem, this spirituality becomes part of the solution through advocacy and presence with those who are suffering and oppressed.

Death by Bread Alone

Dorothee Soelle believes all this senseless striving will cause what she calls "death by bread alone," with bread representing whatever fancy toys, treasures, or dream vacations that someone's striving pursues in their self-defined vision of the perfect life/style. After offering the example of a neighbor who builds the dream house and then freaks out whenever the tiniest little thing happens to damage this prized possession, Soelle explains, "Death by bread alone is the death by mutilation, death by suffocation, the death of all relationships. Bread alone guarantees the kind of death where we can continue to vegetate for a while because the machine is still running, the terrible death by lack of connection: we continue to breathe, keep on consuming, we eliminate, we get things done, we produce, we still mutter words, and yet we are not alive."[29] Striving for the sake of striving negates spirituality and dramatically reduces the value of life itself.

Similarly, in the *Rock That Is Higher: Story as Truth*, Madeleine L'Engle insightfully notes, "All too often we fall for it and go into debt to buy the latest gadget. Whatever it is, it's made to self-destruct after a few years, and it will never help whatever it is that's making us hurt."[30] It's this self-destruction and hurting that lead to death by bread alone. Soelle warns, "The person who lives from bread alone and dies of it, of the bread you cannot live on. This is the death the Bible speaks of; it fears this death and arouses the fear of it—not the exit we mostly associate with death, but the death that is a senseless and empty life, the death amidst absence of relationship, fear, speechlessness, abandonment."[31] Not only do people die from bread alone through futile striving with all of the requisite ill effects from wealth attainment but this same push for economic prosperity also harms the environment, a factor spirituality in the borderlands laments, documents, and seeks to challenge and change.

Moving toward Spiritual Maturity

Spiritual development that moves toward spiritual maturity requires honesty with reality. It engages the inner sense of reflective knowing with the external realities that agree or impact a spirituality of and for justice and peacemaking, a spirituality that can't not also include resistance to *in*justice. Gottlieb prioritizes the importance of being honest during listening and searching for what's actually occurring. He notes, "If we are going to listen and search, we had better take seriously what turns up, no matter how scary it is."[32] With his context of ecojustice in view, Gottlieb emphasizes the importance to "not be afraid of the depths of our feelings about the environmental crisis [or the humanitarian crisis in the borderlands]. While these feelings are painful, they also reveal the depth of our connections to the rest of the world."[33] While he acknowledges "the first temptation is that of despair,"[34] a handwritten note in the margin from an earlier reader of my used copy of a *Spirituality of Resistance* clarifies, "Despair causes us to stop when problems come. Resistance causes us to act." It's a spirituality that engages with the world around us to make a proactive difference for the greater good of Mother Earth and *all* created beings.

Divine Rage

In response to their discontent with the shallowness generated from ceaseless striving and the fallout of injustice in the borderlands, volunteers embrace positive, helpful, and productive actions to transform their anger, frustration, disappointment, and any former naivete or denial through what Valarie Kaur terms "divine rage," a more vocal, aggressive, and engaged variation of baseline discontent. For Kaur, "The aim of divine rage is not vengeance but to reorder the world. It is precise and purposeful. . . . It points us to the humanity of even those who we are fighting." Connecting this rage to the Hindu goddess Kali, viewed as a motherlike figure who also is the goddess of time and death, Kaur points out, "It is only *through* accessing her ferocity that divine rage can take form in the world. Perhaps our task as human beings is to find safe containers for our raw reactionary rage—and then choose to harness that energy in a way that creates a new world for *all* of us."[35] Divine rage is expansive and inclusive. It's also a rage that embraces justice and peacemaking.

Kaur's sense of divine rage includes wide-ranging activist and humanitarian response options, such as what occurs in the borderlands. She writes, "Now I see instances of divine rage everywhere. I see it in the activists who storm the stage at political rallies, disrupt confirmation hearings, and confront senators in elevators. I see it in the indigenous rituals that appear in the wake of atrocities . . . I see it in people who stand up to tell the truth at school board meetings, in workplaces, on social media, and at their kitchen tables." She acknowledges there are numerous ways to respond to injustice without such fiery rage or anger, adding, "But in the case of ongoing social injustices, expressing outrage is often the only way to be heard."[36] Kaur also recognizes that, of course, engaging "divine rage can make people uncomfortable: It can feel disruptive, frightening, and unpredictable. There are those who wish to police such rage in the name of civility. But civility is too often used to silence pain that requires people to change their lives."[37] Divine rage doesn't equate to hate, a distinctly negative response that's completely and totally counterproductive and unhelpful, as MLK famously insisted: "Hate is just as injurious to the person who hates."[38] Hate destroys, whereas divine rage speaks out for justice and peace.

Expressing discontent with injustice in the borderlands through moral outrage in public settings becomes a vehicle for justice and an integral component of a spirituality in the borderlands that responds attentively to in/justice. It's exactly this sense of divine rage that prompted environmentalists to conduct peaceful protests to halt the construction of the junkyard border wall in Arizona in late 2022. Their outraged persistence was rewarded with the news that this ridiculous environmental travesty would be removed.[39] "Again, I looked and saw all the oppression that was taking place under the sun: I saw the tears of the oppressed—and they have no comforter; power was on the side of their oppressors—and they have no comforter" (Ecc. 4:1 NIV).

SPIRITUALITY THAT PAYS ATTENTION TO *INJUSTICE*

Philosophers, followed a bit belatedly by theologians, have long argued that it's the stranger, the other, who offers the genuine opportunity to become a kind, compassionate, loving, caring, and just person.[40] We become our best spiritual selves when we unabashedly invite in those who are different from us. In *Uncommon Gratitude: Alleluia for All That Is,* Benedictine sister Joan Chittister proposes, "The 'other' is the one who teaches us that we are not the whole world. We are only a piece of it waiting for the 'other' to make us more than we were when we began. Alleluia."[41] In particular for spiritual growth, through our presence with those who suffer, it becomes possible to grow in compassion, love, and kindness. It's this presence with the suffering others that serves as a guidon to what's truly meaningful in life. Chittister adds, "Clearly, suffering calls us to conversion, to that change of attitude that softens our hearts to one another and opens our arms to life in all its shapes and forms."[42] In addition, she argues, "Suffering is what puts us in touch with the rest of the human race."[43] To look away, in apathy, disinterest, indifference, or even self-righteousness, is *spirituality in decline,* a reverse spirituality of immaturity rather than of life-giving growth. Chittister explains, "It is suffering that moves us to rethink life, to find other kinds of meaning in life, to realize that life is made up of stages, each different from the last, each one a new challenge—and a new pitfall—as we begin to negotiate the tasks peculiar to each of them."[44] When anyone becomes sucked into the culture of striving, it requires consistent intentionality to physically, mentally, spiritually, emotionally, and holistically step aside from the gerbil wheel and shift gears to being discontent with the shallow, self-centered, striving life and instead move toward care and compassion for the trashed environment and the strangers seeking asylum at our southern border.

Positive spiritual growth requires actively engaging discontent with the superficiality and injustices surrounding paradox (chapter 3) in order to refocus and embrace a spirituality of resistance, which appreciates and respects the precious precarity of all life. In *Dance of the Spirit*, Maria Harris describes as the apt starting point that acts "in response to these lies (and deep down within us we know they are lies), I propose the attitude of disbelief, for it will nurture Awakening."[45] Applying her argument for resistance to gender injustice to the displaced families who've experienced it, Harris specifies, "We must learn to practice *disbelief*. We can say it quietly or we can shout it. But when told we are inferior or unworthy *because we are women*, then we must say something. And in the face of the lies about our spiritual incapacities, there is only one thing to say. And it is 'No, I don't believe that. Not anymore.'"[46] Her gender-focused argument parallels practicing disbelief of the blatant lies surrounding grievous evils, paradox, and bad business in the borderlands, including human and environmental. Disbelief embraces discontent, creating spiritual empowerment to work for the greater good, powered with love and compassion.

Volunteers, advocates, and environmentalists personify their discontent with the shallowness generated from ceaseless striving for the American dream through their presence in love and compassion as they work for justice, embracing actions that gain a more meaningful life. A seventy-five-year-old grandmother who makes regular trips to help migrants and Mexican nationals in Piedras Negras, Mexico, said, "We're so spoiled. You know, our culture is so spoiled." She highlighted the example that she brings thrown-away canned goods, clothing, toys, and other supplies to this Mexico border community as her response to the paradox between the disposable culture in America and her friends in the borderlands. The Texan said she takes a lot of outdated food by US standards, quickly adding, "But they're still good. I don't bring any food down to the border that I wouldn't eat myself." For her, the disjuncture is between spoiled Americans who are too precious to eat foods after the best-by dates, in stark contrast to the families at the border who struggle for the bare necessities for survival. She said, "If you give someone something that they can use and make their life better, even something that might seem very simple, it just warms your heart so much." Disposable America offers a sharp contrast and pointed paradox with the families in the borderlands.

Discontent with striving and with inattention to injustice shapes and reinforces the spirituality of the incensed, disheartened, and compassionate Americans who see the unfairness, inequities, and mistreatment and who also pointedly connect *our* complicity to *their* suffering. Each has their own reasons for why they help the families, but the definitive commonality is the desire to become part of the solution to the clearly dysfunctional grievous evils in the borderlands. Objecting to dysfunctionality in the borderlands motivates their spirituality to engage in practical action framed around humanitarian compassion. Moving toward honesty with reality about the bad business around paradox begins to foster a spirituality of compassionate response that intersects with spiritual hope.

STRIVING AND MIGRATING FAMILIES: INTERSECTION OF HOPE

The intersecting spirituality in the borderlands is that *their* hope can become *our* hope. Liberation theologian Jon Sobrino is well known for his argument that "the [suffering] poor have a humanizing potential because they offer community [instead of] individualism, service [instead of] selfishness, and simplicity [instead of] opulence."[47] He believes those poor people who are suffering, whom he calls the "crucified people," also offer hope. He explains, "Of course it is hope against hope, but it is also active hope that has been demonstrated in work and struggle for liberation.... The very fact that hope rises again and again in the crucified people shows that there is a hopeful current in history available to all."[48] This active hope of the families is a pervasive aspect of spirituality in the borderlands because it exemplifies what's worthwhile in life. Their hope provides a visceral antidotal option to discontent to Americans who are tired of the treadmill connected to perpetual striving. Sobrino explains, "The crucified people offer hope, senseless and absurd, it may be said, 'because it's all they have left,' others may argue. But there it is and it should not be trivialized by other worlds."[49] Futility in striving for justice amid rampant grievous evil pushes the families out of their homelands and onto the migrant trail, where hope is their guide throughout their journey.

There's only so much striving anyone can do to navigate, challenge, and/or overcome when horrific grievous evils run unchecked, particularly for vulnerable women, children, and unempowered marginalized minorities. When striving to survive paradoxical injustice in their homelands becomes no longer tolerable, survivable, or a remote option, the families shift from striving for life in their homelands to striving for life as displaced migrants. They express their discontent with the paradox of bad business in their homelands by making their choice to migrate to the United States (chapter 7), hoping and praying to defy the odds and experience the American myth of being able to live happily and safely ever after. Hope for peace and safety is an integral element in their journey, but it's a very different kind of hope than the American dream striving-for-success hope. Rather, their hope is for life, for themselves and their children. Their hope maintains what Gottlieb proposes is "the steadfastness of hope," which is what he describes as "essential, just because it expresses our capacity to think beyond the pain we ourselves are experiencing in any particular moment and to delight in the prospect that someone, somewhere, can still find happiness."[50] This is the magnitude of hope for a better, safer future that pushes the families out the door and also sustains them throughout their long journey. Despite the inherent risks (chapter 8), the families must at least *attempt* to strive to gain a place and space of safety (chapter 9). When remaining at home is no longer possible, their singular option is to take the chance for a better/safer life, hoping and praying every step of the way toward the strange new land before them.

NOTES

1. Luc Olinga, "FTX Collapse: Sam Bankman-Fried Will Stand Trial in October," MSN, January 4, 2023, https://www.msn.com/en-us/money/markets/ftx-collapse-sam-bankman-fried-will-stand-trial-in-october/ar-AA15Xrm8.
2. *Encyclopedia Britannica*, "Howard Hughes," accessed January 4, 2023, https://www.britannica.com/biography/Howard-Hughes.
3. Henri J. M. Nouwen, *Our Greatest Gift: A Meditation on Dying and Caring* (San Francisco: HarperCollins, 1995), 31.
4. See Allyson Chiu, "Climate Solutions: People Don't Really Talk about Climate Change: Here's How to Start," *Washington Post*, September 16, 2022, https://www.washingtonpost.com/climate-solutions/2022/09/16/climate-change-conversation-action/?utm_campaign=wp_post_most&utm_medium=email&utm_source

=newsletter&wpisrc=nl_most&carta-url=https%3A%2F%2Fs2.washingtonpost.com%2Fcar-ln-tr%2F37f07f7%2F632497aef3d9003c58db65b2%2F601b21b3ae7e8a31ba652c5f%2F31%2F72%2F632497aef3d9003c58db65b2&wp_cu=c69473bc37b1c5a5d5387d9454883ddd%7CBA76FEAA9C964D77E0530100007F5803.

5. Ruether, *Sexism and God-Talk*, 263.
6. Ruether, *Sexism and God-Talk*, 263.
7. Ruether, *Sexism and God-Talk*, 264.
8. Ruether, *Sexism and God-Talk*, 264.
9. Daniel Lombroso, "American Scar: The Environmental Tragedy of the Border Wall," *New Yorker* documentary, YouTube, April 30, 2022, https://www.youtube.com/watch?v=Cx71C4iguuk&t=13s.
10. Sky Island Alliance, "American Scar Post-Film Q&A," YouTube, May 5, 2022, https://www.youtube.com/watch?v=p9xcrXMbd4M&t=1s.
11. Sky Island Alliance, "American Scar Post-Film Q&A."
12. Sky Island Alliance, "American Scar Post-Film Q&A."
13. Melissa del Bosque @MelissaLaLinea, Twitter, 11:41 a.m., November 30, 2022, https://twitter.com/MelissaLaLinea/status/1598009218417983490. See also Melissa del Bosque, "Arizona Governor Builds Border Wall of Shipping Crates in Final Days of Office," *Guardian*, December 11, 2022, https://www.theguardian.com/us-news/2022/dec/11/arizona-governor-border-wall-shipping-containers.
14. Center for Biological Diversity, https://www.biologicaldiversity.org/.
15. See Andrew Christiansen, "Santa Cruz County Sheriff Threatening Action against People Working on Shipping Container Border Wall," KGUN 9 News, December 5, 2022, https://www.kgun9.com/news/local-news/santa-cruz-county-sheriff-threatening-action-against-people-working-on-shipping-container-border-wall.
16. Sky Island Alliance, "American Scar Post-Film Q&A."
17. Sky Island Alliance, "American Scar Post-Film Q&A."
18. Madeleine L'Engle, *And It Was Good: Reflections on Beginnings*, Book One in the Genesis Trilogy, foreword by Rachel Held Evans (New York: Convergent, 1983, 2017), 46.
19. Alice Walker, "To the Editors of Ms. Magazine," in *In Search of Our Mothers' Gardens*, ed. Alice Walker (New York: Houghton Mifflin Harcourt Publishing Company, 1983), 347–354, 353.
20. See Reinhold Niebuhr, *Moral Man and Immoral Society: A Study in Ethics and Politics*, introduction by Langdon B. Gilkey (Louisville, KY: Westminster John Knox Press, 1932, 2001).
21. Audre Lorde, "Sexism: An American Disease in Blackface," in Lorde, *Sister Outsider*, 63.
22. Audre Lorde, "Poetry Is Not a Luxury," in Lorde, *Sister Outsider*, 36.
23. Weil, *Gravity and Grace*, 95.
24. de Beauvoir, *Ethics of Ambiguity*, 75.
25. Kurtz and Ketcham, *Spirituality of Imperfection*, 2.
26. Gottlieb, *A Spirituality of Resistance*, 62.
27. Gottlieb, *A Spirituality of Resistance*, 62.
28. Gottlieb, *A Spirituality of Resistance*, 59.
29. Soelle, *The Mystery of Death*, 118. See also Dorothee Soelle, *Death by Bread Alone: Texts and Reflections on Religious Experience*, trans. David L. Scheidt (Philadelphia: Fortress Press, 1978).

30 Madeleine L'Engle, *The Rock That Is Higher: Story as Truth* (Wheaton, IL: Harold Shaw Publishers, 1993), 272.
31 Soelle, *The Mystery of Death*, 119.
32 Gottlieb, *A Spirituality of Resistance*, 55.
33 Gottlieb, *A Spirituality of Resistance*, 55.
34 Gottlieb, *A Spirituality of Resistance*, 56.
35 Kaur, *See No Stranger*, 133.
36 Kaur, *See No Stranger*, 133–134.
37 Kaur, *See No Stranger*, 134.
38 King Jr., *Strength to Love*, 53.
39 Jack Healy, "Arizona Agrees to Dismantle Border Wall Made from Cargo Containers," *New York Times*, December 21, 2022, https://www.nytimes.com/2022/12/21/us/arizona-border-shipping-containers.html#:~:text=Dec.%2021%2C%202022%20PHOENIX%20%E2%80%94%20Gov.%20Doug%20Ducey,the%20Biden%20administration%20against%20Mr.%20Ducey%2C%20a%20Republican.
40 See Boursier, *Ethics of Hospitality*, 240–244.
41 Chittister and Williams, *Uncommon Gratitude*, 113.
42 Chittister and Williams, *Uncommon Gratitude*, 129.
43 Chittister and Williams, *Uncommon Gratitude*, 130.
44 Chittister and Williams, *Uncommon Gratitude*, 131.
45 Harris, *Dance of the Spirit*, 18.
46 Harris, *Dance of the Spirit*, 18.
47 See Jon Sobrino, *Jesus the Liberator: A Historical-Theological Reading of Jesus of Nazareth* (Maryknoll, NY: Orbis Books, 1993).
48 Sobrino, *Jesus the Liberator*, 263.
49 Sobrino, *Jesus the Liberator*, 263.
50 Gottlieb, *A Spirituality of Resistance*, 56.

CHAPTER FIVE

Chance

Since no one knows the future, who can tell someone else what is to come? As no one has power over the wind to contain it, so no one has power over the time of their death.

—Ecclesiastes 8:7–8a (NIV)

Life is filled with unpredictable chance events, actions, and encounters, sometimes referred to as *luck, fate, karma,* or *providence.* Some are good, some bad. In Ecclesiastes, chance includes the Big-C Chance, *death* (Ecc. 9:11–12), and the little-c chance, small encounters that can generate a positive lucky outcome and others that are unlucky, miserable raw deals (Ecc. 4:8, 5:14, 10:5). Whether small, large, or the ultimate Big-C Chance that signifies death, these interactions are an inevitable part of the human condition and the precariousness of this precious but very fragile life. Navigating these unpredictable experiences interfaces with a spirituality of finitude, the reality of the finiteness of this short life. This sense of finitude permeates the borderlands, where death looms larger than life. Ecclesiastes posits it's how each person responds to chance encounters that contribute or not to finding calm within the storm.

THE UNPREDICTABILITY OF C/CHANCE

The reason chance is termed *chance* is because it's unpredictable. No one has total control over what happens. Accidents occur; that's why they're called *accidents.* It's possible to be prudent, cautious, and extremely careful, but this doesn't guarantee anyone can or will skirt or avoid chance. In her introduction to Hannah Arendt's *The Human Condition*, Margaret Canovan points out that "the other side of that miraculous unpredictability of action is lack of control over its effects." Similar to the unpredictability of C/chance in Ecclesiastes, Canovan explains, "Action sets things in motion, and one cannot foresee even the effects of one's own initiatives, let alone control what happens when they are entangled with other people's initiates in the public arena."[1] Motivational speaker Zig Ziglar was famous for saying, "Luck is where preparation meets opportunity," an idealistic view that resonates with the America-first work ethic. As explained earlier, the wisdom of dissent in Ecclesiastes shows that this optimism works when it works, but many times, it's just not so. Instead, Ecclesiastes points out, "Again I saw that under the sun the race is not to the swift, nor the battle to the strong, nor bread to the wise, nor riches to the intelligent, nor favor to the skillful, but time and chance happen to them all" (Ecc. 9:11 NRSVUE). Sometimes chance interferes, and bad things happen.

Hard work doesn't guarantee a happily-ever-after ride on the merry-go-round or roller coaster of life. Preparation doesn't ensure avoiding some nasty outcomes with chance. For example, I flunked one of the five ordination exams when I was a seminarian preparing for vocational ordained ministry in the Presbyterian Church (USA). It was the easiest one at that. Despite all the advance studying I did to guarantee my success, I flunked one anyway. The committee on preparation for ministry later asked me how I felt about failing one of these exams after I'd retaken it six months later and passed. A committee member quickly explained they wouldn't normally ask someone this, but since I was "so successful" at everything, they wondered how I felt about "failing." I remember responding that between two of these lengthy exams, I'd had a chance encounter with a peer who was in distress and needed someone to be present in solidarity to listen and encourage. Instead of the last-minute cramming that I would've done, I spent time encouraging this friend and future ministry colleague. In addition, I'd also come down with a nasty cold, and I'd spent much of the previous night coughing and not sleeping. With the Ecclesiastes message already in my spirit from previous coursework, I took the "failure" as chance. Similarly, when I attended one of the women's marches that was quickly organized to protest the repeal of *Roe v. Wade*, I tripped on the uneven brick walkway in a city park in San Antonio. I took a hard fall that netted a nasty black eye plus a frozen shoulder that took a year to recover from. I tend toward clumsiness, so I intentionally look down while I'm walking, particularly in unknown territory, so I won't stumble over something. In this case, I'd glanced up to look toward the bandstand area where I'd be meeting a friend, and at this exact chance moment, the brick walkway dramatically slanted at a forty-five-degree angle, my foot went down wrong, and I did a face-plant onto the red brick walkway in this historic old park. It wasn't my fault. I was being cautious, but still chance happened, and I ended up in the emergency room.

Precaution helps to reduce the risk of accidents, just as advance preparation for an exam helps to ensure success, but chance still intervenes. Accidental encounters, large and small, can still cause problems. As Choon-Leong Seow writes in his commentary on Ecclesiastes, "Sometimes accidents just happen, no matter how careful one tries to be. Wisdom may have its advantage, but wisdom guarantees nothing."[2] Prudence, wisdom, and precautionary measures help to a point—but only to a point. I didn't flunk the ordination exam or take a hard fall that netted a frozen shoulder on purpose. I was prepared. I was cautious. Chance happened anyway, and bad things happened. The same concept applies to the families and the chance encounters that contribute to their forced migration, additional chance that harms them during their journey, and the chance that continues to dog them during their application process to receive asylum in this country. They aren't doing bad things or making poor choices. They're not at fault. Rather, they are the recipients of chance after chance after chance.

THE BIG-C CHANCE AND LIVING LIFE WITH THE END IN VIEW

Ecclesiastes wants us to make the most of the small-c chance events because the Big-C Chance, death, is coming for everyone. We don't know what leads up to the Big-C Chance, including the location, context, suffering, or the exact moment, what Ecclesiastes terms the "appointed time" (Ecc. 3:11; see also chapter 6). Despite any survival-of-the-fittest mindset, death is the inevitable, unavoidable, and ultimate reality for all. There are no excused absences from this finite end to all life. Death is the nonnegotiable given of the finite nature of what it means to be human. We're all going to die. Period.

The Big-C Chance is foremost in a spirituality of borders because the families are desperately trying to live much longer lives than what would be

Illustration 5.1 *Rugged Terrain* 7" × 7" black-and-white acrylic painting of the Sonoran Desert with ocotillo cactus and a distant mountain range in the southern Arizona desert, where migrants often lose their way, become disabled, and die alone. Art © Helen T. Boursier.

possible if they remained in their homelands, where a much earlier death would be immanent. For example, Mary, who fled El Salvador, explained, "I left my country because on August 22, they killed my sister with a machete. That's how it happened to her, and that's how it would have happened to me if I had stayed. That's why I'm running. They almost killed me. They beat my son—the gang members. I tried to stop them, but I couldn't. They stole everything from me. I left for the United States."³ With the Big C on the immediate horizon due to extenuating circumstances beyond her control, she looked to the little-c chance risks and chose migration. Although the migrants are seeking to flee death, they end up becoming front and center with the Big-C Chance, death, throughout their migration journey to America.

Big-C Chance is also evident in the spirits of the volunteers, particularly those who help with searches for injured or lost migrants who are traveling on foot through the Sonoran Desert, a large region that encompasses three states in northwest Mexico and sections in the southwestern United States. There are many ways to die in this desert on both sides of the US-Mexico border, including due to human trafficking, being kidnapped for organ donation, falling or being pushed off of a train, dehydration, exposure, hypothermia, flash flooding, hunger, thirst, and becoming disoriented or stranded from an injury in this immense and environmentally harsh desert (illustration 5.1). These risks are factually and experientially documented. In the Sonoran Desert in southern Arizona, Caroline Tracey reports that "the numbers [of migrant deaths] kept going: the forensic office identifying human remains at the [Arizona] border."[4] In fact, southern Arizona has the most documented deaths of "unidentified border crossers," primarily related to the expansion of the border wall that pushes migrants farther out into the desert to cross the international border. Since the Pima County office of the medical examiner began in May 2002 to document the full and partial remains of the deceased, this "office has classified 3,600 deaths in its electronic records system as 'Unidentified Border Crossers.'" Dr. Bruce Anderson, who directs this office's work to identify the remains of these migrants said, early on in this work, he expected the rising number of remains would capture the attention and concern of lawmakers in Washington. But it did not. He said instead it became obvious "that no number of deaths would be high enough to attract Washington's attention."[5] This inattention and lack of concern for so many migrants dying unnamed and often alone in the desert inform the spirituality of resistance in the borderlands, a resistance to death that's informed by a deep appreciation and respect for life—all life.

A GVS Samaritan said her respect for all life that informs her empathy with migrating families goes back to her younger years when she lived in Mexico, where she worked at an educational center from North America that included visiting some of the extremely poor villages and also people living inside cities who were in squatter settlements. She said, "I learned what they're coming from and what they're fleeing, and I can't turn my back on what they're fleeing." When the Samaritans are conducting searches in the desert for injured or disoriented migrants, the volunteer said, "We meet people whose lives are saved. Even if it's just one person that you find who's completely lost and has blisters on their feet. If they kept going, they'd be dead within a day or two." She added, "You just can't turn your back on that." The Samaritans conduct several searches on remote roads each week, looking to chance upon stranded migrants who've fallen prey to chance or Chance in the Sonoran Desert. The GVS Samaritan meeting notes regularly highlight close encounters with displaced migrants. For example:

> Randy drove two searches: Drove Shura and Director of GV concert band (along with his clarinet because he said that the car was too hot to leave it!). East of Sasabe, they found Alejandro, a Guatemalan carrying a cartel-made Mexican ID. He was walking in Mexican desert two days, plus one-and-a-half days in US desert and in bad shape, probably because of bad knees. He could not keep up with his group. He had paid the cartel $3,000 and owed another $12,000 upon arrival in New York City. His initial group included about 300, and was broken into smaller groups of about 15, each traveling with a coyote. [The search team] gave humanitarian assistance, called 911, but they had no [cell] coverage and transported him until they saw a helicopter. Ten to fifteen minutes later, a helicopter dropped down and three agents got out, Alejandro and the searchers got out of the vehicle. BP [border patrol] asked if it was truly an emergency. We said, "Yes, Alejandro was in bad shape." They said "OK," and said we could leave.[6]

It's an ethical choice to dedicate time each week to offer lifesaving humanitarian assistance to stranded migrants, taking their own chance to prevent Chance from happening to others.

Little-c chance and Living Life in the Present

Ecclesiastes wants us to view life with the end in mind. Given that the Big-C Chance happens to everyone, how ought we to live our lives now? Instead of dwelling on the negative aspect of Big-C Chance, Ecclesiastes prefers to concentrate on the little-c chances, these unpredictable interruptions, detours, and changes that swerve in and out of life. Life is tough while we're still alive, and then we die, but the living possess hope, which the dead don't. The one who is alive is *still alive* and therefore has at least a modicum of hope for a better future. Regardless of whatever precarious disruption of chance that someone's in the middle of, there's still hope as long as there's still life, for the living know that they are still alive (Ecc. 9:4). Embracing the present, with respect for the reality of the finiteness or finitude of life, with the inevitable death that comes hopefully much, much, much later interfaces with the perspective each person carries through life, including when the little c's disrupt things and the unexpected discursions from whatever the vision is for happily ever after. The attitude about these little c's has the possibility to make a profound spiritual impact for peace, centeredness, and the ability to make prudent choices in response to the unpredictable chances dropped on them. Or not.

For instance, a *Far Side* cartoon by Gary Larson once depicted how attitude or perspective shapes response amid the downer chances of life. The cartoon featured a man who was pushing a wheelbarrow up a hill, whistling as he carted the heavy load full of rocks. Meanwhile, a personification of the devil was shown poking people with pitchforks. The comic strip essentially said the person whistling didn't understand that he wasn't supposed to be happy in hell. Similarly, Ecclesiastes emphasizes the importance of making the best of your lot in life, including navigating the c-bomb chances that explode around you. While we can't totally avoid or control little-c chance, we can choose our spiritual attitude when chance disrupts our lives, even when a bigger chance hits you in the face, leaving you reeling with what any response could or should be.

Spiritual Maturity Shapes Response

Spiritual maturity shapes response, and response then shapes spirituality, including each person's attitude about how to navigate through each chance. A spirituality of borders directly relates to chance in the broader human perspective because it leans into current circumstances with hope for a better future. There are numerous times, places, and circumstances when the Big-C threat to life can move dramatically close to the present at any given unpredictable chance moment. For example, one of the older nursing students in one of my Introduction to Spirituality classes journaled about the physical struggles he'd been having in the aging process, and he wondered, at age sixty-two, how he'd be able to continue with the demanding work involved in his new profession. He ultimately realized he'd been fighting against the inevitable aging process and instead that he wanted to work on what he termed "leaning into aging."[7] This is the same concept of leaning into chance that provides balance in the spirituality of the families in the borderlands.

Chance before the Journey

The litany of unlucky chance encounters confronting these families, while technically falling under the Ecclesiastes concept of a little-c chance, are so predictably consistent that a quick list of them shows how normative these little-c chance happenings are that force the families to exodus their homelands. Consider, for example:

- Ada: "I saw someone murder a lady. Now they want to kill me."
- Evelyn: "The gangs were extorting money from me—money I did not have. The next step was death."
- Ingrid: "The gangs cornered our son in the bathroom at school during the second recess They said, 'We will murder all three of you. Do not doubt what we are telling you. We have massacred others.'"
- Anderson, sixteen: "The MS13 gang (Mara Salvatrucha) tried to force me to join their gang. I refused. They said they would kill my parents if I did not join their gang. I was obligated to leave my country. I had no choice."[8]

There are so many examples from the families about their chance encounters that generate suffering and force their migration journey. Each story is unique and personal to the particular people whose lives are impacted.

There's also a sameness to the suffering, a repetition of the types of violent chance that force survivors and innocent victims to flee for their lives. Sibia, from Honduras, explained, "Four years ago they killed my daughter's father, and now they persecute us and want to kill us because of some debts he left behind when they killed him. I beg the United State to help me protect my daughter so she can study. She is seven." She added, "I have proof of everything I've said. Her father's name was Josué Castillo Rivera. His death appeared in the papers."[9] A teenager from Honduras, Lorraine, shared the nightmare chance behind her journey to America, saying, "When I reached adolescence, my stepfather wanted to have sexual relations with me. When I told my mother, she intervened, and he beat her. Then he threatened that if we left our country, he would kill us. We were so afraid." She added, "Now we are in this migrant shelter, and members from the cartels come every night and touch the windows. We are so afraid."[10] The little-c chance encounters can quickly intersect with the Big-C Chance. Sometimes the families are suddenly forced to make their decision to migrate. Other times, they endure numerous bad chance happenings in their lives for several years before something snaps in their spirits, and they can no longer tolerate one more grievous evil enacted against them.

Luck or Providential Chance?

The families also experience chance as good luck when they're making their decision to flee. For instance, a mother shared her family's experience after receiving death threats: "We talked as a family about leaving to migrate to the USA, but when we looked outside, we saw gang members surrounding our house. Then we saw a police car nearby, and it also started raining. We took advantage of these chance distractions and left the house." Explaining these chance occurrences literally during the moments they were making the decision to migrant, the mother said, "We know that God Almighty intervened to protect us."

Let Go and Let God

The spirituality of absolute faith in God's care and protection, that the will of God ultimately will prevail, is a scriptural theme in Ecclesiastes, which also emerges through the witness of the families. It's what Diana L. Hayes in *No Crystal Stair* describes in her context of elderly Black women expressing "whenever something goes wrong or someone is burdened more than they feel they can bear, 'You just have to let go and let God.'"[11] Hayes describes the strength and courage it requires to have this deep, abiding trust in God because to "'let go and let God' is to put yourself into the hands of God, even for just a little while, until the challenges of life are more bearable. It enables us to step away from the seeming chaos of today's world and to be at peace for a time while we catch our breath."[12] Hayes matter-of-factly confirms that "there is the liberation that comes from a deeply held faith in a God who saves, a 'wonder-working' God, a God who can make everything all right, who frees us from the many pains and problems of the day and enables us to go on about our business of helping to bring about the coming of the kingdom."[13] It's a freedom of, in, and through faith that the families embody in the borderlands. It's not a fake faith that fosters a fake hope. Rather, it's genuine belief in God and the ultimate care and provision that God absolutely will provide a pathway through the stormy chance (Ecc. 3:17).

COMING TO AMERICA

The families take the monumental risk of chance into consideration before they make the decision to journey to this nation (chapter 8). They ultimately choose to risk the Big-C Chance of death along the migration trail because they believe the American dream mythology personified by the Statue of Liberty and the ideology of welcome: "Give me your tired, your poor, your huddled masses yearning to breathe free." For the departing families, it's not just a physical act of departure but a spiritual yearning. They *need* the myth about America to be true because they need life for themselves and their children. It's an urgent physical need that's undergirded with spiritual longing. Migration is a spiritual decision to go toward the possibility of freedom to live in safety, not unlike the spiritual journey that former slaves in America experienced on the Underground Railroad from the cotton fields in the South to safety and freedom in the North. Why would the families seeking asylum in the United States today feel as if their own journey toward freedom from oppression was any less spiritual?[14]

In striking contrast to the perpetual striving for affluence, money, fame, and glory that's the American way (chapter 4), displaced families are following their inner *spiritual* calling to protect themselves and their families by relocating to a place that offers life. Not necessarily life abundant but bare life, where they can live without fear of death, sexual violence, kidnapping, extortion, and all the other horrors that are their daily reality in their homelands. It's normal and healthy to hope for a safer or better life. Life is supposed to beget life, with each generation providing for a little bit better and safer future for their offspring than what they had experienced, what Simone de Beauvoir describes in the *Ethics of Ambiguity*: "Life is occupied in both perpetuating itself and in surpassing itself." She goes on to say, "If all it does is maintain itself, then living is only not dying, and human existence is indistinguishable from an absurd vegetation."[15] She proposes the whole point of life is literally to create a better life for one's self and those in one's care. For the displaced families, that better life requires migration. Emerald, thirty-four, from Honduras said:

> I'm a single mother with three children. I did not have a job—there are no jobs—so I could not feed my children or give them the opportunity to study. I have no help from anyone. Also, the gangs kidnap children age 10 and under and force them to sell drugs.
>
> They kidnapped us in Mexico, but with God's help we made it to the border. We didn't choose to immigrate because it was something we wanted to do. We immigrated because we had to. It was out of necessity.

This is my message. I hope you take this into account and may God bless you.[16]

The families would agree with Judith Plaskow's assessment that part of trusting God is to do so in the good times as well as in the bad. Plaskow specifies, "I do not know how a monotheist can choose to find God in the dry land and *not* in the tidal wave that destroys it—or only in our power to choose life and not also in our power to *choose*" (see Deut. 20:15 and 19; and chapter 7).[17] The monotheist spirituality of the families embraces the mountains, rivers, desert, monsoons, and the ever-lurking chance of falling prey to the cartels while also always expecting and seeing God present (illustrations 5.1 and 8.1).

SPIRITUALITY OF RESPONSE TO LITTLE-C CHANCE

It's impossible to discount the spirituality of the families from the hopeful witness they bring on their journey. Similarly, it's not unlike what philosopher William Mann highlights in his opening chapter for *Philosophy of Religion: Classic and Contemporary Issues*: "It is difficult to imagine someone who says, sincerely, 'I've just had one of those annoying religious experiences. I do wish I could be free of them. They're so insipid and boring.'"[18] It's much more valid to acknowledge these experiences as being real, impacting, informing, enlightening, and inspiring the actions of the families while also interacting and influencing the spiritual connection in the borderlands. Their response to and through their life-changing chance experiences becomes their spiritual witness.

Their spiritual strength amid the supersized little-c chances that befall them is humbling and uplifting to witness, something that cannot help but overflow and intersect with the spirituality of the volunteers and advocates who interact with them, contributing to a distinct spirituality in the borderlands that has a calm, peace, and centeredness despite the swirling little-c chances that create chaos. A volunteer with the GVS Samaritans remembered a time when he was with a search team, and they came across two men, with the very large man carrying the smaller one. Describing the scene, the volunteer said, "We sat the smaller man in a chair and pulled his shoes off. The bottom of both of his feet were raw and he could no longer walk. I started getting things ready to do some first aide for the blisters, which is a really difficult task to do and not fun for the patient or the caregiver. It just takes time." This volunteer explained that after he'd had laid out everything he needed on some towels, he went back to the vehicle to get antibiotics and some bandages. The volunteer said, "When I came back, the big man was washing the injured man's feet. His hands and fingers were stiff, but I could not believe how gentle he was." The volunteer said his church has a foot-washing ceremony on Maundy Thursday during Holy Week, adding, "But on that day, I really learned foot washing. I think the migrants we encounter can't do what they do without experiencing the profound. That doesn't mean they have seminary education. But they have a strong faith that somehow or other with God's help, they're going to get out of the terrible situations that they have in their home communities and find something better." For nones living in cynical a/religious America, the beautiful spirituality of the families, while sometimes initially unexpected, always ultimately uplifts, shapes, and inspires spirituality in the borderlands.

Describing her time with the families in Matamoros, Mexico, during MPP, a volunteer wrote, "They are also tremendously vulnerable to assault, kidnapping and rape. The camp is dark at night and there is no protective fence. People who mean to harm these families and individuals can stroll in and out of the camp at their leisure and there is little being done to prevent children from disappearing or from gang members terrorizing asylum seekers as they wait for doors to open again. While we felt no threat in the camp, there was an uneasy calm. We were aware that we were only safe because the organized crime in the area allowed it—not because we were in control."[19] The volunteer added, as her group was leaving the camp, she spoke with a reporter

> who had been sitting and speaking with a woman outside her tent. She had just been served a simple breakfast prepared over campfire by her new asylum-seeking friend. We decided the camp and the people in it were like the little flowers or grass that finds a way to grow between cracks in cement sidewalks. They are trying to grow between the uninhabitability of their home countries and the wall that is MPP. They have nowhere to go, but they cling to hope and faith and a rather fierce will to survive and thrive.[20]

She closed her reflections saying, "How very human of them."[21] Their striving for life is exactly that: very, very human.

The profound spirituality among the migrating families isn't dissimilar to what Nazi concentration camp survivor Viktor Frankl describes in his classic *Man's Search for Meaning*. He said, "The religious interest of the prisoners... was the most sincere imaginable. The depth and vigor of religious belief often surprised and moved a new arrival. Most impressive in this connection were improvised prayers or services in the corner of a hut, or in the darkness of the locked cattle truck in which we were brought back from a distant work site, tired, hungry and frozen in our ragged clothing."[22] Amid the indescribable suffering and chaos, with the abiding trust in the presence of the Living God, spirituality can, and does, permeate the horrifying little-c chances of life, offering genuine comfort and redress from fears of the Big-C death. Suffering through the storm is not and cannot be separated from spirituality in whatever context suffering occurs. Suffering, as Frederick Schmidt Jr. explains in *When Suffering Persists*, "is inevitably a part of everyone's emotional, spiritual, and intellectual pilgrimage," interwoven elements of a person's spirituality.[23]

Spirituality through little-c chance that nets suffering is evident in the witness of each family. For instance, Maria from Honduras explained the series of chances that led to her displacement in a migrant shelter in Nuevo Laredo during MPP. She said, "The gangs stalked and threatened me. Then they stalked and threatened my daughter. We had to leave our country." They traveled with Maria's two-year-old daughter through Mexico. She summarized her predicament: "Ugly things happened to me in Mexico. When we finally got to US immigration, my children were happy. But it only lasted a little while. They told my daughter she had to enter the USA alone. They sent her to detention. Alone. I had never been separated from my daughter. I experienced such sadness. Then they deported her to Honduras." "Ugly things" is often code for rape, which, as Rabbi Lia Bass describes, is "a violent act, an act of establishing authority and power through fear."[24] This rabbi adds what too many of the families experience firsthand: "Rape is about power, but it will never secure the power that the rapist seeks."[25] The families will press on, as Maria explained the small-c chance that continued to impact her migration journey. After she decided to wait with her young son for their asylum appointment, immigration promptly walked them back across an international bridge connecting Laredo, Texas, and Nuevo Laredo, Mexico, and dumped them at Mexico immigration, where they were left to fend for themselves. Maria said they were fortunate to find space in a church-sponsored shelter for migrants in what is considered one of the most violent and dangerous cities along the Mexico side of our southwest border.

Despite all the hardship and the various chances that were completely beyond her control, her spirituality centers on gratitude for God and also confidence that all will be well. She said, "We have a roof over our heads at the shelter for immigrants. We are in a very dangerous area, but we trust God. All will turn out well. I will miss my daughter, but God will see that all is well."[26] Trust in God through the middle of the muck and the worst possible chance encounters is a common theme among the displaced families. While detained inside GEO Karnes, a mother wrote that the trip was more difficult than she'd expected and also very different from what the guide had said it would be. She explained that she still has so much fear, particularly that she will fail her asylum hearing and then be deported. Nevertheless, she emphasized, "I trust in God. God is able. God never disappoints us. God is love."[27]

In the middle of the myriad of harsh chance encounters that are out of their control, the depth of faith that flows through the spirituality of the families in the borderlands is beautiful to experience. It also offers a soothing balm for the cynicism of a/religious nones who interact with the families. A Texan who volunteered periodically at the migrant encampment in Matamoros during MPP described a border trip when the small group she led visited with the families there who struggled to find ways to work so they could provide for families during the interminable wait for legal permission to enter the United States. The volunteer remembered, "Many were discouraged to find they often do not get paid for their labor. They have no legal recourse, no enforceable rights in Mexico. They are vulnerable to abuse by employers and even if they are paid, they are then subject to extortion from criminal cartels," adding, "I was surprised to hear the casual tone in the voices of the people with whom we spoke as they described their problems. They experienced these issues in their home countries, in the countries through which they traveled to get to this point and they encounter these same issues in Mexico."[28] This periodic volunteer mentioned their struggles because she "was impressed at the will of so many to persevere and to try to create some semblance of normalcy in a desperate circumstance." She mused, "I wonder if I would have the same tenacity of spirit if the shoe were on the other foot."[29] Their spirituality trusts God, which prompts them to cry out to God to lift them out of each unpleasant chance that befalls them. There's definitely a casual way they talk about the myriad of unjust chance events, but they're also simultaneously asking and expecting God to intervene.

Of course, for a person of faith, as Rabbi Beth Singer argues, "It makes sense that a religious woman experiencing gut-wrenching pain would pray to God."[30] Just as a woman in a biblical story "prays to better understand her pain," the migrant families have the same intensity and depth to their suffering before, during, and after migration. Each new little-c chance brings them back to God to recenter their spiritual well-being in their deep and abiding faith. This steadfast faith through the small-c chance permeates spirituality in the borderlands. As with any of the sheroes of faith in the biblical text, the expectation is that when they pray, God will answer *immediately* and without delay.[31]

Each prayer is a sense of heartfelt spiritual renewal and also a declaration of faith, not dissimilar to the historic creeds of the Christian Church such as the Apostles' Creed or the Nicene Creed. Similarly, Rabbi Abraham Joshua Heschel explains in *God in Search of Man: A Philosophy of Judaism*, "The moment we utter the name of God we leave the level of scientific thinking and enter the realm of the ineffable. Such a step is one which we cannot take scientifically, since it transcends the boundaries of all that is given."[32] In other words, it's by reaching out to God through the simplest of prayer that merely mentions the name of God that spirituality moves forth from the inward self to the outward power of the presence of something greater than anything this earth has to offer. It's a cry out to the possibility for this Something to use their super powers to rescue us from the little c's and to keep the Big C off in the distance. This belief, faith, and confidence in God comforts, uplifts, encourages, and inspires the faithful families in the borderlands, overflowing to the volunteers who assist them. A Catholic sister reflected about when an uneducated migrant mother shared that she was about to be deported. The sister remembered, "The mother said she would be okay and that she was in God's hands. She's uneducated, so it will be extra hard for her. She brought one child with her and has three at home. I was struck by her peacefulness. I was more upset by the deportation news than she was. I was really struck by her faith. It is really coming from her heart with deep trust in God. It is not just talk; there is a genuine trust that speaks to me."[33] It's an inspiring spirituality that overflows into the volunteers and advocates who have the privilege of accompanying the families at any point during their migration journey.

Where some volunteers are deeply moved by the profound faith of the families in their response to the litany of little-c chance that assaults them, others are spiritually centered in their role with the families because they sense their own luck or little-c chance of simply being born on the northern side of the US-Mexico border. As a GVS Samaritan said, "I volunteer because I always think it could have been me. It's a lottery that we won to be born in the United States. No one gets a choice to where they are born, so it's pretty simple for me. I would hope if I was ever in a horrible situation, someone would help." She explained that her desire to assist the families is based on the simple reality that she could be the one in their shoes, but she happened to win the lottery and be born in the United States. The various small-c chance encounters that bring the families and the volunteers together intersect with time and the timing that affects when to migrate and also when and where to volunteer.

NOTES

1. Hannah Arendt, *The Human Condition*, 2nd ed., introduction by Margaret Canovan (Chicago: University of Chicago Press, 1958, 1998), xviii.
2. Choon-Leong Seow, *Ecclesiastes: A New Translation with Introduction and Commentary*, vol. 18C of The Anchor Bible (New York: Doubleday, 1977), 327.
3. Mary from El Salvador while staying in a migrant shelter in Nuevo Laredo, Mexico, during MPP, November 4, 2019.
4. Caroline Tracey, "'The Numbers Kept Going': The Forensic Office Identifying Human Remains at the Border," *Guardian*, September 19, 2022, https://www.theguardian.com/world/2022/sep/19/arizona-migrants-remains-border-forensics?CMP=Share_iOSApp_Other.
5. Tracey, "'Numbers Kept Going.'"
6. Green Valley-Sahuarita Samaritan meeting highlights, October 3, 2022. See "Maps and Reports," Green Valley-Sahuarita Samaritans, https://www.gvs-samaritans.org/maps--reports.html; see also Lane Van Ham, *A Common Humanity: Ritual, Religion, and Immigrant Advocacy in Tucson, Arizona* (Tucson, AZ: University of Arizona Press, 2011).
7. Student, Introduction to Spirituality, The College of St. Scholastica, 2022; shared by permission.
8. Excerpts from migrant testimonies from Guatemala, El Salvador, and Honduras while they were staying at a migrant shelter in Nuevo Laredo, Mexico, during MPP, December 4, 2019.
9. Sibia from Honduras while waiting in Nuevo Laredo, Mexico, during MPP, November 19, 2019.
10. Lorraine, thirteen, from Honduras while in Nuevo Laredo, Mexico, during MPP, December 4, 2019.
11. Hayes, *No Crystal Stair*, 51–52.
12. Hayes, *No Crystal Stair*, 53.
13. Hayes, *No Crystal Stair*, 54.
14. See Thomas A. Tweed, *Crossing and Dwelling: A Theory of Religion* (Cambridge, MA: Harvard University Press, 2006), 125.
15. de Beauvoir, *Ethics of Ambiguity*, 89.

16 Emerald, thirty-four, from Honduras while staying at a migrant shelter in Nuevo Laredo, Mexico, during MPP, November 13, 2019.
17 Plaskow, *Coming of Lilith*, 137.
18 William E. Mann, "The Epistemology of Religious Experience," in *Philosophy of Religion: Classic and Contemporary Issues*, ed. Paul Copan and Chad Meister (Malden, MA: Blackwell Publishing Ltd., 2008), 9–22, 10.
19 Rio Valley Relief Project, "Resilience of the Human Spirit."
20 Rio Valley Relief Project, "Resilience of the Human Spirit."
21 Rio Valley Relief Project, "Resilience of the Human Spirit."
22 Viktor E. Frankl, *Man's Search for Meaning*, foreword by Harold S. Kushner (Boston: Beacon Press, 1959, 2006), 34.
23 Schmidt Jr., *When Suffering Persists*, 2.
24 Rabbi Lia Bass, "Vayishlach: No Means No," in *The Women's Torah Commentary: New Insights from Women Rabbis on the 54 Weekly Torah Portions*, ed. Elyse Goldstein (Nashville: Jewish Lights Publishing, 2000), 87.
25 Bass, "Vayishlach," 88.
26 Maria from Honduras while in a migrant shelter in Nuevo Laredo, Mexico, November 5, 2009.
27 Mother from El Salvador, "Expectations," Art Inside Karnes, July 27, 2016.
28 Rio Valley Relief Project, "Resilience of the Human Spirit."
29 Rio Valley Relief Project, "Resilience of the Human Spirit."
30 Rabbi Beth J. Singer, "Toldot: Rebecca's Birth Stories," in *Women's Torah Commentary*, ed. Cynthia A. Culpeper (Nashville: Jewish Lights Publishing, 2000), 76–77.
31 Singer, "Toldot," 76–77.
32 Heschel, *God in Search of Man*, 102.
33 Sister Denise, Art Inside Karnes Field Notes, July 16, 2016.

CHAPTER SIX

Time

For everything there is a season, and a time for every matter under heaven.
—Ecclesiastes 3:1 (NIV)

Time or timing plays a significant role in spirituality in the borderlands, for the families and also for the volunteers, resonating with the viewpoint Ecclesiastes takes on time. In particular, Ecclesiastes emphasizes there's a "time for everything" (3:1–8). This Jewish Scripture poetically expresses that every aspect of life is constrained by time, and this time is something only God knows, controls, and understands. Time itself is sacred, not just the high holy events or liminal moments. All time is holy because time is always God's time.[1] It's never ours. Time is sacred, but it's also part of the human condition. Situations vary in life, which contributes to how and when time holds greater or lesser significance. There also are particular times when there's an unprecedented urgency that impacts how it feels like it's being measured. At times, it passes painfully slowly, and other times, it races by much too swiftly. Despite whether fast or slow, time has a limited supply, which makes it a finite measure for life. There's only so much time, which makes time particularly significant for spirituality in the borderlands. Time never ceases. It's always turning to the next moment.

TIME: TURN! TURN! TURN!

The words from the opening verses of chapter 3 in Ecclesiastes were immortalized by folk singer Pete Seeger, who wrote "Turn! Turn! Turn! (To Everything

There Is a Season)." Seeger based his song lyrics on Ecclesiastes 3:1–8 in the late 1950s, and it was first recorded in 1959. The Byrds made this timeless classic popular, particularly after this group sang it on the *Ed Sullivan Show* on December 12, 1965.[2] Ecclesiastes, as in the song that Seeger wrote, is an ancient poem about time:

> There is an appointed time for everything. And there is a time for
>   every matter under heaven—
> A time to give birth and a time to die;
> A time to plant and a time to uproot what is planted.
> A time to kill and a time to heal;
> A time to tear down and a time to build up.
> A time to weep and a time to laugh;
> A time to mourn and a time to dance.
> A time to throw stones and a time to gather stones;
> A time to embrace and a time to shun embracing.
> A time to search and a time to give up as lost;
> A time to keep and a time to throw away.
> A time to tear apart and a time to sew together;
> A time to be silent and a time to speak.
> A time to love and a time to hate;
> A time for war and a time for peace. (Ecc. 3:1–8 NASB)

Ecclesiastes isn't saying that all of these times are okay. Rather, the point is that these times exist. It's not meant to be taken as, for example, there's a time for war that's acceptable, okay, or even blessed by God, and that there's another time when there should be peace. It's more about stating a fact regarding an observed reality: there's a time when there is war, and there's another time when there is peace. It's an affirmation about the reality of the inevitable existence of, in this example, war.

In the context of this wisdom literature that's seeking to discern the meaning of life, why bad stuff happens, and how to make the best of life despite the bad business and chances that befall someone at any given moment, this poem on time synthesizes observations that there are various times in the cycle or seasons of life. The point is that we're circumscribed by time. Our lives are ordered or arranged by appropriate times, but the irony is we're trapped "under the sun" in finite time. In addition to being limited in our view or perspective, we also have the constraint of time. Immediately following the poem on time, Ecclesiastes points out that God has placed eternity within our hearts (Ecc. 3:11). The problem is mere mortals can't fathom or begin to understand exactly who or what God is or is about. Time relates to the sense of wonder Rabbi Heschel emphasizes and the importance of slowing down and taking time to recognize, see, feel, and experience even the tiniest bits of time. For Heschel, "The ultimate insight is the outcome of *moments* when we are stirred beyond words, of instants of wonder, awe, praise, fear, trembling and radical amazement; of awareness of grandeur, of perceptions we can grasp but are unable to convey, of discoveries of the unknown."[3] It's not just the whopper chunks or landmark events in time that are profound. Often, spirituality is situated in the minute details, literally in the split seconds and miniscule precious moments within the Big Picture of Life.

TIME ITSELF IS UNCONTROLLABLE

As with chance, time is something that remains out of our control. The clock ticks on, the calendar steadily moves from one week to the next, flipping the pages from one month to another, as time marches on. We can't slow it down or speed it up. Time is nonnegotiable. There are sixty seconds in every minute, twenty-four hours in every day, seven days in every week, fifty-two weeks in every year. Period. After a delayed departure for an airplane flight from one city to another, the pilot might say, "We'll try to make up some lost time in the air." It isn't time that will be changed. Rather, it's the speed of the plane interacting with the elements in the air that will "make up" the time. Time itself ticks on at exactly the same pace. Even though we change the time on our watches, or it's automatically done on a smartphone, when we make a cross-country flight from the East Coast to the West Coast, setting our watches ahead or back doesn't really *change* time. Even with the concept of time travel, like in the popular *Back to the Future* science-fiction movie trilogy where actor Christopher Lloyd portrays the character Doc, who builds a time machine, the characters travel back and forth through time during this series, but time itself remains unchanged. Time remains a slowly progressing constant. It's only when it interfaces with grievous evil (chapter 3), chance (chapter 5), and/or choice (chapter 7) that time takes on additional significance related to profoundly good or bad ramifications.

Chronos or *Kairos* Time

Whether it's understood as the time on the clock, cell phone, or wristwatch of the here-and-now human time (*chronos* in Greek) or as the Big Picture time that only God can know (*kairos* in Greek), time plays a significant factor in chance (chapter 5) and choice (chapter 7). We're all going to die, but it's the time/timing that remains unknown and TBD. Ecclesiastes isn't saying that not knowing or not being able to control time is divine determinism, which would mean humans are no more than puppets on a string with God as the marionette master. Rather, Ecclesiastes shows it's simply that time is God's time (*kairos*) and God's plan versus our knowing in linear human time (*chronos*). We're to do our job, and God will do God's job. Is there indeterminacy? Is it up to God? Up to us? We can't know. For Ecclesiastes, knowing we can't know the time or timing, and also that we can't know how much we control through our choices, ought to make us even more careful about the choices we do make, particularly because there isn't an unlimited amount of time for each human life. Rather, each lifetime is finite, constrained within the confines of the finite linear nature of *chronos* time.

THE FINITUDE OF TIME

The essence or nature of time intersects with spirituality in multiple ways, including revisiting finitude and the finite nature of being human, a recurring theme in Ecclesiastes, which poignantly impacts spirituality in the borderlands. Everyone lives in a particular time, and the only time each person has to live exists or occurs between their time of birth and their time of death. What anyone accomplishes occurs within the time frame of their particular finite lifespan. When it comes to time, humans really have *a spirituality of finitude* because of this limited or finite nature of being alive. The finitude factor of the limited lifespan shapes who we are, what we dream about doing, the choices we make, and the risks we're willing to take along the journey to gain whatever it is that we're hoping to be, or do, or achieve. Time is the heartbeat of life because each person only has so much. This temporality factor is what Martin Heidegger famously argues in *Being and Time* forms the basic *primordial meaning* of the essence of being. He terms it a "time reckoning" to confront the reality of the limited lifespan remaining before each person.[4] The finish line is always out there, hovering on the horizon, where life no longer is and where the possibility for being or doing more no longer exists. It doesn't matter who a person is or what they do, Ecclesiastes consistently points to death as the commonality, the great equalizer, and that which absolutely no one escapes (Ecc. 9:11). This finite nature is integral to spirituality in the borderlands because the limitedness of time is ever-present in the precariousness of the displaced families who daily experience this very unpredictable life. Time alive matters because life is shorter than anyone ever expects, and it always inevitably ends with death. The clock seems to tick faster and faster the older we get. Time is short; life quickly flies by.

The families are desperately seeking asylum in order to avoid early death. The reality of ultimate impending death relates to the time factor of spirituality in the borderlands because it's part of the inevitable human condition. Time and death directly intersect. Heidegger discusses how this finitude factor, the ultimacy of death, is the key aspect of human *temporality* and the limited time we have left for this human life.[5] To reiterate an earlier point, Ecclesiastes doesn't want to emphasize the death aspect so much as life with the reality of death in view. The reality of death offers a perspective on each person's remaining life. For instance, our adult son recently shared that his wife didn't appreciate it when he used his age and the average life expectancy of a white male in America to factor in how many weekends he has remaining in his life. He said he didn't factor this to be morbid. Rather, he wanted to get a sense of how many more weekends he has left to spend time doing the things he loves. He wanted to know how much fun time he has left. It's not a morbid focus on death but the time factor of life. Similarly, Heidegger explains, "Holding death for true (death *is* just one's own) shows another kind of certainty, and is more primordial than any certainty which relates to entities encountered within-the-world, or to formal objects; for it is certain of Being-in-the-world."[6] The focus is on life, with the parameter of death in the distant timeline view.

Heidegger notes it's a "temptation to overlook the finitude of the primordial and authentic future and therefore the finitude of temporality," but it's not helpful.[7] Instead, he suggests living into what he terms "everydayness," which represents the same ol' stuff (SOS) of daily life. Ecclesiastes sees these SOS moments as the preciousness in life because it's the little moments that make up each person's life.[8] Everydayness is how each person chooses to live their life. With the little moments gaining momentum to become minutes, hours, days, months, and then years, it's this everydayness that

Illustration 6.1 *Disengaged* 11" × 15" blue charcoal portrait against patterned paper of a migrant child living with his family in a migrant encampment in Matamoros, Mexico, December 15, 2019, during MPP. Traumatized by all that had happened to him, this child remained off by himself and disengaged from the education activities that Team Brownsville was facilitating with the children in the borderlands. Art © Helen T. Boursier.

is life. For Heidegger, it's by measuring time in the moments, seasons, and historical eras, such as the current postmodern condition, that provides the public and private personification of a particular time. For Heidegger, it's always been the case that a thing has always had "'its time' attributed to it."[9] Using the term very differently than Kierkegaard, Heidegger still makes a connection between time and spirituality, pointing out, "History, which is essentially the history of spirit, runs its course 'in time.' Thus 'the development of history falls into time.'"[10] Of course, time includes the past, present, and future. Time also factors in with why and when the families flee and also why and when volunteers and advocates are available to offer assistance.

TIME AND MIGRATION

When the families share their experiences of suffering, time always is of critical importance, including specifying time before they migrate, the timing of momentous events along their migration journey, and the various logjams during their formal process to request asylum (illustration 6.1). For example, Juanita arrived at the US-Mexico border with her six-year-old son when family separation was making headline news, and CBP took her son from her a few hours after they arrived to this country to seek asylum. When I asked her what she expected would happen when she arrived to the United States, she said, "I was hoping to get to the United States to stay with my brother for protection. I had no idea this would happen. My brother didn't know I was coming until I called him when I arrived in Reynosa [Mexico]." She started weeping as she said, "I woke up one morning and left. The problem that I had there was too great. It forced me to leave. I had no time to plan. I left in emergency."[11] Time intersected with chance and grievous evil, prompting her urgent exodus. Regardless of the context, the fleeing families always specify some aspect of time. For example:

- "April 23, 2011, is the date a lady never forgets, when a person without scruples, a person without morals nor ethics, abused me."[12]
- "I have been a victim of extortion since 2013. The gangs force me to pay different amounts. The amounts and dates vary. They take everything I have."[13]

- "When I left the bank at 1:20 in the afternoon, gang members escorted me back inside and forced me to withdraw 28,000 lempiras [$1,148 US], leaving me nothing. It was extortion money for my son to protect his life and to keep him out of the gang."[14]
- "I decided to leave my home December 7, 2015, when I received a death threat."[15]
- "We decided to leave, my son and my niece, because they assassinated my husband. We left from our country August 3, 2015, without knowing what to expect."[16]
- "The trip began at 3 a.m. I arrived at immigration twenty days later."[17]
- "Our daughter made the trip with me. She is two and a half years old. We walked. It took twenty-two days."[18]
- "My trip began June 29, 2015. We left at five in the morning. My trip lasted fifteen days."[19]
- "After thirty-five days of traveling through the mountains in Mexico, we arrived at immigration in the United States."[20]
- "We experienced twenty days of suffering. Then the *hielera* [cooler or refrigerator; a CBP border facility]. Then they brought us here to family detention."[21]
- "We arrived October 2, 2015, thirteen days ago. I trust in God to leave here *soon*."[22]
- "I arrived in the United States on Saturday morning. I spent three cold days in the refrigerator: cold, tired, dehydrated, and fearful."[23]
- "We were in the *hielera* two days. Then they took us to the dog kennel. We were there five days. We did not bathe. It was terrible for me all that happened there."[24]
- "My son and I spent twenty-four hours in the *hielera*. Then we spent two days in the *perrera* [dog kennel]. I thought it was a dog kennel. It looks like the one near where I lived in my country."[25]
- "I finally spoke to my son on the telephone eighteen days after immigration took him from me in the *hielera*. My son is six years old."[26]
- "We arrived October 17, 2019. We had our first court date yesterday, December 3, 2019. The judge did not approve our case. They walked us back across the bridge. They left us at the Mexico immigration station."[27]

- "We have been hungry for three months, sleeping on the floor in a shelter for migrants [in Nuevo Laredo, Mexico]."[28]

When the witness of the families is inserted in the *Time* poem in Ecclesiastes, it serves as midrash, which shows the cycle of time in the migrants' lives:

There is a time to tolerate unavoidable suffering, and another season
   to stop enduring every injustice under heaven:
A time to be born, and a time to choose life;
A time to work (when there's work available), and a time to relocate
   to another country in order to provide for the family (when
   there's no work available);
A time to do anything possible to care for your children, and a time
   to swim across a forbidden river if that's what it takes to get your
   children to safety;
A time to sleep under cactus during the walk across the desert, and
   a time to flag down a passing car because you're afraid you're
   going to die from hunger and thirst;
A time to weep in bitter anguish, and a time to laugh;
A time to mourn for those in your homeland you've left behind, and
   a time to dance in anticipation of reuniting with other family
   members in America;
A time to flee from an abusive relationship, and a time to gather
   your children and walk to America;
A time to embrace your family tightly, and a time to let go and let
   God;
A time to seek asylum, and a time to fight for the safety of your
   children;
A time to keep the few belongings you have in a backpack, and a
   time to sell everything else to pay for the journey to America;
A time to wear your shoes until the soles rub through and blisters
   form on your feet, and a time to wear the same clothing without
   washing them for two or three months during the migration
   journey;
A time to keep silence while hiding in fear from the cartels, and a
   time to speak up boldly during the asylum interviews;

A time to love your children so much that you will do literally anything to ensure their safety and wellbeing, and a time to reject every grievous evil under the sun;

A time for acknowledging the war in your household or homeland will never ever end, and a time to migrate so that you can live the rest of your life in peace. (midrash on Ecc. 3:1–8)

A notable difference between the midrash and the Ecclesiastes version of time is the point that there never, ever is an acceptable time to remain in the doormat position of domestic violence, extortion by the gangs, or any form of bad business or grievous evil. Rather, it's always time for the families to ensure the safety and well-being of themselves and their children. The time is always now to say no to violence, no to extortion, and no to any form of physical, emotional, or spiritual mistreatment. The time to interrupt, disrupt, and leave is always when a threat to life says the time is *now*.

TIME AND GRIEVOUS EVIL

Time intersects with spirituality in the borderlands when grievous evil, through harsh policies and practices, forces the families into stressful and often inhumane circumstances. Time crawls by as the families wait interminably to receive formal due process to enter the United States, which nearly always means living in extremely harsh conditions where their lives are at risk from the myriad ways to die in the borderlands mentioned earlier. It's never safe to linger in publicly accessible places and spaces along the northern Mexico border, where women and children remain extremely vulnerable to the worst possible grievous evil.[29] This slow-motion waiting for official admission permission makes time feel as if it's at a standstill. The clock doesn't seem to move forward, with the days, weeks, and months melding together as one slow, horrible moment. The same standstill of time occurs for the families and individuals locked inside detention facilities. Time stands still as the detainees are left to wonder, worry, and fear about what happens next, with the looming possibility of deportation.

The mothers and children who were detained during the family detention era struggled to balance the interminable waiting for a positive outcome on their asylum hearings and fear beyond all fear that their request would be denied, with immediate deportation the next day. The waiting is spiritually painful because many of them also are enduring forced separation from the family members they traveled with who were sent to different detention facilities, such as an eighteen-year-old adult son or daughter or a husband who would've been put through the immigration system individually without the supporting family members they'd traveled with. In addition, many are also longing to reunite with family members they've been separated from for many years and the dear ones they're hoping and praying to gain permission to reconnect within the United States. In one sense, time seems to be at a standstill, but the moment the worst possible bad news arrives—deportation—then that same clock shifts into anxiety overdrive.

Spirituality That Comforts and Encourages

Spirituality is their one comfort, encouragement, and solace through the time tedium. During the two years I was a volunteer at GEO Karnes, the staff chaplains there held chapel services that began just as we were winding down from the morning session for Art Inside Karnes, and we attended the prayer and praise service multiple times. It was difficult to understand any of the words in the songs because the music was super loud, and the acoustics were horrible in the gymnasium where the families sat on bleachers for the service. Nevertheless, what you could experience was the deep faith that radiated forth through their facial expressions and body motions. The mothers sang with gusto, using their bodies to express their devotion and depth of faith. There was a beautiful feeling of the presence of the Divine among them as their distress in their circumstances radiated through the music. They also lifted their voices loudly during the time of prayer. It wasn't a unison prayer with everyone carefully citing the same words aloud or silently together. Rather, each person spoke their prayers aloud, simultaneously, with their words gathering speed, vigor, and intensity as the prayers continued. Their spirituality was palpable during this sacred time, despite their grievously evil family detention. The profound beauty of this spiritual experience overflowed to the staff and volunteers who witnessed the spirituality of the families.

In comparison, during the same time frame when I was volunteering at the family detention center several times a month, I was the lead pastor of a hundred-member church. The contrast between the expression or feeling of absolute, total commitment, belief, and faith in God that the families readily expressed was a stunning, striking, and sharp difference to that of the congregation I pastored. My experiential observations about my congregation's relatively cool faith didn't and doesn't differ from the postmodern perspective explained earlier. I recently was reminded of this contrasting spirituality during a sermon I heard preached to a mainline, predominantly white, fairly affluent congregation located in my community. The preacher focused on trusting God when trauma hits, such as a cancer diagnosis, divorce, or losing a job. The preacher emphasized the connection that these traumas in affluent America often did not increase one's spirituality or confidence in God. Instead, a chance or grievous evil was more likely to generate the tendency to turn away from God in disbelief or doubt. This sermon reminded me again of the pointed difference between typical spirituality in mainline America and the depth of faith many of the displaced families maintain in the trenches of time-delayed justice. I didn't have to preach or teach or remind these displaced mothers and children who were suffering through long-term family detention to have faith and to believe that God would make the way clear and care for them. They already believed this without any reservation, without any doubt. Time might have felt like it was standing still during their lengthy detention, but God was very present and very real.

It was humbling to witness the unwaning faith in and steadfast love for God. Despite this arduous wait in family detention, or later during MPP, their spirituality remained steadfast, with unwavering faith in the God they trusted to set them free. When the families are in the depths of despair, they never fail to invite God into their pain. Their faith gains strength and sustains them "through the valley of the shadow of death" (Ps. 23: 4) that hoovers around them. American spirituality or faith, in contrast, often falters. The spirituality of the families sustains them in the present and offers hope for a better future.

PRESENT TIME CONNECTS TO THE FUTURE

Bonhoeffer wrote to his dear friend Eberhard Bethge about time, faith, and his long-term detention prior to his execution by hanging shortly before the end of World War II. Bonhoeffer wrote, "Everything has its time, and the main thing is that we keep step with God, and do not keep pressing on a few steps ahead—nor keep dawdling a step behind." He termed it "presumptuous" to desire or expect "to have everything at once." Citing Ecclesiastes, with everything having a season, and excerpts from the poem on time (Ecc. 3:1–8),

Bonhoeffer wrote about his confidence that "God gathers up again"—despite all the bad that is happening in our lives, God is still there.[30] Instead of clinging with longing to the past, Bonhoeffer advises trusting God in the present to bring someone safely forward into the future.

Time in the present eventually connects to time in the future. Nazi concentration camp survivor Viktor Frankl writes about the significance of faith and the role of spirituality to move prisoners from the horrors of the present into the possibility of a future, despite the fact that these prisoners knew that their internment was indefinite at best and moving toward an early death at worst, living in a "provisional existence."[31] Despite this unspoken interminable detention, not dissimilar to what immigrant detainees experience in this country, Frankl said, "The prisoner who had lost faith in the future—his future—was doomed. With his loss of belief in the future, he also lost his spiritual hold; he let himself decline and became subject to mental and physical decay."[32] It's not an automatic given that spirituality can sustain anyone or everyone through the horrors of displacement, but when spirituality is the go-to, it can, does, and will infuse the displaced with inner spiritual strength.

The time factor of long and uncertain waiting for an unknown and unspecified future freedom generates way too much time to think, to feel, to regret, to second guess previous choices, and to fear the future. In this season of waiting—whether in a detention center lockup, migrant shelter, huddled up alongside the southern side of the US-Mexico border, or while waiting to learn of a possible cancer diagnosis or other trauma on this side of the international border—time creates a gaping hole to think, to feel, and to mourn for lost minutes, hours, days, weeks, months, and years. It's the time to ask what Joan Chittister calls "some of the most basic questions of life.... 'What am I doing and why am I doing it? Who profits from what I do and who does not?'" Chittister suggests that asking and responding to these "questions alone could change the world." At a minimum, they refocus our thoughts, feelings, and choices to consider what matters most now as we live into the Big Picture of Life. Chittister proposes these questions "bring us to the mirror of the world and ask us what we ourselves have done to make the world better or worse."[33] In other words, time is the place for spirituality because it's a time for reflecting on the most important people, issues, concerns, feelings, remembrances, and dreams of this life. Faith enters in because it offers a glimpse of hope into a future beyond the trauma, beyond grievous evil, and beyond present suffering. With spirituality entering in, time becomes a bridge to a better future.

VOLUNTEERS: TIME INTERSECTS WITH CHANCE, OR CHANCE INTERSECTS WITH TIME

Time intersects with chance, and sometimes chance intersects with time, to mobilize volunteers for their participation with displaced migrants in general and justice in the borderlands in particular. In my case, time and chance intersected at the time I chanced to be serving as a pastor in a connectional denomination when I was asked to chair the regional committee on mission, justice, and outreach. Time and chance also factored in because it was the time when large numbers of unaccompanied minors were arriving at the southwest border, followed by young mothers traveling with children. This country responded with a series of grievous evils against these displaced children and families.[34] Time and chance essentially created a global mission on a very local scale for anyone living moderately near the southwest border. In response to time, chance, and US grievous evils against the families, beginning in November 2014, I began visiting detained families in the detention center located seventy miles from my home. Then we hosted families overnight in our home once they were released from detention and given permission to continue on their journey to families already living in the United States. Four months later, I volunteered to do art as spiritual care with the children inside the GEO Karnes detention center, and through chance, or a divine providence miracle, my request was approved (see Introduction).[35]

Time and chance intersected to create what, in retrospect given the supertight nondisclosure and nontransparent DNA of ICE, was a miraculous time of spiritual care with the families. While it was a miracle we had this art ministry with the families inside a for-profit immigrant family detention center for nearly two full years, it also was possible because of the time commitment of the three volunteers who facilitated it. So, yes, there was this phenomenal and unusual chance, but we also dedicated our time to be there, as the volunteer chaplains committed their time month after month to be present. This intersection between time and chance with willingness for what Bonhoeffer terms "responsible response" is integral for why, when, where, and how volunteers, advocates, and environmentalists engage for justice in the borderlands.[36]

Time for Retirement Provides Time for Response

For many volunteers and advocates, retirement provides the time for compassionate volunteer work. For example, a GVS Samaritan who has been volunteering in various capacities to assist displaced migrants in the Sonoran Desert since 2005 explained his long-term time connection: "My father was a pastor on [Indigenous] reservations in the USA, so I saw the great disparity in living styles, living standards, and living possibilities. I never lost that understanding as we [he and his wife] spent our professional lives in Asia where we saw the same thing. And so, in retirement, we thought, 'Well, why would we stop now?'" He explained, "This is, we think a very valid way to express loving your neighbor as yourself (Lev. 19:18), and that keeps us going." He added, "And the spirit of the group is contagious. It also keeps us going." The wife of another couple who retired to the Green Valley-Sahuarita area said they "came to live peaceably on the border." Her husband added, "We didn't have much of a plan. We did know we wanted to do something hospitable . . . we knew we would do some volunteer work." He explained they've kept their time "open-ended" to be available and that now they're "getting much busier than we had planned, but it's been a really good experience." They have the time in their retirement, and the opportunity is literally just around the corner.

Time and chance also intersected for a winter-Texan retired couple who lived in Colorado and migrated south to spend the winter in Brownsville, Texas. Their southern border migration chanced to coincide with when the Trump administration used MPP to close the border to asylum seekers, forcing them to remain on the southern side of the US-Mexico border. In response to time and chance and grievous evil (MPP), Team Brownsville began facilitating their phenomenal assistance to provide compassionate response to the families who were stranded long-term just across the international bridge in Matamoras, Mexico. The winter Texan explained, while she was living in Colorado, she'd chanced on a newspaper article there about Team Brownsville, and she immediately talked to her friends about taking Christmas Eve food and supplies across the border from Brownsville to Matamoros. She remembered, "I was so excited. I thought, 'Oh, I can't wait to get there and be part of it in Brownsville.'" She shared a memory of a particular time when she crossed the Gateway International Bridge from Brownsville to Matamoros with Team Brownsville and someone in the group had played a ukulele for the children at the migrant encampment. The children joined in and sang along with the music. This winter-Texan volunteer sighed as she remembered, "Oh my gosh, if you wanted to feel the Spirit of God, I mean, I felt it at that moment. It was so precious and so kind." She explained from that point on, the time she spent volunteering with the families "took on a whole lot more of a spiritual meaning to me." She said she also sought "to understand who they are and what they are going through."

Time and Chance Also Prompt a Spiritual Passion for Ecojustice in the Borderlands

Time, chance, and his spiritual passion for ecojustice intersected for a videographer who continues to document the environmental destruction created by the expansion of the Trump border wall along remote sections of the Arizona-Mexico border. John Kurc said, "I ended up here, you know, it was an accident, basically." He explained he was in Phoenix on another assignment, and he had "a few extra days to kill and I rented a car." It was during the time when there was a lot of negative public and political rhetoric about the southern border. He elaborated, "The American public was being told that you're being invaded, and I was like, 'Okay, where's the cartel? Where are the humans being smuggled?'" He went to the border to see for himself. He said, "And I saw none of that." However, he did see the Army Corps of Engineers "was literally blowing off the tops of mountains along the borderline." He emphasized, "I was horrified with the devastation of this incredible desert. Every day there would be three or four more blasts, and three or four more huge scars in the earth. Then my mission was to start documenting this ecocide." Kurc explained he "wanted to show people how wrong it was and how senseless it was." He said he expected to "kind of poke my nose around for three weeks," but it became his passion and mission to use drone photography to document this time and season of eco-injustice in the borderlands. He added, "I'm out here every day, for every blast. They told me they don't like it. They don't want us to see what's going on, what they're doing."[37] Nevertheless, his spiritual passion for ecojustice motivates why he chooses to spend his time and retirement resources to witness and document the eco-injustice. A similar passion for ecojustice erupted in response to Ducey's container wall at the Arizona-Mexico border (illustration 4.1), with protestors literally stopping the construction of this environmental travesty.[38]

TIME AND FORCED DISPLACEMENT

The same time frame that forced violence on the environment also created havoc with displaced families, becoming a catalyst in time to propel volunteers to response. For example, a physician became proactive for humanitarian response when the Trump administration initiated its family separation fiasco in the spring of 2018. The physician connected with a pro bono immigration attorney to organize a public-protest witness event outside of the CBP processing facility located in McAllen, Texas. Referred to by the families as *la perrera* (the dog kennel) because of its fully enclosed caging that resembles the actual dog kennels in their homelands, the physician-attorney organizer duo chose to stage their protest there because of its notoriously bad reputation among the families and the press.[39]

The physician said, "It wasn't until family separation happened that I learned that there was this whole complex of what happens to children when they come to the border without their biological parents. It was something that had been litigated for decades before, as a justice issue that the government was incessantly out of compliance with." She explained that until the official Trump policy was launched, she had no idea that these violations had been long ongoing against unaccompanied migrant children detained in US custody. She emphasized, "It was all very new to me, and it was flabbergasting." When she chanced to learn about this from a pro bono attorney who'd led teams of volunteers to collect testimonies from unaccompanied migrant children while they were detained in US custody, including inside the *perrera*, the CBP facility in McAllen, to support litigation against the US government when it was out of compliance with the Flores Settlement Agreement, the physician said she remembered "being appalled" when she had this initial conversation with the pro bono attorney who explained all this grievous evil to her. The physician said, "I felt like, at that time, and in conversations since, that we had a real responsibility to take advantage of the moment." There was heightened interest in concern over families being torn apart at the border during the time of Trump's family separation policy, so it seemed to be the appropriate time to draw attention to the larger issues surrounding immigrant children when they are detained in US custody. Time and chance intersected with grievous evil in the borderlands. It became self-evident that it was past time for change.

TIME FOR CHANGE

Time marches on, but time itself doesn't automatically change what happens. Change requires intentionality. It requires action to make that change happen during any given time of injustice. Choosing how to respond, how to make change happen, is one of the slivers of control Ecclesiastes offers, explained in more detail in the next chapter. We're not necessarily stuck with exactly how things are at this time. We can choose our response to work toward something better. Some choose to work for justice, while others disregard or dismiss the grievous evil and go on with life as normal. For instance, lack of time is one of the many excuses my clergy colleagues gave for why they didn't/don't do more preaching, teaching or compassionate response on immigration, even though all of them are located within a short drive to a gateway city where there is a myriad of options of how to provide direct assistance with the families.[40] For the religious, spiritual leaders in my geographic time and place, they have "no time" for immigrant justice. However, as Ecclesiastes makes clear, everyone has the exact same amount of time. Everyone has the same twenty-four hours, the same seven days a week, and the same fifty-two weeks in each year. Ecclesiastes points to the consistency of time. There's a soothing repetitiveness to the rising and setting of the sun and the cycle of the seasons through each year. Time isn't the issue. Rather, it's how each person takes the time they have and chooses to use it wisely, prudently, and without squandering it away.

Our Time Is Now

While Ecclesiastes offers these times without judgment, it does say that there absolutely is an offsetting good to balance out the bad. In the larger scheme of this wisdom of dissent genre, by pointing out the better, positive, or preferable side of the time equation, there's the option to initiate actions to foster a balance point back toward the *good* when whatever chance timing kicks in the *bad*. Choosing the time to say no to bad business in all its forms is always the appropriate time, for the families to flee and also for the volunteers, activists, and environmentalists who passionately respond. Enough is enough. The time is always *now* to challenge and change grievous evil, working to bring into being a more just and peaceful world.

Chittister eloquently highlights, "Ecclesiastes is quite clear: the first thing a person is meant to understand is that there is no such thing as being 'born out of time.' Our time is now. The era into which we are born is the era for which we have responsibility, the era for which we are meant to be blessing." She believes the connection to each person's responsibility for response is "sobering." Chittister stipulates, "Whatever is going on now—ethnic slaughter, unjust international business policies, the false god of militarism, the sexism of the churches—is our affair. What we want to have happen in these arenas we must make happen in our own."⁴¹ The time to sow change is now. It's each person's responsibility during the particular time or season where the chance or accident of birth places them. There's never an acceptable time for silence or inaction in the face of grievous evil. Spirituality in the borderlands embraces the timing of *now*. Now is always the appropriate time to work for justice.

Of course, there's never been a time or season in history when wanting something to change was effective in and of itself for that change to happen. Consider any given bad business, injustice, or grievous evil that's ever occurred anywhere, such as freedom from slavery, Apartheid, and the Holocaust; votes for women; racial, gender, sexual orientation, and reproductive justice; ecojustice; or challenging and changing the direct link between systemic racism in America and exclusion from asylum at the US-Mexico border.⁴² It's the spirituality of the people who act intentionally for justice that gradually transforms the evils of bad business into new life. Change requires people to make the choice to work for something different. This is the time factor of spirituality in the borderlands. Chittister argues, "Change, real change, the kind of change that touches the soul as well as the environment, is not instantaneous. It is slow and labored and painful. It does not come easily. It exacts a price; it demands a dull commitment. Ecclesiastes in its commitment to the singular process of preparedness is very clear about that."⁴³ Spirituality in the borderlands acknowledges this intersection between time and chance, or perhaps between chance and time, while also affirming that any sort of response that moves bad business toward a better future begins with choice. What's your choice to make for justice in the borderlands, and are you willing to make it?

NOTES

1. Abraham Joshua Heschel, *I Asked for Wonder: A Spiritual Anthology*, ed. Samuel H. Dresner (New York: Crossroads, 1983, 2002), 33.
2. *The Ed Sullivan Show*, "The Byrds 'Turn! Turn! Turn! On the Ed Sullivan Show,'" December 12, 1965, YouTube, August 16, 2021, https://www.youtube.com/watch?v=W3xgcmIS3YU.
3. Heschel, *God in Search of Man*, 131.
4. Heidegger, *Being and Time*, 278.
5. Heidegger, *Being and Time*, 378.
6. Heidegger, *Being and Time*, 307–310.
7. Heidegger, *Being and Time*, 379.
8. Heidegger, *Being and Time*, 422.
9. Heidegger, *Being and Time*, 471.
10. Heidegger, *Being and Time*, 480.

11 Cited in Boursier, *Desperately Seeking Asylum*, 87.
12 Mother, Art Inside Karnes, "My Case for Asylum," November 2, 2016.
13 Mother at the Greyhound bus station in San Antonio, November 16, 2020.
14 Mother at the Greyhound bus station in San Antonio, April 15, 2019.
15 Mother, Art Inside Karnes, "My Courage," January 13, 2016.
16 Mother, Art Inside Karnes, "*Ya! Me Voy!*" (Enough, I go!).
17 Mother, "My Journey from There to Here," Art Inside Karnes, September 9, 2015.
18 Mother, sharing her story with a visitor volunteer while she was detained inside GEO Karnes, December 10, 2014.
19 Mother, "My Journey from There to Here."
20 Migrant from Honduras while stranded in Nuevo Laredo, Mexico, November 27, 2019.
21 Mother, "My Journey from There to Here."
22 Mother, "Timeline: The Big Picture," Art Inside Karnes, October 14, 2015.
23 Mother, "Timeline: The Big Picture."
24 Mother, "My First Seven Days in America," Art Inside Karnes, October 26, 2016.
25 Mother, "My First Seven Days in America."
26 Mother at a Sanctuary Church in San Antonio during family separation, July 13, 2018.
27 Mother at a migrant shelter in Nuevo Laredo during MPP, December 6, 2019.
28 Emerald, migrant shelter in Nuevo Laredo, Mexico.
29 See Helen T. Boursier, ed., *Rowman and Littlefield Handbook of Women's Studies in Religion* (Lanham, MD: Rowman and& Littlefield, 2021), 231–262.
30 Dietrich Bonhoeffer, "To Eberhard Bethge [Tegel] 18 December 1943," in Bonhoeffer, *Letters and Papers from Prison*, 169.
31 Frankl, *Man's Search for Meaning*, 67–68.
32 Frankl, *Man's Search for Meaning*, 74.
33 Joan Chittister, *There Is a Season*, art by John August Swanson (Maryknoll, NY: Orbis Books, 1989), 102.
34 See Boursier, *Ethics of Hospitality*; *Desperately Seeking Asylum*; and *Rowman and Littlefield Handbook of Women's Studies in Religion*.
35 For a detailed case study on Art Inside Karnes, see Boursier, *Arts as Witness*, 87–103, 121–134. See also Helen T. Boursier, "The Power of Hope: Art inside an Immigrant Family Detention Center," *The Arts in Religious and Theological Studies Journal* 29, no. 2 (May 2018): 50–67.
36 See Dietrich Bonhoeffer, *Ethics*, vol. 6 of *Dietrich Bonhoeffer Works*, ed. Clifford J. Green, trans. Reinhard Krauss, Charles C. West, and Douglas W. Stott (Minneapolis: Fortress Press, 1941, 2005).
37 John Kurc, "American Scar Post-Film Q&A."
38 See Caleb Newton, "Protesters Shut Down Illegal Border Wall Construction by GOP Governor," Bipartisan Report, December 11, 2022, https://bipartisanreport.com/2022/12/11/protesters-shut-down-illegal-border-wall-construction-by-gop-governor/.
39 See Project Lifeline, https://projectlifeline.us/. See also Boursier, *Desperately Seeking Asylum*, 180–182.
40 See Boursier, *Willful Ignorance*, 99–156.
41 Chittister, *There Is a Season*, 17.
42 See Boursier, *Willful Ignorance*, 23–53.
43 Chittister, *There Is a Season*, 54.

CHAPTER SEVEN

Choice

Better is the end of a thing than its beginning; the patient in spirit are better than the proud in spirit.
—Ecclesiastes 7:8 (NRSVUE)

Learning how to navigate the liminal differences between two apparently equal grievous evils requires identifying and affirming the nuanced variables regarding which option is slightly better than the other. Against the backdrop of the *better-than* statements of Ecclesiastes (7:1–10), this chapter considers what ultimately is better than something else as displaced migrants make their difficult choices and also why volunteers, activists, and environmentalists make their relatively easy decisions to be present through witness, advocacy, and compassion in the borderlands.

BETTER-THAN CHOICES IN ECCLESIASTES

The better-than statements in Ecclesiastes are about relative goods, something that's a smidge better than something else. Better-than decisions prioritize choice but in relationship with risk (chapter 8) and the hoped-for gain (chapter 9). Sometimes the contrast is literally between being dead or alive (Ecc. 4:2–3). Other choices relate to comparing certainty with uncertainty (Ecc. 4:6), or the practical reality of what's more profitable for financial gain—being safer while working or traveling—or life in general, because "two are better than one" (Ecc. 4:9). The migrating families might not know or speak the words of Ecclesiastes, but their lives during forced migration reflect the actuality of the better-than statements. In Ecclesiastes, it's all about what's slightly better, if only as a relative good, since these better-than choices are slightly preferable to the not-so-nice alternative. It's rarely an easy or obvious decision. The comparisons in Ecclesiastes aren't prescriptions for what's always the best choice. Rather, they simply show the importance of carefully considering how, when, and/or if something is slightly better than something else. In Ecclesiastes, some of the relative goods include that it's better to have a patient spirit than to be prideful (Ecc. 7:8) and also that the end of something is better than the beginning because you know the outcome. It'd be nice to know the outcome of something *before* starting off on a venture or journey, particularly for migrating families, because then it'd be possible to judge whether or not everything's going to work out well. For example, a teenage girl who made the migration journey through Mexico with her mother shared their horrible experiences, writing, "Maybe it is better to die in your own country than to die in a place where you have no family, where there are missing bodies, or the animals ate them." She added, "Yes! It was a very bad trip!"[1] The relative good comes into play because, of course, it's impossible to know the outcome of anything before someone even begins whatever project, process, relationship, or journey.

Two Are Better than One

Ecclesiastes sees that two are better than one because the buddy system works in life just as it does in underwater diving when the buddy is there to keep their partner safe, including picking them up if something goes wrong. It's also a truism that two bodies are warmer than one and also that there's strength in numbers. Without a second, when someone falls down, the buzzards or cartels will get them, or they'll die from dehydration and exposure. The migrating mothers have often remarked on how it was better to travel with a larger group or at least with a teenage son for protection against rape. There's safety in numbers, which explains the popularity of the migrant caravans that wind their way through Mexico. It's also better to memorize the telephone numbers of family members and travel without a cell phone than to risk the cell phone falling into the hands of the cartel, who would then use it to extort money from family members living in America in exchange for the lives of the displaced migrants. When time and chance bring grievous evil, the families must choose their better-than and hope and pray for the best.

CHOICE

GRADUAL OR ABRUPT FORCED "CHOICE"

Sometimes grievous evils put gradual pressure on the families, such as verbal and emotional domestic abuse that increases in regularity and intensity or extortion threats that begin with small amounts of money as payment to ensure a child doesn't get pressed unwillingly into a gang, with extortion gradually increasing until there are no more funds available. Others have the grievously evil choice suddenly before them when they chanced to witness or survive a violent crime or when they receive outrageous extortion demands with death threats if they fail to pay the amount that dramatically exceeds any possibility to come up with the required funds.

Chance and grievous evils frequently force the families to make the difficult choice to migrate now, in this particular urgent moment. They don't have the luxury of procrastination or delay. In his *Letters and Papers from Prison*,

Illustration 7.1 *Stuck in Mexico* 15" × 11" mixed-media collage portrait of a four-year-old whose family was stuck at a migrant encampment in Matamoros, Mexico, December 15, 2019, during MPP. The collage includes elements of the art/reflections created by mothers and children while they were detained at GEO Karnes, including their testimonies for asylum.

Bonhoeffer reflects on what he sees as "two ways of dealing physically with adversities. One way, the easier, is to try to ignore them.... The other and more difficult way is to face them deliberately and overcome them; I'm not equal to that yet, but one must learn to do it, for the first way is a slight, though, I believe, a permissible, piece of self-deception."[2] The families must face their adversities head-on, including those who are gradually experiencing bad business, whether physical or emotional abuse, lack of work that begets lack of food, or paying extortion money to the gangs in order to keep their children safe (illustration 7.1). The slower or gradual suffering from bad business provides a longer on-ramp to the decision-making road that leads to forced migration.

Less-Horrible-than *Non*choices

Compared to the better-than statements in Ecclesiastes, the choices that displaced migrants must make are more aptly termed *less-horrible-than non*choices. Gloria from Honduras, who has children age twenty, fifteen, and eight said she left her country "because they killed my brother-in-law, and they said I would be next. I had no choice. I took my eight-year-old daughter and fled from our homeland."[3] It's not a first choice to leave everyone and everything familiar behind, but it's *less horrible than* remaining. There are multiple painful choices to make, most when there seems to be no better-than choice because all of the options are so horrible, beginning before departure and continuing throughout their journey to asylum. Elsa from Honduras said, "It was better to file a complaint to take the chance that my local police department is corrupt, with the possibility that they would protect us, than to say nothing and suffer the inevitable consequences—death—because I witnessed my brother's beating. To do something is better than to do nothing."[4] Evelyn from El Salvador said, "It's better to take the risks along the journey than to stay and wait for the gangs to kill my children."[5] The decision to leave home, with the necessary physical departure that brings separation from beloved ones, creates a searing rip in their spiritual wholeness.

In my journal reflections following the Art Inside Karnes exercise "From Tears to Joy" that I facilitated with the mothers, I reflected about their physical and spiritual tears as they processed their separation from their beloved family members. One mother expressed her pain in being forced to leave her son behind with her mother—taking only her daughter with her. She hopes one day her son will understand and forgive her. She's hoping to work in the

United States to then help him join her. She left with her daughter because her mother's companion was after her—clearly sexually implied but not stated. After sharing their traumatizing domestic and sexual violence experiences, the mothers always added, "I cannot return to my country." One wrote, "It broke my heart into one thousand pieces to leave my mother." A mother who was being extorted for money from her tortilla-making job, otherwise they would kill her son, wrote, "My son is my life." Most included something specific about their faith and trust in God.[6] The option to freely choose, even between two *non*choices, provides spiritual empowerment because choice offers at least *some* personal agency. Some choice is better than no choice.

PERSONAL AGENCY AND FREEDOM OF CHOICE

All of the better-than statements in Ecclesiastes point to the importance of human agency to choose, the basic human right for freedom of choice. Freedom of choice, even for the most miniscule of options, is empowering because it provides the invaluable benefit of personal agency. It's through choice-making at all levels, large and small, that individuals gain freedom through that choice. It's mine or ours to make, not yours to tell me/us what to do. Pastoral care theologian Donald Capps explains, "There are no set formulas for freedom, but we do have choices. We are not without some freedom to choose what we will or will not do."[7] Chance also factors in because there are clearly many things that happen in life that are beyond personal control, particularly as it relates to grievous evils and the injustice these exacerbate. It's also important to make carefully measured choices that consider previous experiences while prioritizing the urgency of the present moment.

Empowerment through personal choice and individual agency mingles with the innate normal human desire for something better. Joan Chittister describes this as the desire to go "underneath the facades of life, in the bottomless center of ourselves, [is where we] can, if we listen, hear the sirens cry. They enchant us, seduce us, tempt us, promise us that there is more to life than what we now have. Most of all, they tell us over and over, the more is within our grasp."[8] In the Global North, too often this siren pushes the urgency of choice to overproduce, overwork, and overgrasp for the brass ring (chapter 4). It's what Chittister explains pushes people toward the ever-present desire to make the choice of "striving for an invisible finish line, a sun-covered summit, a grail in the life that, once we reach it, we are certain we will bring with it not only present satisfaction but perpetual peace as well. We live wanting to get it right. We go on searching for the secret to having it all."[9] This forceful inner push for success is a very different sense of choice than what the families face when bad business confronts them with direct threat-to-life choices that then force them to flee their homelands or choose to remain and die.

For the families, more of this internal siren's call is always safety for their children first and secondarily safety for themselves. This inner spiritual siren directly shapes their choices. For the families, theirs often is a *non*choice in the same sense as the depressing 1982 film *Sophie's Choice*, starring Meryl Streep, who plays a Polish refugee during World War II. When Streep arrived at Auschwitz with her two children, the Nazi guards gave her the "choice" of which one to send to the gas chamber and which one the Nazis would send to a children's camp. This is the same sort of distressing less-horrible-than *non*choice that the displaced families regularly must make.

These migrating mothers and fathers don't want to leave a child behind in their homeland, often under the care of an aunt or an older sibling. But it's frequently a less-horrible-than *non*choice many must make. Sometimes it's because they can't afford travel costs for everyone in the family, and/or a particular child is most at risk of early death if the child doesn't migrate to a country far away. It's always a *Sophie's Choice* less-horrible-than decision. For example, a mother from Honduras wrote about her migration journey while she was detained inside GEO Karnes. After explaining some of the horrifying experiences that had occurred during her overland journey from Honduras to America with her youngest son, she explained, "The journey was not difficult because of my faith. I trust God." She emphasized, "The difficult part was leaving behind two sons. Lord, protect my two sons in Honduras."[10] Forced separation is an agony that rips through their souls every step of their journey. Their spiritual anguish touches the hearts of the volunteers and advocates because it's such a deep, abiding, familial love that engenders empathy and compassion. *Their* spirituality inspires *our* response.

THE MORAL CHOICE TO INSTILL STRONG SPIRITUAL VALUES

There's also a strong parallel to gendered disparity and the fight for the dignity and personal agency for all women and the fight for and right to dignity for all displaced migrants, particularly the many females of all ages but also the males who've chosen to follow a spirituality that embraces morally, biblically grounded ethics and a sense of accountability to family and the Creator God. One of the often overlooked choices the migrating families have is their decided choice to instill strong moral values in their children. For instance, while detained inside GEO Karnes, a mother wrote a symbolic letter to the children she'd had to leave in her homeland:

Letter Home

To my children:
    You are my treasure.
        So special.
    You are the love of my life.
        My three children.
    You are a gift from God.
I taught my children your ways God.
    To respect.
    To love.
    Not to take things that are not theirs.
I taught my children your principles.
    Your values God.

        *

We must instill in our children:
    Principles.
    Values.
    Love.
So they are
    Good and respectful children.
Who grow up to be
    Good and respectful adults.[11]

This choice to embody and instill ethical values has consequences. Because the mothers and fathers, guardian aunties and uncles, or older siblings raising younger brothers and sisters *choose* to live moral lives for themselves, their families, and the children under their care, they are at greater risk in their homelands to becoming recipients of bad business and grievous evils from the gangs. Nevertheless, their inner moral compass refuses to be dissuaded or coerced by the gangs. No means no. They choose to stand firm, guided by a strong spiritual conviction that guides their deliberate choice to lead moral lives, which then puts them at great risk for immoral governments, gangs, and cartels.

More Difficult Choices the Displaced Families Must Make

Once grievous evils and horrid chance obligate the families to make the *non*choice of forced migration, the difficult choices range from who stays and who goes to the mode and route of travel and a myriad of better-than choices between two less-horrible-than other choices throughout the journey. Writing on behalf of her family who left Honduras because gangs killed the father's brother and then threatened to kill the extended family too, the fourth-grade daughter wrote, "We threw everything away and left our home. We traveled by bus to Guatemala, but when we crossed into Mexico, the police took money from my father because my brother didn't have a passport." She added, "There was no time to get one!" It's better to leave without official paperwork in place than to remain and wait to be killed. When the family arrived at the US-Mexico border, other migrants warned them not to cross, but the daughter emphasized, "We had no choice."

Risk (chapter 8) contributes to making the choice between less-horrible-thans. In this instance, it was better to risk crossing the Rio Grande River than to risk surviving the cartels who fight for control over access to the river on the Mexico side of the southwest border. She reiterated, "We had no choice, so we crossed, but immigration ruined all of our happiness. They put us in a prison for fifteen days, wearing the same clothes. We did not bathe for six days. Then they sent us back to Mexico." The families weigh and pray each choice, trust God through the process, and then call on God to protect them when more bad things happen to these good people. This daughter closed her written testimony with "We ask God to please let us be able to live in the United States. God is able."[12]

"Bad Parents"

While they're suffering emotional and spiritual distress over the physical separation from the beloved family members to whom they'd had to say goodbye in their homeland, a public anti-immigrant narrative often portrays them as "bad parents" because they "choose" to leave children behind or because they "choose" to send children on ahead alone. This negative rhetoric disregards that their painful decision is never without personal, emotional, and spiritual pain, for the parents and also for their children.[13] The "bad parent" label also misconstrues the reality about the less-horrible-than *non*choices these families are forced to choose between. This misperception of the families relates to the well-known opening line in chapter one of the classic feminist text *The Second Sex*, where Simone de Beauvoir writes, "One is not born, but rather becomes, woman."[14] Beauvoir makes her case for how culture and the choices of those around them, by males and females, create the gendered expectations of who and what females are and do, which parallels how public rhetoric erroneously creates what it means to be a migrant. However, this forced-on-them description by passionately dispassionate and often antagonistic strangers living in an affluent receiving nation is made externally, without ever being empathetically present with the families.

Similar to Beauvoir's argument that the stereotypical passivity "that essentially characterizes the 'feminine' woman" in her context "is a trait that develops in her from her earliest years," there's much stereotyping of migrants by receiving nations. Beauvoir adds it's "false to claim that therein lies a biological given; in fact, it is a destiny imposed on her by her teachers and by society."[15] Likewise, displaced migrants are the recipients of a parallel false claim that sees them in a decidedly disparaging, noncomplimentary light, largely related to the difficult less-horrible-than *non*choices they've had to make. Just as Beauvoir argues that becoming a woman signifies the expectations society imposes on them of what cultural expectations require for what it means to be a woman, so, too, the migrating families are defined by what a receiving nation says about them. This misplaced image is pressed on them from the outside, just as it was forced on them to make a series of difficult choices before and during the journey to safety in another country. Spirituality in the borderlands seeks to refute or dispel the racist derogatory public and political anti-immigrant rhetoric about being so-called bad parents. Instead, a spirituality of dissent shows the reality of the difficult choices displaced families must make to avoid a *more-horrible-than* early death.

Trauma and Choice

The families are making all of these challenging choices amid extreme trauma. Something traumatic is always the catalyst for why they migrate: no work, no food, no safety, no peace, no life. Once they make their difficult choice to migrate, they must continue to navigate new *non*choices throughout their journey to America, using their spiritual resilience and courage to confront one trauma after another. As trauma specialist Judith Herman explains, "Traumatic events are extraordinary, not because they occur rarely, but rather because they overwhelm the ordinary human adaptations to life. Unlike commonplace misfortunes, traumatic events generally involve threats to life or bodily integrity, or a close personal encounter with violence and death. They confront human beings with the extremities of helplessness and terror, and evoke the responses of catastrophe."[16] Herman explains that when traumatic events occur, like those that force the families to choose to migrate, "the human system of self-defense becomes overwhelmed and disorganized."[17] These soon-to-become displaced families must make difficult choices while they are, as Herman explains, "traumatized people [who] feel and act as though their nervous systems have been disconnected from the present."[18] Within this space of traumatized disorientation with the Big Choice for migration forced on them externally by people, events, and chance circumstances outside of their control due to the grievous evils pressed on them, the families exercise a modicum of control by choosing the less-horrible-than option.

How well the families navigate these little choices depends on their spirituality and resilience. As Herman notes, "Only a small minority of exceptional people appear to be relatively invulnerable in extreme situations."[19] Everyone is more vulnerable during extreme situations. Migration is one of those extreme contexts, even in the best of circumstances. Relocating from one safe place to another safe place, as in from one city or state within this country to another, is difficult enough. Relocation is dramatically more stressful when it's forced on someone due to external circumstances. It's particularly stressful when a fleeing migrant is headed through dangerous territory toward an unknown place where there will not be open arms to receive them and where the welcome mat will not be out. There's nothing fun, easy, or desirable about walking overland through the length of Mexico, often carrying small children, only to be forced to remain in Mexico in a makeshift shelter or migrant encampment, then to languish in line for days, weeks, or months while waiting for Title 42 to lift so they may gain admittance to the United States to pursue an asylum claim.[20] Nothing about this process is easy-peasy. Every aspect requires an internal spiritual calling, the muse for a safe and peaceful life.

LEANING INTO FAITH

The families lean into their faith as they make their difficult choices, trusting in what Madeleine L'Engle envisions: "The promise is that not only can we bear the dark night, but that dawn will come."[21] For the mothers and fathers, migration is a frequent better-than choice these ethically grounded, moral people must make. As Evelyn from El Salvador explained, "In my country there are many violent deaths every day. They kill children, young adults, every day. Boys and girls, male and female. The members of the terrorist structures kill indiscriminately without remorse." She said she left for the well-being of her children so that they "will have the hope for life when they get safely away from the gangs." Despite all the risks involved, this mother of three said, "It's better to take the risks along the journey, than to stay and wait for the gangs to kill my children." As is typical of the families, she ended her witness with "I ask God to protect us."[22]

As the families make their various difficult choices, they're embodying what Lorde would say means to "live a considered life. The necessity for that consideration grows and deepens as one faces directly one's own mortality and death."[23] It's this ever-present sense of an impending early death and the fragility of their mortality that strengthens the migrant's resolve to make the journey and to press on to the eventual goal of safety in America. Overcoming the stereotypical expectations of females who become migrants shapes the better-than choices that the migrating women and girls must make.

BETTER-THAN CHOICES OF WOMEN AND GIRLS

Women and girls too often set off on the migration journey because of the violent death of a spouse or parent and/or because of extreme domestic violence that includes wife battering and rape of the mother and the girls, which too often elevates to femicide. I've never spoken with a migrant mother who didn't personally know a close friend, family member, and/or neighbor who was the ruthless victim of femicide, killing females because they are female.[24] Their fear is justified. Their fear is real. With her emphasis on women, Lorde explains in the *Cancer Journals* that it's only when "we open ourselves more and more to the genuine conditions of our lives, women become less and less willing to tolerate those conditions unaltered, or to passively accept external and destructive controls over our lives and our identities."[25] It's never a good decision to put up with domestic violence at any level, and when it includes rape or probable femicide, women choose migration as the definitive better-than to allowing themselves or their daughters to being repeatedly subjected to rape, child molestation, and/or incest. A thirteen-year-old from El Salvador who was traveling with her mother said, "I left my country when I turned thirteen. My stepfather beat me. Often. Now he wants to rape me. He hit my mother too. He said he would kill us if we left the house. We cannot return to El Salvador. Our lives are in danger. He will kill us. I don't want to suffer more. I don't want him to rape me. So we left. We trust God to protect us."[26]

Women and girls quickly realize, as Herman points out, "in rape they are not only violated but dishonored. They are treated with greater contempt than defeated soldiers, for there is no acknowledgment that they have lost in an unfair fight. Rather, they are blamed for betraying their own moral standards and devising their own defeat."[27] In addition to rape being acknowledged on a global scale as a gross human rights violation, this crime against women is supposed to net, as Herman notes "(at least in theory) the same gravity as other war crimes."[28] The decision to flee sexual violence that often leads to femicide is, to use a colloquial expression, a no-brainer. When there's no place to remain safely, the obvious choice is to go. Fleeing becomes an urgent physical, emotional, and spiritual necessity.

SPIRITUAL ANGUISH EXACERBATED DURING MPP

During the extended time frame while the families were forced to remain in Mexico after the Trump administration implemented MPP and soon after used the COVID-19 pandemic to enact Title 42 to further impede the US and international laws that provide protection for displaced migrants, pregnant women and mothers of young children became so desperate that they chose to hang on to a blow-up raft similar to what people use in a swimming pool and float across the Rio Grande River from Mexico to the United States. While this was happening along the Texas-Mexico border, it netted more of the "bad parents" criticism from Americans. However, as a missionary who maintained a ministry of solidarity with the families throughout MPP and the COVID-19 pandemic exclaimed, "These women cannot swim! How desperate do you have to be to fling yourself onto a tiny raft when you are nine months pregnant?"²⁹ The self-righteous Americans who've condemned these desperate parental actions had no concept of the less-horrible-than choices the families were faced with throughout the duration of MPP. It's better to send a child alone to American and risk arriving and staying alive than to remain in Mexico and die young at the hands of the cartels who traffic the families for drugs, sex, and body parts. While clearly not a good choice to float across the river on a toy raft when someone can't even swim, the mothers believed it was better than haplessly waiting to be kidnapped, tortured, and/or killed.

MPP intensified the less-horrible-than choices at the border. For instance, Karla from Honduras said she and her son were trying to reconnect with her husband and daughter who were already living in the United States. When they arrived at US Immigration to request asylum, she said immigration gave her two choices: "(1) return to Honduras or (2) wait in Mexico for an asylum hearing." She said it was "very painful" to be so close to her daughter and to be denied. Karla added, "I cried and cried." She opted to remain in Mexico, explaining, "It is better to wait the long months until my case for asylum comes up than to give up and return to my country." Karla added, "In truth, what we are going through is very painful."

VOLUNTEERS AND ADVOCATES: THE CHOICE TO BE PRESENT

It is better to go to the house of mourning than to go to the house of feasting, for this is the end of everyone, and the living will lay it to heart. Sorrow is better than laughter, for by sadness of countenance the heart is made glad.
—Ecclesiastes 7:2–3 (NRSVUE)

Whereas the families often don't have a choice of whether or not to migrate because their circumstances frequently are forced on them by externally caused grievous evils and bad business beyond their control, the volunteers do have the flexibility and freedom to choose to be present in solidarity with the families. Volunteers and advocates in the borderlands understand exactly what Ecclesiastes means when this wisdom literature makes the better-than comparison between going to a house of mourning or to a house feasting, effectively saying it's better to go to a funeral than to a wedding (7:2). It might seem like an unlikely opposite to draw attention to, but it's a better-than comparison that focuses on what really matters most in life. Being present together with people who are suffering begets a unity of purpose through the mutuality of comfort, compassion, and solidarity amid pain and loss. The house of mourning / house of feasting contrasts the intensity of what really brings meaning to life. It might rarely come down to the choice between these two exact contexts, a funeral or a wedding, but the point stands that it's much more meaningful to spend intentional time in solidarity through suffering, dying, and death than it would be to invest the same energy in a frivolous activity.

Spirituality in the borderlands embraces this better-than, opting for solidarity with those in the house of mourning over meaningless feel-good time-wasters so typical of American leisure life. Engagement with the families in the borderlands brings satisfaction through time well spent compared with detachment into frivolous pursuits. Their choice to be present with the families resonates with the Rascal Flatts song "Feels Like Today," where a friend reflects on going to the funeral of a close friend who was a "good man" but who never really fully lived his life. The refrain repeats this funeral-goer's goal to embrace and live life right up to the moment "when the sand runs out."[30] Such close encounters with death reshape what's genuinely worthwhile in life.

The Choice to Accompany

Two volunteers who'd lived and worked in the Philippines during their career years at the time when the Marcos regime was very cruel said they "saw evidence of a lot of torture of people who came from the hills. And so we identify very much with these migrants now who are coming out of such terrible situations. How can you turn your back on them?" For this couple, it's their intentional choice to be in solidarity by being present with displaced migrants. Similarly, a Roman Catholic sister who serves on the IWC leadership team said she began her assistance with the families in late 2014 when there was a rapid increase of mothers and children seeking asylum in the United States from the violence in their homelands, primarily Guatemala, El Salvador, Honduras, and Mexico.[31] Since San Antonio is a gateway city from the smaller cities along the Texas-Mexico border, many of the families traveled through on the way to their families who were already living in cities across the United States. The sister explained, "These are my brothers and sisters, and they're going through this time, and it's important to be there with them, to *accompany* them." She reiterated, "I use the word *accompany* when I greet them. I don't ask them how I can help them. I ask them, 'Is there some way I can accompany you? Is there some orientation, perhaps, that I can be with at this point?'" She said that, of course, this all-volunteer organization offers all sorts of practical assistance to the families traveling through, but it's most important for this sister to focus her time on accompanying them, being with them spiritually, emotionally, and/or physically.[32]

Reorganizing, Relocating, and Reprioritizing

Volunteering also includes the choice to reorganize their lifestyle to be able to spend time with displaced families in the borderlands. A volunteer started helping displaced migrants when she and her late husband retired, and they started spending the winters in Arizona during the late 1990s. She said her husband wanted to go south to golf. This snowbird from Minnesota remembered, "We lived on a golf course. I don't play golf. I don't play mahjong. I don't go to art classes. I read a lot. I can read a book a day, which is wonderful, but there's only so much of a book a day that you can stand." She said she learned about a meeting with a group that assisted migrants, GVS Samaritans. It was being held at a nearby United Church of Christ (UCC) church. She explained that NAFTA "had only recently been signed, which meant, because US farmers were being subsidized by the American government, but Mexican farmers weren't being subsidized by their government. Consequently, Mexican corn cost more than the corn imported from the US into Mexico." In the language of Ecclesiastes, this chance change in the international market generated bad business that immediately began harming Mexican farmers. The Arizona snowbird explained, "So the Mexican farmers were going broke very quickly." Her succinct description is exactly what happened, which precipitated the increase in migration soon after NAFTA began.[33]

This volunteer from Minnesota explained she attended the meeting to learn about the Samaritans who conducted organized searches in remote areas of the Sonoran Desert about an hour south of Tucson toward the Arizona-Mexico border. The Samaritans travel in a four-person team that includes the driver, someone with medical skills, a Spanish speaker, and a "gopher" to assist as needed. Following the meeting, she spoke with one of the core volunteers who'd started this group of Samaritans that still has a home base at a UCC church, Good Shepherd United Church of Christ. She remembered thinking or saying, "Well, I don't know if I want to do anything religious because I'm kind of sick of churches saying they will do something, and then they collect money and go away." After receiving assurance that this wouldn't be a concern with the pastor or with the interfaith group of religious and nonreligious people who were just beginning to organize this group to assist displaced migrants, this retired Arizona snowbird decided to begin helping with the seven or eight people who conducted these searches in the desert. She said, "I dragged my husband along, off the golf course, to go do this." She continued to volunteer for several more years during her snowbird days. Time and chance intersected in her life, and she chose to respond to the opportunity.

For a lifetime Episcopalian and native-born Texan who helps migrants and Mexican nationals in Piedras Negras, Mexico, it comes down to choosing to be present in love. She said, "It's like the line in the song: 'They will know we are Christians by our love.' I'm not an evangelist type of person, but I do know how to love, and that's what I try to do. When I help someone, I try to demonstrate that you gain something in your heart by helping somebody else." Her moral compass is simply to help someone. Period. It doesn't matter which side of an international border they live on or what their immigration status is. She said, "I want to see God's work being done." She explained she goes with a group who helps in Piedras Negras "to see the needs that they have, and try to help them with that." When I responded, "It sounds so simple and almost humanitarian or egalitarian in the sense that they're human, I'm human, you're human," the volunteer responded, "That's what I mean. Humans are humans." This volunteer's choice is to connect in relationship with what Hannah Arendt terms the "web of human relationships," which is what happens when someone makes the choice to be present with the families in the borderlands.[34] It's a choice that contributes affirmatively to spirituality in the borderlands as humanity is mutually affirmed and reaffirmed. Difference and "otherness" meld into humans helping humans.

A rabbi who's filling an interim position at a synagogue in southern Arizona said the choice to respond is just that—a choice to response. He said while he "wouldn't want to compare myself in any way shape or form with Rabbi Heschel," he went on to explain that after Heschel had marched for justice with Martin Luther King Jr. and others in Selma, Alabama, he was asked, "'Where do you find time to pray?' He [Heschel] said, 'I prayed with my feet.'" The interim rabbi in Arizona added, "And that's the challenge I think we all face is to put our faith into practice and to practices." He admitted that putting beliefs into practice has always been "difficult in religious life... especially in so many divided religious organizations." There's a distinct connection between this "difficult in religious life" choice and those disaffiliated with religion who opt to choose in favor of solidarity with displaced families in the borderlands.

Refuting "Bad Choices"

Volunteers also intentionally refute the negative immigrant narrative by humanizing the families through sharing their experiential witness in the borderlands. Instead of denigrating parents for making difficult choices to protect their children, border spirituality uplifts the ethical and spiritual strength of character of the displaced families. The questions for reflection regarding the authority of the source parallel what Plaskow suggests for gender justice and apply equally for a spirituality of dissent that challenges any anti-immigrant rhetoric, policies, and/or practices: "Who is speaking? Who decides? Who has the power to decide? Who's included in the conversation? Who is being addressed? Who decided that the glory of women is inside? Who decided that men and women complement each other and this is who men are and this is who women are? Have women been part of the three-thousand-year conversation through which those rules have been defined?"[35] Who has the authority to denigrate the difficult choices the families must make? Who has the authority to make the choice in favor of one asylum claim for safety while outright rejecting the equally fervent request of another? Who decides that the right to life for an "economic migrant" is less worthy than the request for the safety of an asylum seeker? Who decides when/if one displaced migrant is more or less valuable as a human being than a resident American? Border spirituality embraces a hope and a future that prioritize the right to life for all, including displaced migrants and at-risk-for-extinction migratory animals.

The *Nonchoice* of Volunteer Choice

For some volunteers, choice seems more like a *non*choice. A pro bono attorney who spends her retirement educating and advocating on behalf of unaccompanied migrant minors detained in US custody said, "It never occurs to me not to do it, okay. I don't have a choice. I am positioned to do this. Therefore, I must do it." She reflected on the opportunities she'd had early in her retirement to lead investigation teams to support possible litigation against the federal government if it was found to be out of compliance with the Flores Settlement Agreement in its (mis)treatment of unaccompanied migrant children while they were detained in US custody. After describing the work she'd facilitated on various trips when she'd led volunteer teams of physicians and attorneys to interview unaccompanied migrant children while they were detained in various government-funded facilities across the United States, she concluded, "That's who I am. That's what I do. I just don't feel like I have a choice."

I felt a similar sense of *non*choice when I had the privilege of facilitating art as spiritual care inside Karnes. Each time my security clearance was reauthorized, it reenergized my zeal to spend as many days as possible with the families before the security clearance expired. It felt like a *non*choice to make the 140-mile roundtrip visit to the detention center to spend a day with the detained mothers and children. Of course, I actually had a choice. But, as with the pro bono attorney, I couldn't *not* go and *not* be present when I had the skills and permission to be present with the families inside Karnes.

Another reason behind the *non*choice of choice is the ever-present consensus of volunteers regarding their responsibility to make an ethical response to injustice in the borderlands. As this religiously disaffiliated attorney explained,

> I believe deeply that we come into this world all the same. And but for the grace of God go I, including that I was born white, in a middle-class home in the United States of America, and also that there were all sorts of benefits in life that I was given. I understand that people just like me, in the United States and everywhere else, aren't as lucky as I was to have all I have from the accident of birth, to have and be like I did. I believe that everybody deserves the same dignity, and everybody deserves the right to be safe and to have enough to eat and to have a good place to sleep and to be able to have relationships that comfort them and care for them.

For clarity, she added, "I don't think everybody has to have what I have. That's not what I'm saying. But I am saying that all people deserve the right to have life, and to have life doesn't mean to just exist." She explained she grew up in a Jewish household post–World War II that was situated in a Catholic neighborhood in Indianapolis. She had socially liberal parents who were engaged in racial justice and other equality concerns. She said, "Social justice has always been part of the vocabulary in my house. I grew up with the sense that people betrayed their neighbors by not taking care of them."

Following the formation in advocacy for justice from her childhood, she chooses to work for justice in the borderlands. She elaborated, "What I'm saying is that you don't turn your back on what's happening right next to you. We have a responsibility to pay attention to what's going on around us, and to take action. If we see things that violate the order of how they should be, it's a no-brainer." She added, "And I'm not talking about Trump. I'm going back to [the mid-1990s] when I first became aware of how we treated kids (unaccompanied migrant children detained in US custody). It's a no-brainer to say you're turning your back and allowing innocent children to be treated that way. Whatever that way was, it's never been doing what we're supposed to be doing." She said once someone stops turning their back and really looks at the mistreatment of children in the borderlands, then it changes them into someone who can't not do something. This retired immigration attorney said the easy part is *not* to look, *not* to try to see the truth about injustice in the borderlands. However, once someone seriously engages and sees the reality of the suffering from grievous evils and bad business, it changes the "choice" of nonresponse to the *non*choice of mandatory response. She reiterated, "It's easy not to look, but it's not right."

INTERNATIONALLY BLENDED SPIRITUALITY

The intersection of choice in the borderlands, the forced *non*choice of migration and the myriad difficult choices thereafter—some using their individual freedom from chanced choice but still others forced on them as more *non*choice by grievous evils in the borderlands—intermingles with the choice and *non*choice of volunteers and activists who work in solidarity together with the displaced families. The combination of these two very different sets of choices creates a distinct spirituality of dissent through solidarity in the borderlands. It's a unique spirituality that differs from what spirituality is for just the migrants or just the volunteers and advocates. When these very different contexts intersect in the borderlands, a spirituality emerges that becomes an entity of its own, similar to the uniqueness that forms in a long-term covenant relationship, such as a longtime marriage or lifelong best friends. One without the other is just one part of the equation, whether that's one spouse or partner without the other spouse or partner or one best friend without the other. Each component of the friendship or marriage is unique in and of itself, something that's very different individually from what forms together through the longtime union, longtime covenant relationship. This same concept occurs in the borderlands when the spirituality of the displaced migrants mingles with the spirituality of the volunteers in solidarity with them. Together is better. Together is stronger. Together is the freely chosen better-than. Together is the heart of this unique spirituality that cannot exist one without the other. These are two parts in one blessed whole. It's a better-than spirituality that also includes risk.

NOTES

1. Teenage daughter while detained inside Karnes with her mother, "My Journey from There to Here," September 9, 2015. See also Boursier, *Ethics of Hospitality*, 141.
2. Bonhoeffer, "To Eberhard Bethge [Tegel] Advent 2 [2 December 1943]," in Bonhoeffer, *Letters and Papers from Prison*, 159.
3. Gloria from Honduras in a migrant shelter in Nuevo Laredo, Mexico, during MPP, November 5, 2019.
4. Elsa from Honduras while in a migrant shelter in Nuevo Laredo, Mexico, during MPP, November 5, 2019.
5. Evelyn from El Salvador while at a migrant shelter in Nuevo Laredo, Mexico, during MPP, November 13, 2019.
6. "From Tears to Joy," Art Inside Karnes, August 24, 2016.
7. Donald Capps, *The Poet's Gift: Toward the Renewal of Pastoral Care* (Louisville, KY: Westminster John Knox Press, 1993), 167.
8. Chittister, *There Is a Season*, 1.
9. Chittister, *There Is a Season*, 1.
10. Mother from Honduras, "My Journey from There to Here," September 9, 2015.
11. Mother, "My Love Story," Art Inside Karnes, February 10, 2016.
12. A fourth-grade daughter from Honduras writing for the Fuentes family while in a migrant shelter in Nuevo Laredo, Mexico, during MPP, November 5, 2019.
13. For an excellent narrative about a migrant who traveled alone to rejoin his parents in America, see Javier Zamora, *Solito: A Memoir* (London: Hogarth, 2022).
14. de Beauvoir, *Second Sex*, 283.
15. de Beauvoir, *Second Sex*, 294.
16. Judith Herman, *Trauma and Recovery: The Aftermath of Violence from Domestic Abuse to Political Terror* (New York: Perseus Books, 1992, 1997, 2015), 33.
17. A Harvard clinical psychiatrist, Herman draws her argument from the testimonies of combat veterans and survivors of incest, rape, and political terror. Herman, *Trauma and Recovery*, 34.
18. Herman, *Trauma and Recovery*, 35.
19. Herman, *Trauma and Recovery*, 58.
20. Camilo Montoya-Galvez, "The Facts about the Legal Battle over Title 42 and What Its End Could Mean for US Border Policy," CBS News, January 2, 2023, https://www.cbsnews.com/news/title-42-what-its-end-could-mean-us-immigration-border-policy/.

21 Madeleine L'Engle, *A Stone for a Pillow: Journeys with Jacob*, Book Two in the Genesis Trilogy, foreword by Rachel Held Evans (New York: Convergent, 1986, 2017), 231.
22 Evelyn, Nuevo Laredo, Mexico, November 13, 2019.
23 Audre Lorde, *The Cancer Journals*, foreword by Tracy K. Smith (New York: Penguin Books, Random House, 1980, 2020), 50–51.
24 See Boursier, ed., *Rowman and Littlefield Handbook of Women's Studies in Religion*, 231–246.
25 Lorde, *Cancer Journals*, 50–51.
26 Lorraine from El Salvador while in a migrant shelter in Nuevo Laredo, Mexico, during MPP, November 13, 2019.
27 Herman, *Trauma and Recovery*, 67.
28 Herman, *Trauma and Recovery*, 238.
29 Alma Ruth, interview with the author, September 10, 2020; cited in Boursier, *Willful Ignorance*, 75.
30 Wayne Anthony Hector and Stephen Paul Robson, songwriters, "Feels Like Today," sung by Rascal Flatts, Lyric Street Records, 2004.
31 The Interfaith Welcome Coalition assisted 138,584 migrants traveling through San Antonio between January and September 2022. Email update, November 9, 2022.
32 See Boursier, *Desperately Seeking Asylum*, 161–166.
33 See Miguel A. De La Torre, *Trails of Hope and Terror: Testimonies of Migration* (Maryknoll, NY: Orbis Books, 2009); and Vincent De La Torre, *Trails of Hope and Terror: The Movie* (Centennial, CO: V1 Educational Media, Inc., 2018). Available at https://www.trailsofhopeandterrorthemovie.com/about.html.
34 Arendt, *Human Condition*, 183–184.
35 Judith Plaskow response to an interview with Hava Tirosh-Samuelson and Aaron W. Huges, "An Interview with Judith Plaskow June 24, 2012," in *Judith Plaskow: Feminism, Theology, and Justice*, ed. Hava Tirosh-Samuelson and Aaron W. Hughes (Leiden, the Netherlands: Brill, 2014), 119–120.

CHAPTER EIGHT

Risk

Send out your bread upon the waters, for after many days you will get it back. Divide your means seven ways, or even eight, for you do not know what disaster may happen on earth.

—Ecclesiastes 11:1–2 (NRSVUE)

The choices that migrants, volunteers, and advocates make collectively shape spirituality in the borderlands that necessarily includes weighing, praying, and dealing with risk, a theme Ecclesiastes also addresses in its pragmatic considerations about what brings meaning to life. Risk for the families is about navigating choices forced on them through grievous evils, while volunteers and advocates freely and intentionally choose when, where, and how to engage various risks. This chapter weaves the themes in Ecclesiastes with the words and witness of displaced migrants who take calculated risks to save their lives. It also considers the often gutsy actions of volunteers and advocates, informed by their spiritual moral call, that are inspired and shaped by the courageous spirituality of the displaced families whom they stand in solidary with and the precious precarity of the natural environment in the borderlands.

RISK IN ECCLESIASTES

When Ecclesiastes advises, "Send out your bread upon the waters, for after many days you will get it back. Divide your means seven ways, or even eight, for you do not know what disaster may happen on earth" (11:1–2), it's recommending taking calculated risks that could generate tangible future benefits. To "cast your bread" means to put the options out there for future possibilities, not necessarily expecting everything to come to fruition, but it's at least putting it out there and giving it your best effort so that "after many days" the efforts will prove worthwhile as you "get it back." Ecclesiastes immediately follows up by advising using some prudence when taking risks by diversifying the options to avert the unpredictable and unlucky chance disaster that may occur. Not dissimilar to the advice a financial planner or stockbroker might give to diversify options and not to put all the investment eggs in one basket. It's still important to put funds aside for the future, but putting all the money in a single venue is overly risky and even foolish. If something happens to the one single investment, everything is affected.

Risk isn't just a money matter. Risk is a reality that touches literally every aspect and age of life. Chance is often chance because it includes a risk factor. It's risky to hop in the car to drive from point A to point B, just as it's risky to travel by train, plane, or ship. It's risky to smoke cigarettes, drink alcohol, eat too much sugar and/or too much salty fast food. Every medication includes its litany of risks, as does each medical procedure. It's risky to leave home and go to college, to a vocational training school, or to serve a stint in the military. Life is risky. Risks are everywhere. Even in a moderately safe and healthy nation like the United States, there's no escaping risk. The only way to really live life is to learn how to navigate the possibility of risk with a modicum of discernment that requires varying levels of bravery and courage.

Generosity despite Risk

Ecclesiastes suggests that risk-taking is a necessary aspect of life, including taking risks with doing something to contribute to the greater good of humanity and the entire created order, even when this includes taking some financial risks by spending funds that otherwise could be designated to save for a house, a college education, or retirement. Ecclesiastes scholar Seow proposes it's important "to take some risks in doing good, for even in those seemingly frivolous deeds one may find some surprising rewards. It's not that one must put out something to get back more later on, nor that one should give in order to receive. Rather, all may not be lost in spontaneity. One should throw away a good deed and not worry about the consequences, for the consequences of human actions are often contrary to expectations."[1]

Risk-taking intersects with spirituality in general, and spirituality in the borderlands in particular, because it requires faith, trust, courage, and a strong moral compass to navigate the minefields during the risk-taking. It's by taking these calculated risks that it becomes possible—not guaranteed but possible—to gain more meaning in this repetitive, sometimes senseless, and futile life. It's an important and necessary component of spirituality to be a generous giver, despite the threat of risk. Seow explains, "One should give freely—not just to a few, but indeed to many—even if one does not know that terrible things may happen in the future. Presumably terrible tragedies may strike; the economy may collapse. No one knows if or when a misfortune may happen. Generosity ought not to be kept in abeyance in anticipation of possible tragedies ahead."[2] Participating to make a difference to challenge and change present injustice is better than worrying about the risk of losing or spending future retirement funds.

Risk and Retirement Funds

The retired attorney who led teams to collect testimonies from detained children as part of the Flores Settlement Agreement accountability mentioned in the previous chapter explained she was "uniquely suited" to do this important volunteer work. She reiterated several times that she wouldn't *not* go because there was no compensation or even reimbursement for her travel expenses. She explained, "I didn't have an employer. I wasn't working in that type of paying job. So I'm supposed to say, 'Well, I can't do this. I can't go to Homestead, Florida, because it costs three thousand dollars [to cover airfare and hotel]? I'm not going to say, 'I'm not going to do it because it's expensive.'" There are expenses that accompany the deliberate choice to be present in solidarity with displaced migrants, which adds another risky choice of whether or not to spend money to challenge and change the bad business surrounding migration in the borderlands. This retired attorney explained, with who she is and what her skill set includes, there are expenses that come with her particular sense of call to be present in solidarity. The seventy-year-old retiree explained,

> I spent a lot of my retirement money doing this. So what if, when I'm older, I don't have money. I had it when I needed to do it. What am I going to do, not go take care of kids because I might need my money, because I might live to one hundred? I mean, you don't make your decisions that way. If you believe in social justice, and that you're called to do it, then you just do it. And if you pay a price for it, that's just the cost of admission.

The price, cost, or risk differs from what someone else might need to do, but there always are costs involved. Spirituality in the borderlands includes this generosity of spirit to happily spend the time and money necessary to assist the families and also to work for ecojustice in the borderlands.[3]

TAKE CALCULATED RISKS

The wisdom of Ecclesiastes prioritizes taking calculated risks but taking some risky action nonetheless. *Not* taking necessary risks won't change current circumstances, for "whoever observes the wind will not sow, and whoever regards the clouds will not reap" (Ecc. 11:4). Standing around watching the wind or staring at the sky isn't helpful. Inaction won't solve problems or move the issue forward. Standing around twiddling your thumbs doesn't fix anything. Ecclesiastes goes on to recommend, "In the morning sow your seed, and at evening do not let your hands be idle, for you do not know which will prosper, this or that, or whether both alike will be good" (11:6). Just as Ecclesiastes advises prudence in weighing difficult choices (chapter 7), this wisdom literature also advises cautionary discretion in risk-taking.

Mitigating Risk

Ecclesiastes connects its rationale for forward progress, doing what needs doing even if there's some risk involved, with relying on a strong inner moral compass. The nature of the finiteness or finitude of being human is that it's impossible to know an outcome in advance, but that doesn't mean someone should remain in a terminal point of inertia, unwilling or unable to do that risky thing that's before them. Ecclesiastes advises, "Just as you do not know how the breath comes to the bones in the mother's womb, so you do not know the work of God, who makes everything" (11:5). Confidence in the inner moral voice provides the courage to press on with the race that is before you.

Mitigating risk for the families often means splitting up and sending part of the family ahead to prepare the way for the rest of the family to join later. For example, Luis, the father of two girls and a boy, left his wife in Honduras with the two youngest children while he traveled to America with their oldest daughter, age thirteen. He said, "We go ahead to find work so we can bring my wife and our other children to join us in America."[4] Ideally, the front-runners would arrive safely and then provide an easier, less risky future journey for the rest of the family. It certainly isn't ideal to separate the family, but that's sometimes prudent to reduce the overall risk of harming the entire family.

FEAR AND RISK

Fear is another normal aspect of the human condition. Even in a democratic nation where life is moderately safe and well-ordered, the precarity of human life includes chance, fears, and risks. Sometimes it's the result of unpredictable chance that increases risk and produces the automatic fear reflex, what's often called the fight-or-flight response, a basic survival element to overcome the precarious fragility of life. Other times fears creep into the spirit due to uncertainties about the normal frailty of human life. Fears are wide-ranging and all-encompassing, including social fears of judgment, failure, and vocational or relational rejection. People may have a fear of heights, spiders, snakes, tight spaces, and/or wide-open spaces. Others have a fear of public speaking, aging, outliving retirement savings, personal safety for self and children, and losing a relationship. Parents fear their children will die before they do, and children fear their parents will die an early and/or painful death. It's also common to harbor fear of major medical issues like diabetes, stroke, heart attack, Parkinson's, Alzheimer's, and cancer.

Everyone has some deep fear that festers inside, holding them back from leaning into being fully present in the moment. Generally, people are always worried about something that might happen in the immediate or distant future. Personally, I've long harbored a fear that I'd die young of cancer because three members of my immediate maternal family did when they were fifty-nine, sixty-one, and sixty-three. When my mother radically surpassed all of them with her recent ninetieth birthday, I've come to realize that I might've wasted some unnecessary fear on dying young. Instead, I might need to now worry about the risk of living too long instead of too short.

Fear stymies spirituality when someone holds back from taking action because of worrying about taking a risk. Anxiety keeps people trapped inside the fear box. Instead, as psychiatrist Viktor Frankl writes about his experience of enduring years of suffering in Nazi death camps in his book *Man's Search for Meaning*, he calls "the last of the human freedoms" how each person chooses to respond.[5] What are the internal and external options available as possibilities for response amid the grievous evils, chance, and risk? There's always something that can be done internally and spiritually but also externally through solidarity with those around you. The invitation is to risk response despite anxiety or fear.

ANXIETY VERSUS FEAR

Fear differs from anxiety. Many of the aforementioned fears, including my own fear of getting cancer and dying young, are really anxiety, not fear. Reflecting on fear in her *Cancer Journals*, Audre Lorde writes, "I live with the constant fear of recurrence of another cancer. But fear and anxiety are not the same at all. One is an appropriate response to a real situation which I can accept and learn to work through just as I work through semi-blindness. But the other, anxiety, is an immobilizing yield to things that go bump in the night, a surrender to namelessness, formlessness, voicelessness, and silence."[6] Similarly, in the *Courage to Be*, theologian Paul Tillich also distinguishes fear from anxiety because the former has a specific thing that's the reason for the very real fear, whereas anxiety is more broad-based and general.[7]

Not all fears are created equal. It's one thing for a volunteer to risk feeling foolish due to speaking mediocre Spanish in public or traveling in remote sections of the desert while searching for stranded migrants, but the fear factor rises exponentially for the families who harbor fear of starvation, mutilation, torture, rape, and death. The families may have daily anxiety about the threat to life in their homelands, but that steps up to fear when general violence becomes specifically targeted directly against them or a family member. The ultimate fear is the Big-C Chance, death. Tillich argues, "The fear of death determines the element of anxiety in every fear. Anxiety, if not modified by the fear of an object, anxiety in its nakedness, is always the anxiety of ultimate nonbeing. Immediately seen, anxiety is the painful feeling of not being able to deal with the threat of a special situation. . . . It is the anxiety of not being able to preserve one's own being which underlies every fear and is the frightening element in it."[8] Perpetual risk keeps migrants living in the turbulence of fear and anxiety, which turns them inward and outward: inward through their courage and faith and outward as they cry out to God for intervention to carry them safely through their valleys while they walk in the shadow of death (Ps. 23).

The anxiety the families experience is what Heidegger would argue "discloses, primordially and directly, the world as world."[9] In other words, it's anxiety that makes the reality of fear real. Anxiety, rather than being inappropriate or misplaced with fear, actually gives fear substance and makes fear real. Fear exists because of anxiety. Anxiety that produces fear or fear that creates anxiety can produce inertia. Fear that immobilizes isn't helpful. It won't reduce or mitigate the thing that's creating the fear. What's generating the very real fear needs to have a spiritual and/or practical action as intervention that seeks to discern what's really happening. Then discernment considers the various choices for how to manage anything that's possible to be managed so that there's at least some control over the fear-generating beast. Sometimes fear is a reality that keeps someone sharp when danger is immanent, but other times fear is what Heidegger calls a "State-of-Mind."[10]

Fear as a State of Mind

Heidegger suggests the way to navigate fear is to consider three aspects: "(1) that in the face of which we fear, (2) fearing, and (3) that about which we fear."[11] By considering these three interrelated aspects of fear, it becomes possible to modify or reduce fear. He proposes it's by looking "*in the face of which* we fear" that it becomes less "fearsome,"[12] which resonates with the Ecclesiastes perspective to be prudent in taking risks, including navigating the inevitable fears that go with each risk.

Whether it's called *fear* or *anxiety*, both of these intense emotions, feelings, and very real sense of being are about what's happening or what's about to happen. Fear makes the fearful thing real. As Heidegger writes, "Fear is a fearing *in the face* of something threatening—of something which is detrimental," as in something very bad that will cause tangible harm.[13] Fear is how someone knows something's wrong, that something harmful is poised and ready to threaten their safety. For example, Heidegger proposes that "anxiety is not only anxiety in the face of something, but, as a state-of-mind, it is also anxiety about something."[14] It's by having anxiety about that horrible thing we fear that we come to realize what matters most. Fear is grounding because it provides a vivid picture of what's most important to us.[15] If we weren't afraid of the consequences to X, then that X wouldn't matter in the first place, and we wouldn't feel fear. It's the fear that pushes people to be decisive about the choices they must make, selecting between the less-horrible-thans in life.

More than a State of Mind

Fear in the face of risk is much more than a state of mind on the migrant journey. A seventeen-year-old unaccompanied minor male migrant said, "The path of immigration is very hard, difficult. I do not recommend it to others. I've been more scared than at any other time in my life." He added, "Detention is a horrible experience. Many good people have very negative experiences with US Immigration. The officers are mad at us, and they treat us very badly. There is much discrimination against migrants in the USA." Despite this quick series of risks, he added, "I give thanks to God at all times. God has the power to provide for our safe arrival to the United States."[16] David, a father from El Salvador traveling with his son Daniel, age five, shared their similar experience:

> We earned our way, working along the journey. We risked our lives and suffered daily. We crossed rivers and muddy swamps, walking for hours and hours to get to a safe place. We endured hunger and thirst; we slept in very ugly and very cold places, underneath bushes [illustration 8.1]. We endured the cold through the night and early morning, and we also were mistreated by people along the way. But always we maintained our faith that God would take care of us and protect us from all the dangers and all the evil.
>
> These have been long and difficult days for me, but even more so for my son, who is age five. He misses his mother and brothers. We are going ahead to get things settled, and then my wife will join us with our other two sons.
>
> We also received mistreatment at US Immigration, sleeping in the cold *hielera*. They did not show compassion for the children, and they did not give us our rights to call an attorney. They just returned us to Mexico, exposing us to all kinds of dangers.[17]

After his quick summary of the grievous evils they'd suffered on their journey, he promptly gave thanks to God for the unexpected opportunity to stay in a migrant shelter. He said, "God is the one who accompanies us. Without God, we are nothing. God is love."

Fears of Female Migrants

For female migrants of all ages, fear as a state of mind to survive the gender-based risks is even more challenging because they are interminably confronted with the misogyny, gender suppression, oppression, and sexual violence they're desperate to leave behind. Gender-based fear is normative, as Lorde reflects: "As women we were raised to fear. If I cannot banish fear completely, I can learn to count with it less. For then fear becomes not a tyrant against which I waste my energy fighting, but a companion, not particularly desirable, yet one whose knowledge can be useful."[18] It takes tremendous fortitude, guts, gumption, and spiritual centeredness for the more vulnerable female migrants to assess the radical risk factors at home and also along the migrant trail.

Fear also points to temporality and the finiteness of this precious and precarious life. This temporality factor, when it intersects with anxiety and fear, offers a forward sense of possibility. No one wants to stay stuck in the space and place of fear. The desire to live in peace—not in fear—sets the wheels in motion to begin to do what needs to be done to get out of the place and space of fear. Fear can also be the catalyst for courage to risk-taking the necessary actions to move toward a safer life, a better being, a hope for the future.

THE REALITY OF DEATH

The reality of death resurfaces here because it intersects with risk and the ever-present threat to life. Living with the reality of death in view can be empowering when it shapes choices to overcome fear and navigate risk, whereas considering risk alone, as its own entity or category, could become an immediate blockade because of the anxiety and fear that automatically seem to go with risk. Bringing in the death check as part of risk management isn't necessarily a downer. Rather, when the reality check of death enters into the risk-reflection equation, it becomes an energizer and motivator to do something to overcome the risk at hand.

Whether it's dealing with fear of dying from cancer, a common enough fear in America, or the double fear of dying the families have as they weigh the risks between dying at home or dying on the migration trail, dying is still dying. It's through taking a chance with risk that it becomes somewhat possible to imagine a possible new future (illustration 8.1). Lorde comes to the conclusion in her journey with cancer that "I was going to die, if not sooner than later, whether or not I had ever spoken myself. My silences had not protected me." She emphasizes, "Your silence will not protect you." So, too, the families come to terms with risk and make the decision to act.[19] Lorde's assessment that "the transformation of silence into language and

Illustration 8.1 *Camping Alongside the Rio Grande* 9" × 12" black-and-white acrylic painting based on a photograph by Kay Geurin of the Rio Grande River in Piedras Negras, Mexico, April 9, 2022, where migrants sleep in the shadow areas underneath the bushes along the riverbank. Art © Helen T. Boursier.

action is an act of self-revelation and that always seem fraught with danger" parallels the risk reality of forced migration and the moral responsibility for our compassionate response.[20] Weighing the pros and cons and reflecting on risk, at home and on the journey, lead to saying what needs to be said, which then launches the families to act. With Ecclesiastes and its Jewish roots in view, Rabbi Heschel emphasizes that "a Jew is asked to take a *leap of action* rather than a *leap of thought*," which includes moving beyond the present to consider doing what needs to be done.[21] It's through the deed, the doing, that it's possible to become aware of what really matters in life. It's through the doing that something better, different, new can happen.

Risk Offers Hope of Resurrection to New Life

In *Figuring the Sacred: Religion, Narrative, and Imagination*, Paul Ricœur calls future hope "the passion for the possible [which] implies no illusion."[22]

He's referring to the possibility of Christian resurrection, but his description whereby "all resurrection is resurrection from among the dead, that all new creation is in spite of death" parallels the early death the families are hoping to navigate for renewed life on the other side of this Big Risk, which would provide a resurrection of sorts from immanent early death to hope for new life in America. From the perspective of resurrection from death to hope for new life, Ricœur proposes, "Seen from the standpoint of hope, life is not only the contrary of but the denial of death; this denial relies on signs, not on proofs. It interprets in a creative way the signs of the superabundance of life in spite of the evidence of death."[23] Instead of denying death, hope lives into the reality of death while also pursuing life in the present. Hope engenders empowerment to act in the face of great risk.

Ricœur explains that hope has an *irrationality* because it steps outside present risk of death and seeks a "superabundance" that survives and thrives to overcome risk of death now.[24] Hope keeps hope alive. Carlos, a sixteen-year-old who traveled as an unaccompanied minor, said, "I have spent many nights sleeping outdoors in the cold, especially in the mountains. I have crossed through puddles, paddocks, and rivers, and I have suffered despair. But thanks to God I am hoping to be reunited with my mother, who is in the United States. I thank God for giving me the patience and the strength to move forward. I thank God for keeping me healthy. God is strong. Thanks to God we are alive."[25] Even though he's sharing this while living in a cramped migrant shelter located in one of the most dangerous cities for migrants along the northern Mexico border and after being deported from the United States, hope still keeps his vision alive for resurrection from risk to new life with his mother in America.

Staying with the parallel of Ricœur's resurrection theme and a resurrection to life from the risk of death, Ricœur proposes, "The passion for the possible implies no illusion; it knows that all resurrection is resurrection from among the dead, that all new creation is in spite of death. . . . For seen from the standpoint of hope, life is not only the contrary of but the denial of death; this denial relies on signs, not on proofs. It interprets in a creative way the signs of the superabundance of life in spite of the evidence of death."[26] Navigating risk offers hope for life, but the only way to do this is to act. Standing still, frozen in fear, will not make the risk disappear.

Furthermore, Rabbi Heschel explains it's through doing deeds that a person's heart and life are made manifest. What someone "may not dare to think" becomes real through taking the risk to do that thing that seems too crazy to even think about doing. It's through the doing that "the heart is revealed."[27] Taking action, despite the fear and inertia of anxiety, is the definitive test. It's also the ultimate risk to act when there's such risk, but it's only through doing that the risk is mitigated and that fear has a hope of receding. The clock ticks on. The only time we have to navigate fear and mitigate risk is now. Our time is always now, today, in the present to choose our better-than and run with it through the risk to the hopeful gain (chapter 9).

Risk That Warrants Credible Fear

Asylum seekers must prove their lives are so at risk that they have *credible fear*, the technical term the US government uses to determine whether or not there's sufficient evidence to prove that someone has over-the-top fear that will end in a quick death if they were to remain in their homeland. "We live in a very dangerous country" is insufficient. Technically, US Immigration specifies it must be "fear of persecution, fear of torture, and fear of return."[28] It can't be fear from living in risks related to a particularly harsh environment where homicide and femicide deaths are dramatically higher than in other unsafe nations. Even when *everyone* in a country, region, or household is at greater risk than what's normative in other nations, an asylum seeker must prove that the *everyone* risk is specifically directed at them.

Government agents determine if these fears are legitimate, a determination that's notably variable, subjective, and biased through an anti-immigrant interpretation by the particular immigration official who conducts the initial screening at the border and/or the judge who later makes the final determination. For example, a Salvadoran father who'd traveled with his wife and children explained the asylum interviews for the credible fear screening when they arrived to the border and requested asylum. They'd been at a shelter for migrants in Nuevo Laredo, Mexico, since they arrived at the border on October 17, 2019, and the family finally had their first appointment with the courts to request asylum on December 3, 2019. The father explained, "We told the judge that 'Yes, we feared for our lives.' My wife said the same thing. They would not listen. They refused our claims. I think they want me to have missing body parts or of my children." He added, "We have so much fear, and the judge does not care. We are in anguish."[29] Theirs is an anguish that resonates with beloved Christian author Madeleine L'Engle, who points out in *Sold into Egypt: Journeys into Human Being*:

> We don't "get over" the deepest pains of life, nor should we. "Are you over it?" is a question that cannot be asked by someone who has been through "it," whatever "it" is. It is an anxious question, an asking for reassurance that cannot be given. During an average lifetime there are many pains, many griefs to be borne. We don't "get over" them; we learn to live with them, to go on growing and deepening, and understanding, as Joseph understood, that God can come into all our pain and make something creative out of it.[30]

The families endure many harsh risks and horrific grievous evils before they arrive to request asylum here, which remain part of their life's memories that contribute to their spiritual formation. As the multiple testimonies from the families included earlier indicate, the depth of loss, pain, suffering, and fear that force the families out the door to seek safe haven in the United States is *credible*. Following Tillich's argument, their general anxiety about the possibility of harm becomes specific fear that can then "be met by courage."[31] It's never anxiety or regular fear that pushes the families onto the migration trail. It's always an intense fear that's fear beyond all fear. Such intense fear that generates agony necessitates finding the courage to continue to do what must be done to remain alive.

COURAGE

Courage is one of the primary benefits of chance and the grievous evil that forces the issue of risk. There must be opposition for courage to be necessary.[32] Courage confronts fear in the journey to taking a risk. Courage can't be separated from what it means to be alive, nor can being alive be disconnected from courage. Courage needs the reality or fact of the finitude factor of life because it's the threat of *nonlife* that emboldens courage to act in the face of risk. Tillich proposes, "Courage can show us what being is, and being can show us what courage is."[33] Courage overcomes the reality of fear in risk through faith in a higher being. In *Dynamics of Faith*, Tillich argues what displaced families know through experience: it's not possible to "replace faith by courage, but neither can one describe faith without courage."[34] In his closing synthesis in his treaties on courage, Tillich emphasizes that *"the courage to be is rooted in the God who appears when God has disappeared in the anxiety of doubt."*[35] The families consistently embrace such courage as they rise to the challenge of risk after risk. It's a courage that inspires spirituality in the borderlands through the dedication, strength, and bold actions these families show in the face of great risk.

Courage and the Families

Courage is a prevalent theme in conversations with the families and also in their written testimonies. The families wouldn't survive their journey to America without courage. It's part of their fortitude to overcome adversity through each risk factor they must take on. For example, a mother from Honduras said, "My courage is why I am here." After considering making the journey, weighing the risks between staying and going, she said, "It took courage to leave my grandparents, to leave my mother, and to leave my brothers and sisters." Leaving her family and country "because of the delinquency," she said she wants to give her daughter a better future and to reunite with her father, who's already living in America. She said, "I knew I was embarking on a difficult trip, long and dangerous with many risks." Her courage, fortitude, and faith amid risk is clear in her statement that "it was very difficult giving birth to my daughter in the mountains during the journey. Danger was everywhere." Reflecting on her courage while detained inside GEO Karnes, she added, "It took courage to spend Christmas without family, locked up, far from home." She concluded, "My courage is why I am here. My courage is keeping me strong." Her courage remains alive through the possibility of reunion with her father, brother, and niece in America. She said, "I want to be surrounded by people who love us very much."[36]

Similarly, a mother from El Salvador who said she made the journey for her daughters explained, "It took courage to leave my home. It took courage to pass through all the tribulations along the journey." Sharing her story while detained inside GEO Karnes, she added, "It takes courage to endure the current situation here in family detention. My prayer is that we may continue quickly on our journey to family. Nothing is impossible for God."[37] The mothers express their particular vulnerability and their added risks while traveling alone through unknown territory, foreign places, and "knowing no one to depend on." The intersection of courage with overcoming fear in the face of extreme risk while leaning into their faith cannot not impact the volunteers and advocates who interact with them in various capacities. The faith of the families amid grave risk is awe-inspiring and humbling at the same time. For instance, after spending a day with the families doing Art Inside Karnes, my journal entry synthesizes the profundity of their spirituality of courage through risk:

> Thankfulness to God is pervasive throughout their reflections. A mother who left two sons behind said it's her faith in God which makes everything different in her life because "God is the most beautiful thing that has happened to me" and she adds that "it is not difficult" [to make the journey] when one has faith in God." Gratitude is given "for the opportunity to be in this country," for "health and safety," and even though "no one can sleep and you are tired, but God cares for his children and protects them always."
>
> Faith in God also is a consistent theme in their closing advice for other women who are thinking about making the trip: "Recommit to the Christian faith" (before you make the journey). In the middle of "fear beyond all fear" and "fear so intense and twenty days of suffering" a mother said it was only through the strength of God that they "were able to persevere." Another said after having had the experience of making the journey her advice is for other mothers to carefully consider the risks they'll put their children under along the journey. Another said that the trip was much more difficult than she'd expected and that she learned "that in this life there are risks and that with God there are no borders" Their ultimate fears remain that they will be barred from entry to the United States, and once here, that they would be deported and forced to return to their home country. A detained mother wrote, "I do not want to return for I have great fear that they will kill us." Amidst the physical suffering of the journey, the greatest sense of loss is their homes and their families, as one detained mother wrote, "God demonstrated to me on the walk that the family is most important of all."[38]

Spirituality Empowers Courage

The families consistently lean into their spirituality to move with courage through each risk. Reflecting on her journey to the United States, a mother wrote:

> *God Is with Us*
>
> God helped us to arrive safely.
> God gives us life.

> God gives us light.
> God is our Pastor.
> God is with us.
>
> Without God
> We are nothing.
> God gives us
> > Life
> > Health
> > Strength.
> God helped us to arrive here
> > Safe.
> God is with us.
> > Always.[39]

Amid extraordinary life-threatening risks, the mothers and fathers steadfastly claim that their courage and strength come from God, but they also attribute their courage to their children, who are their motivation to get to a safe place.

RISKS FOR VOLUNTEERS AND ADVOCATES

The risks that volunteers and advocates take pale in comparison to what the families must survive. Whereas the families tackle Big Risk after Big Risk, which often are literally about life and death, the lowercase little-r risks that the volunteers take are generally emotional, relational, financial, or time investments that don't create a direct threat to life.[40]

Retired Presbyterian minister and one of the original organizers for the Sanctuary Movement, Reverend John Fife explained the risks he chose to begin taking in the 1980s with the rapid increase in migration from El Salvador and Guatemala, work that eventually led to Southside Presbyterian Church in Tucson becoming "the first in the nation to declare itself as sanctuary for Central American refugees."[41] The work continued to evolve as the US government changed its enforcement policies for migration through the US-Mexico border, which is when, he explained, they "moved to humanitarian aid in the desert and everything that's involved." He said his faith-based response to risk was influenced by the "almost total failure of the church in

Europe in the 1930s and 1940s to protect the Jewish refugees who were fleeing the Holocaust in Nazi Germany," which, he explained, "put the faith question directly to me." Rev. Fife said he took it as his pastoral responsibility to educate his congregation about migrant matters, which included responding to the reality of risk in their process of response. He said it was "a serious responsibility" to preach, teach, and lead his congregation to respond with compassion, including and despite the risks involved. He added, "So I spent a lot of time, years and years, decades in that discipline" of studying ancient texts to faithfully preach, teach, and lead his congregation. He concluded, "The evidence from the history of this church [Southside Presbyterian Church, Tucson, Arizona] and what this congregation did accomplish and continues to in the desert now, in the borderlands."[42] The risks vary, but they are very much present as the work and witness continue.

Some risks are taken with a group that journeys together to assist the families or protest an environmentally unjust border wall, but other risks require individual discernment and individual response to act or not. For example, an Arizona resident who regularly volunteers with migrant assistance shared about when she helped two lost migrants who were looking for their pickup connection in a remote section of the Sonoran Desert. The resident said,

> We saw migrants in this area several months ago. They had telephone trackers. I was walking my dog when these two guys just seemed to come up out of the ground. You've seen what it's like out here now, there really isn't any coverage to hide (see illustration 5.1). They needed a place to get picked up. You cannot do this as a member of an assistance group (or everyone gets in trouble). It's something you choose to do on your own, but even still, [it's a risk so] caution is very important. I'm married to someone who has a green card (and could get deported if he was caught aiding and abetting migrants). I talked to the two guys and also to their contact. I directed them to a particular row of mailboxes. I offered to drive them there, but they walked on their own. I asked them to leave me a sign that they got picked up. They didn't, but they were gone.[43]

During an explanation about assisting displaced migrants in the desert, another volunteer interjected to clarify when risk oversteps the boundary with prudence, saying, "You do not want your house to be known as a 'safe house.' When we help a migrant, we tell them, 'We're happy to help you, but please don't tell anyone that we've helped you.' The last thing you want is coyotes to start dropping people off at your house."[44] Not all risks are created equal, and some volunteers are willing to take much greater risks than others. The key is for each person to find the sweet spot matching their gifts with their skills, interests, passions, and risk-taking comfort level.

Emotional and Relational Risks

A Team Brownsville volunteer who participates in a small group in his community, Retired Old Men Eating Out (ROMEO), said, "Many of the guys, not most of them but many, are very, very much entrapped in the MAGA (Make America Great Again) world. I have to be careful to start bringing *that* up [his volunteer work at the border] because I basically would be shunned." He clarified, "A lot of these people, they're my friends, but I just don't go there [discuss immigration] with them because I know how they would react." Another Team Brownsville volunteer interjected, "Some of the people living where we live really hate, absolutely hate what we do—vocally so. Others ignore it." This volunteer continued, "And so it's difficult to know how to respond, when people say, 'Well, how was your day? What did you do today?' You're trying to pick words that are not going to raise a ruckus with whoever you're talking to because it does, it does often here." The volunteer added, "I don't like to hide it. I don't, I wear my Team Brownsville shirts. Everybody knows what I do. I'm proud of what we do. But sometimes you just can't talk about it."

When there's an immigration-related news headline that "everyone is talking about," then these volunteers who live in a retirement community near the Texas-Mexico border emphasized, "We cannot even skirt around the edges and talk with the others. Absolutely not. We can't say a word about it." A Team Brownsville core team member who has an only child, now an adult, who was a strong supporter of the president who instigated MPP, said his son is "very angry at what I do, and it's caused a big division in our relationship, which breaks my heart." These aren't life-threatening risks, but they are deeply wounding spiritually, emotionally, and relationally.

Risk Discernment

In describing the risky options for how volunteers assist migrants through the various outreach choices facilitated through the GVS Samaritans, a volunteer said that there is absolutely black and white, yes and no, and right and wrong regarding what to do and what *not* to do when helping migrants, particularly as it relates to what's legal. However, there's also room for discernment because "it's going to be more squishy than that. And more uncertain than that. And you're going to have to kind of have a meeting with yourself and say, 'Well, how risk-averse am I? How risk prone am I, and how much out of my comfort zone am I willing to go or *not* willing to go?'" The volunteer said that regardless of the responses in the meeting you have with yourself, there's something for everyone to do: "Actually, there's still room for you, even if you're very risk-averse and not willing to push the boundaries. There's still a place for you."[45] During the same Zoom group interview session, another volunteer said a spiritual leader in the group "is always quick to say, 'We're not going to tell you what to do. You have to choose your own line.' I think that's quite a strong message for people to stay involved. We're not going to set rules or boundaries for you. You have to decide for yourself." To paraphrase MLK, spiritual character grows not during the times when life is easy-peasy. Character-building and spiritual growth emerge when that same person is willing to stand up and be counted "at times of challenge and controversy."[46] When there's a higher risk factor, courage intersects with faith and integrity to embrace spirituality, which acts for justice and peacemaking.

Not every risk is for every volunteer or every advocate. I've attended various public witness events, some that became somewhat loud, rowdy, and a little bit too unruly for me, others that were much more within my comfort zone. While I'm not comfortable with a public action in a federal court or facing off with CBP at a border detention facility, I was very comfortable serving as a volunteer chaplain inside a for-profit detention center; visiting shelters for migrants located in Nuevo Laredo, Mexico, which many migrants term "the most dangerous city" along Mexico's northern border, where we could literally feel the eyes of the cartel watching us; and using my mixed-media artwork as illustrations and public witness, despite the extreme vulnerability I felt/feel in each instance. For each volunteer and advocate, part of their spiritual journey in the borderlands is to figure out just what they are ready, willing, and able to do, not only physically but also spiritually and emotionally.

Whatever their level of Big-R Risk or little-r risk, volunteers and advocates embrace it with empathy, which comes from being present in solidarity through accompaniment with the families. Such close connection through direct presence includes what Valarie Kaur describes as "deep listening [that] is an act of surrender," which Kaur explains creates the "risk [of] being changed by what we hear." Volunteers and advocates in the borderlands choose to be intentionally present in solidarity with the families despite the personal, relational, emotional, and spiritual risks. These interactions generate empathy through presence that includes careful listening, which Kaur explains "is cognitive *and* emotional—to inhabit another person's view of the world is to *feel* the world with them."[47] While the families have little to no control over the capital-R Risks they must overcome, the comparative little-r risks that volunteers and advocates typically take with empathy come with a significant amount of freedom of choice regarding what types and how much risk they are ready, willing, and able to take.

Rabbi Heschel proposes, "The seriousness of doing surpasses the sensitivity of our conscience."[48] There are an unlimited number of possible outcomes, good and bad, positive and negative, that can come from the choices people make in response to risk. Heschel points out that the problem is and will always be each person's limited amount of wisdom, which also resonates with Ecclesiastes. Each volunteer has to figure out that spiritual place and space for which risks they're ready, willing, and able to take. My personal mantra that pushes me a bit further along the risk-factor measuring stick, empowering me with the *will to do*, is reminding myself, "No guts, no glory."[49] What I mean by that is if there are no guts in me, then there's no glory for the families, meaning honoring their lives by being fully present and bearing witness.

CONSEQUENCES OF RISK IN THE BORDERLANDS

The grievous evils that befall migrants as a consequence to risk-taking are devastating to the families, often generating a litany of extreme outcomes. The harsh consequences contribute to the unique spirituality in the borderlands, impacting the families most directly but also the volunteers and advocates who are in solidarity with them. For instance, a GVS Samaritan volunteer remembered finding a child's backpack just inside the gate in the fence around her property where she lives at the edge of the desert. It contained a water bottle, toilet paper, three wraps, a partial bottle of alcohol, a rose, a four-inch-tall plastic bag that had cracker crumbs, and a pair of boy's underwear. She said, "I was devastated. I called out, but no one answered. I look as these as sacred items, and I think of this boy often."[50] This missed opportunity to meet, greet, know, and possibly assist this unknown migrant boy is the sort of spiritual connection that regularly occurs in the borderlands, integrating acts of compassion, kindness, hospitality, care, and welcome, despite the risks, through the mutuality of action, ours with theirs—the volunteers with the displaced migrant families.

It's this mutuality in action through the risk, and often because of or despite that risk, that creates what Hannah Arendt describes in the *Human Condition* as "consequences [that] are boundless, because action, though it may proceed from nowhere, so to speak, acts into a medium where every reaction becomes a chain reaction and where every process is the cause of new processes."[51] Arendt argues that this mutuality through action inevitably and necessarily "always establishes relationships and therefore has an inherent tendency to force open all limitations and cut across all boundaries."[52] Spirituality in the borderlands embraces relational mutuality through the risk, moving together toward the possibility for gain.

NOTES

1. Seow, *Ecclesiastes*, 343.
2. Seow, *Ecclesiastes*, 343.
3. See, It's Going Down, "Protests along Arizona Border Halts Construction of Governor's Wall of Shipping Containers," December 6, 2022, https://itsgoingdown.org/protests-halt-contruction-shipping-container-wall/.
4. Luis from Honduras while in a migrant shelter in Nuevo Laredo, Mexico, during MPP, November 5, 2019.
5. See Frankl, *Man's Search for Meaning*.
6. Lorde, journal entry June 20, 1980, *Cancer Journals*, 7.
7. Paul Tillich, *The Courage to Be* (New Haven, CT: Yale University Press, 1952), 36.
8. Tillich, *Courage to Be*, 38.
9. Heidegger, *Being and Time*, 232.
10. Heidegger, *Being and Time*, 179.
11. Heidegger, *Being and Time*, 179.
12. Heidegger, *Being and Time*, 179; italics his.
13. Heidegger, *Being and Time*, 391; italics his.
14. Heidegger, *Being and Time*, 232.
15. Heidegger, *Being and Time*, 180.
16. Daniel, seventeen, from El Salvador while in a migrant shelter in Nuevo Laredo, Mexico, during MPP, December 4, 2019.
17. David from El Salvador while staying in a migrant shelter in Nuevo Laredo, Mexico, during MPP, December 4, 2019.
18. Lorde, *Cancer Journals*, 8.
19. Lorde, *Cancer Journals*, 13.
20. Lorde, *Cancer Journals*, 14.
21. Heschel, *God in Search of Man*, 283.
22. Ricœur, *Figuring the Sacred*, 206–207.

23 Ricœur, *Figuring the Sacred*, 206–207.
24 Ricœur, *Figuring the Sacred*, 205–206.
25 Carlos, sixteen, from El Salvador while at a migrant shelter in Nuevo Laredo, Mexico, during MPP, December 4, 2019.
26 Ricœur, *Figuring the Sacred*, 206–207.
27 Heschel, *God in Search of Man*, 284.
28 US Citizenship and Immigration Services, "Questions and Answers: Credible Fear Screening," May 31, 2022, https://www.uscis.gov/humanitarian/refugees-and-asylum/asylum/questions-and-answers-credible-fear-screening.
29 Father from El Salvador while in a migrant shelter in Nuevo Laredo, Mexico, during MPP, December 4, 2019. His wife shared a similar story of anguish in her written testimony. See Helen T. Boursier, "Call to Accountability: Women's Studies in Religion Critiques State Culpability to Feminicide through Border Controls and Exclusion from Asylum," in Boursier, *Rowman and Littlefield Handbook of Women's Studies in Religion*, 76.
30 Madeleine L'Engle, *Sold into Egypt: Journeys into Human Being*, Book Three in the Genesis Trilogy, foreword by Rachel Held Evans (New York: Convergent, 1989, 2017), 185.
31 Tillich, *Courage to Be*, 39.
32 Søren Kierkegaard, *Purity of Heart Is to Will One Thing: Spiritual Preparation for the Office of Confession*, trans. Douglas V. Steere (New York: Harper and Row Publishers, 1956), 173.
33 Tillich, *Courage to Be*, 2.
34 Tillich, *Dynamics of Faith*, 120.
35 Tillich, *Courage to Be*, 190; italics his.
36 Mother from Honduras, "My Courage," Art Inside Karnes, January 30, 2016.
37 Mother from El Salvador, "My Courage," Art Inside Karnes, January 13, 2016.
38 Helen T. Boursier, personal journal reflecting on Art Inside Karnes theme "My Journey from There to Here," September 9, 2015.
39 Maria, "My Journey from There to Here," Art Inside Karnes, March 15, 2016.
40 For examples of various levels of legal risk for volunteers in the borderlands, see, Amy Knight, "The Borderlands Forum: Humanitarian Aid in the Borderlands," Border Community Alliance, June 22, 2022, https://vimeo.com/726106679.
41 Madeline Hilf conducted the interview with Rev. John Fife as part of her academic project with Fordham University; shared by permission.
42 Madeline Hilf conducted the interview with Reverend John Fife as part of her academic project with Fordham University; shared by permission.
43 Helen T. Boursier, Field Notes, vol. 7, 80–81.
44 Boursier, Field Notes, vol. 7, 62.
45 See "Welcome, Volunteers!" Green Valley-Sahuarita Samaritans, https://www.gvs-samaritans.org/volunteer.html.
46 King Jr., *Strength to Love*, 26.
47 Kaur, *See No Stranger*, 143.
48 Heschel, *God in Search of Man*, 284.
49 Boursier, *Arts as Witness*, 250–251.
50 Boursier, Field Notes, vol. 6, 136.
51 Arendt, *Human Condition*, 190.
52 Arendt, *Human Condition*, 191–192.

CHAPTER NINE

Gain

Light is sweet, and it pleases the eye to see the sun.
—Ecclesiastes 11:7 (NIV)

Gain is another pervasive theme throughout Ecclesiastes as it seeks to discern *yitron*, the benefits or gains in the balance sheet of life. Ecclesiastes considers gain in regard to practical, tangible, or economic benefits that give someone a specific advantage, surplus, or profit (i.e., Ecc. 1:3, 3:9, 5:9, 5:16, and 7:13). It also examines the ethical sense of what's valuable, beneficial, or worthwhile in giving meaning to life (i.e., Ecc. 2:11, 13; 10:10, 11).[1] With the possibility of gain in view, Ecclesiastes considers what's the appropriate portion or lot someone could or should expect as their allotment while living this one and only life "under the sun" (i.e., Ecc. 2:10; 3:22; 9:6, 9). In weighing the options and determining if something is a beneficial gain, Ecclesiastes makes better-than comparative analyses through the choice process (chapter 7). A gain is worthwhile in comparison with something else that, all things being equal, is *less good* or less beneficial.

The primary concern for determining if something is a gain is if it contributes to a meaningful life, which Ecclesiastes addresses in six categories: life in general, wisdom, justice, work, pleasure, and miscellaneous.[2] If something provides a modicum of meaning over something else, then it counts as a gain. A gain is only a gain when people accept this as their portion or lot in life, not in a passive sense that would turn someone into a doormat to be downtrodden such that grievous evil prospers. Rather, accepting a gain as a gain means to embrace the present with gratitude and recognize the beneficial good that's there. The pervasive sense of gain that begets gratitude in Ecclesiastes also contributes to spirituality in the borderlands.

Ecclesiastes considers the ethical or justice aspect because sometimes a portion or lot in life is what someone receives, regardless of whether or not it's sufficient, fair, equitable, or deserved. Each person gains a particular amount, large or small, and then it's up to each individual to figure out how to make the best of it. Of course, there are also choices (chapter 7) and risks (chapter 8) to consider moving from a portion or lot that's imbued with grievous evil (chapter 3) to a place of safety with the basic gains of water, food, clothing, shelter, and health. In *The Ethics of Ambiguity*, Simone de Beauvoir explains, "The characteristic feature of all ethics is to consider human life as a game that can be won or lost" while also teaching and learning what it means to gain the various benefits in life.[3] The gains in the borderlands, small and large, contribute to spirituality in the borderlands.

GAIN IN THE BORDERLANDS: BIG, BIGGER, BIGGEST

Not unlike little-c chance and Big-C Chance, there's a wide range of gain/Gain that impacts spirituality in the borderlands, including lots of small-g gains along the way. The initial Big Gain is a sojourner's safe arrival to the US-Mexico border. Their Bigger Gain is admittance through the tightly guarded southern gate, gaining temporary legal status and permission to pursue the Biggest Gain: long-term safety for themselves and their families, which ultimately will enable them to live in peace.

There are three primary categories, types, or levels of gain that contribute to spirituality in the borderlands (fig. 1), paralleling Maslow's famous hierarchy of needs. Clearly the obvious primary goal for the families is their safe arrival to reunite with family members who are already living in the United States. They need safety from the harm they're fleeing, followed by basic human needs such as water, food, clothing, shelter, and health so they can live the rest of their lives in peace. Reaching the border alive and well is a phenomenal major safety gain, but there also are little gains along the journey that the families must achieve in order to clear the gauntlet of immigration protocols to pass through the maze that leads to receiving temporary legal status to pursue their asylum claims on US soil.

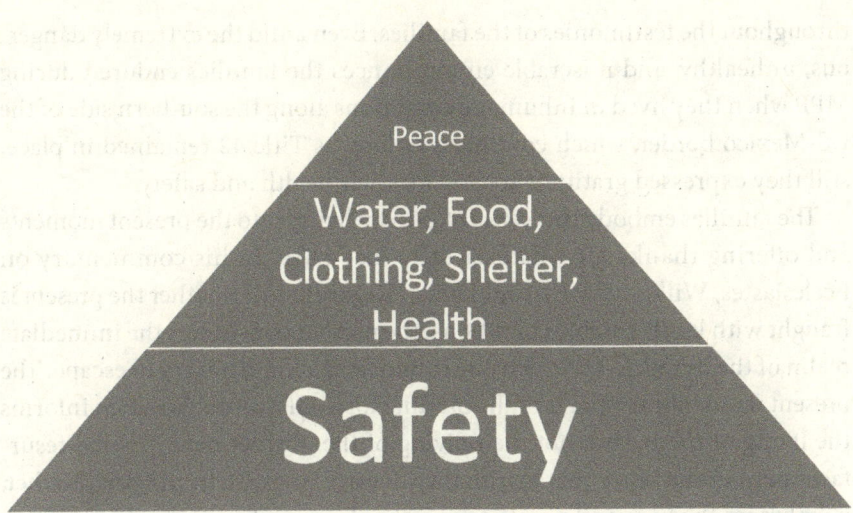

Figure 1 Hierarchy of needs for displaced families.

First and foremost, the families seek to gain and maintain safety. Next, the families want and expect to work for their basic needs so they can provide for the safety and well-being of their own family. Gratitude gains momentum when the displaced families attribute each little gain as a gift from God. They realize, as Simone Weil argues, that "impossibility is the door of the supernatural. We can but knock at it. It is someone else who opens."[4] The families experience firsthand the impossibility of safety. The someone else who opens the door for many of the families is God. Hence, even the smallest gains along the journey to safety in America bring them some peace, some gratitude, and even some joy (chapter 10). It's their gratitude for each and every gain, large and small, that permeates spirituality in the borderlands. Their gratitude is contagious.

GAINING GRATITUDE

Given the ethical, theological, and foundational Hebraic belief in Ecclesiastes that God is God, each gain includes a theological perspective: gratitude for the gifts of God for the people of God. Gain contains gratitude for the portion or lot each person receives and acknowledgment that each gain is a gift from God. This same sense of gratitude for each gain, large and small, is evident throughout the testimonies of the families. Even amid the extremely dangerous, unhealthy, and miserable circumstances the families endured during MPP when they lived in inhumane conditions along the southern side of the US-Mexico border, which continued as long as Title 42 remained in place, still they expressed gratitude to God for their health and safety.

The families embody this sense of gain by living into the present moments and offering thanks for whatever little they have. In his commentary on Ecclesiastes, William Brown highlights, "Regardless of whether the present is fraught with less favorable conditions, the present constitutes the immediate realm of the living, from which one cannot and should not try to escape. The present moment carries a morally binding force all its own. Wisdom informs the living of *these* days, not the reliving of the 'former days.'"[5] Time resurfaces here in the sense that spirituality doesn't languish in the past. Rather, it embraces the here and now. Ecclesiastes places such a strong emphasis on embracing the present because it's the here and now where each person lives their lives, not reflecting on the past or having anxiety about the unknown future. Now is life, in this present context. This moment, today, now, is where each person lives their life. Gratitude in the present, appreciating life now, profoundly influences spirituality in the borderlands. Gaining gratitude is contagious.

When advocates and volunteers see or experience this from the families, as they often do, it deeply touches their spirits and calls them into a stronger desire to be centered in gratitude in their own lives. As Bonhoeffer writes in *Letters and Papers from Prison*, "In the midst of all our hardships we keep experiencing an overwhelming kindness and friendship."[6] It's a cognitive choice to look for and acknowledge the little gains while awaiting, pursuing, hoping, and praying for the Big Gain. For example, while residing in a cramped migrant shelter in Nuevo Laredo, Mexico, during MPP, Claribel from Honduras said, "Yes, things are very bad. Like all of us here at the migrant shelter, we are looking for material things: food, clothing, shelter, safety for our children. But we have not forgotten God's plan." This mother added, "I walk with my three-year-old boy, and we have suffered a lot, but I also have seen the hand of God. God has kept the desire in my heart to reunite with my husband in the United States so we can be a family together. It is through the goodness of God that we will be together again. May God bless you and me."[7] Again, gratitude is contagious. Gratitude is a decided spiritual gain in the borderlands that the volunteers experience through the families.

VOLUNTEERS: GAINING BY DOING

Gain comes through doing something tangible to help, even when that help seems to come too late. For example, a GVS Samaritan volunteer described pulling into a circumventuous road off the beaten path in the Sonoran Desert when they found a dead body. There was no sign of foul play, and the man had been dead for three to four hours. It was too late for his life, but there were still options to provide gains. Two volunteers stayed with the body, and two went to find help. The family couldn't afford to have the body sent back, so the Samaritans paid for him to be cremated. A Samaritan volunteer explained, "The son works as a cab driver in Los Angeles, and he sent a lovely note thanking us for caring for his father. A Samaritan wrote back to tell him that if he ever came out this way, they would show him where they found his father's body."[8] The father gained dignity after his death, the son gained closure that his father's remains were compassionately cared for, and the Samaritans gained spiritual affirmation from their ethical humanitarian actions.

Team Brownsville Example

A Team Brownsville core team volunteer beautifully expressed the mutuality of gain in the borderlands. After hosting a displaced family in his home in Brownsville, Texas, he posted on Facebook:

> After 10 days living with me, the beautiful family from Venezuela is off to Denver. I thank everyone who donated for the bus fare, cell phone and money for food. They told me to thank all of you. I tried my best to get them to feel at home and feel human again after three months of hell trying to get here. I especially tried hard to provide the 7-year-old boy what a normal childhood should be like. I took him to the zoo, park, beach, and he especially liked the carrousel at the mall. I made sure he had all the cupcakes and juice boxes and tried to spoil him as much I could. I got him tons of toys of course. Several of my friends came to the house to donate items. This family was in awe about how many of you stepped in to help. The whole experience gives me such hope for humanity. The boy and I were inseparable. I adored him. He is like the perfect son I never had. Playing around I would ask him if he would stay with me. He always responded very politely "I need to think about it." When we went to buy the tickets for the bus he said "don't buy mine yet because I haven't made my decision." When they left his dad texted me that the boy cried as they drove away. I cried also of course. I will truly miss them, but mostly little Manuel.[9]

This example resonates with what so many volunteers gain along the borderlands through whatever interactions they have with the families.

Pro Bono Example

A pro bono attorney said she gains the most from the families when she's using her skill set and experience to collect their affidavits with their testimonies of mistreatment by government officials. She clarified, "I don't feel spiritual when I'm working; I just feel busy. I feel immersed. But I also feel like I'm doing something to help." It's through the doing that her spirituality gains affirmation that she's where she could and should be. Occasionally, amid the flurry of being busy helping displaced families and children, her spirituality is reaffirmed by theirs and vice versa. She remembered a mother with a small child who'd been in a holding center for migrants for way too long per US laws, while others around her had been processed and released. The authorities didn't have documentation on her child, so there'd been interminable delays. The pro bono attorney remembered, "This mother was crying. I looked at her, and I asked, 'Do you believe in God? Do you believe in Jesus?' She said, 'Yes.' I asked, 'Do you believe if I tell you that I'm going to get you out, and that I believe in God and Jesus, that I will get you out?' And she said, 'Yes.' I said, 'Good.' So I used her belief to give her strength to tolerate her circumstance. And then, of course, I worked hard to get her out." The attorney added, "It didn't happen immediately, but this mother and child did gain their release."

The pro bono attorney remembered another time when she was collecting testimonies from children detained in Tornillo, Texas, which the media referred to as the "tent city in the desert."[10] She was interviewing a seventeen-year-old boy who'd been in detention for ten months. She said detention is often harshest on the younger children, but this "big kid was suffering more." The pro bono attorney said she kept a large silver medallion of Our Lady of Guadalupe in her pencil box, explaining, "It's not a religious thing for me," but she kept it with her because it was a gift from a dear friend. As she was taking her supplies out to do the interview, the teenager saw the medallion and asked if he could touch it. She told him he could hold it as long as they were together, but then he'd have to return it to her. She explained, "He changed. He held that medallion in his hand, and he changed. He felt resilient. He felt hopeful. His body language changed, and the tone of his voice changed.

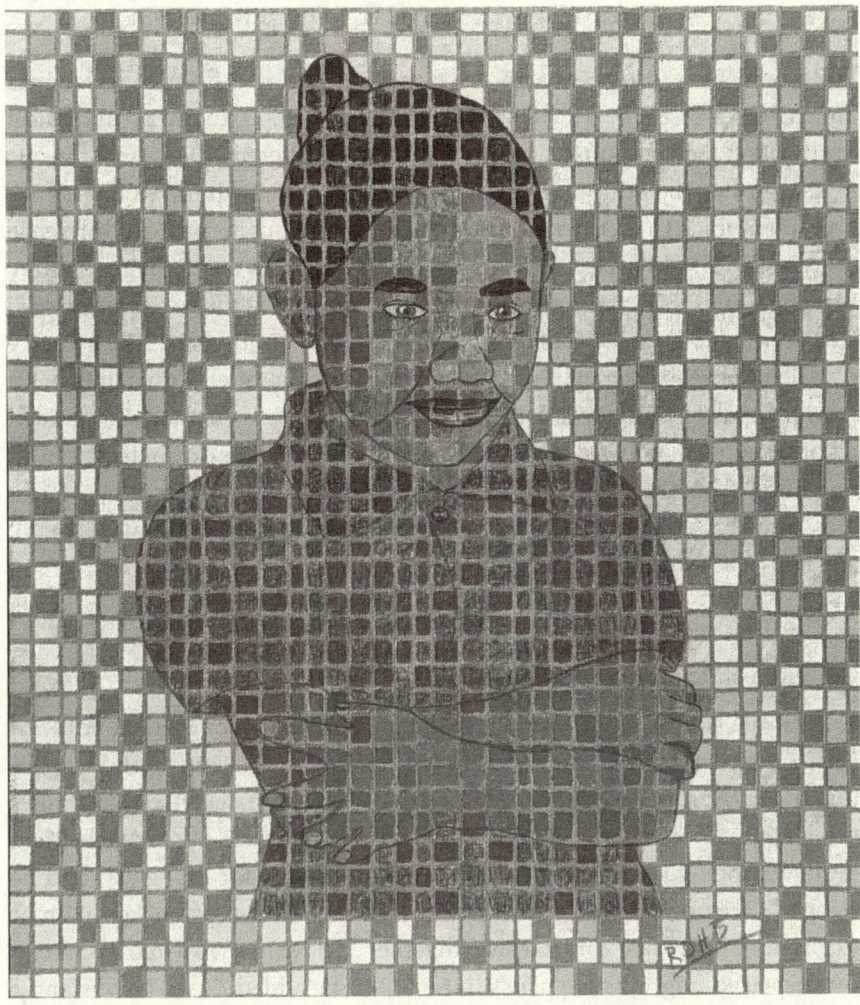

Illustration 9.1 *Vulnerability* 11" × 14" colored pencil portrait on yellow and green patterned paper of a migrant girl in Matamoros, Mexico, December 15, 2019, during MPP. Art © Helen T. Boursier.

When it came time to go, I didn't have to ask for it back. He handed it back to me. He was in a different place. He'd been moved by his own deep faith." His gain was to remember the strength of his own spirituality, and the attorney gained reaffirmation of her spiritual calling to collect the testimonies of children who are detained in government custody. She gained the reminder of why she does what she does.

INTANGIBLE GAINS IN THE BORDERLANDS

Philosophy likes to argue that it's the face of the Other, as Emmanuel Levinas famously expressed, by which people are most challenged to live a truly ethical life through their response. The one who is most different, the stranger in our midst, pushes the ethical envelope through how we respond to the invitation to embrace this Other, not despite difference but because of difference (illustration 9.1). In his essay "Ethics as First Philosophy and Religion," Jeffrey Bloechl argues that "the good life consists in managing this activity and passivity on the complex field of economic, social and political life. The primary occasion in which we feel this challenge is the encounter with someone in need, where a face alone is often enough to call forth a response visibly guided by prior education and experience."[11] For those who are disinterested in or unwilling to embrace the face of these others in the borderlands, it becomes a massively missed opportunity for gains in tangible, ethical, moral, personal, and spiritual growth.

Gaining Solidarity

A Roman Catholic sister, a nun who often volunteers alongside nones with IWC to assist displaced families who travel through the Greyhound bus station in San Antonio, said the first word that she uses to describe the families is *solidarity*. The sister said, "I see it continually. They look out for each other. Yesterday one guy didn't quite have enough money for his ticket, and he went to a friend, who took the last bit of coinage out of his pocket in order to give it to him to be able to travel together." She said the solidarity among the displaced migrants happens all the time. She added, "I see it constantly. They're concerned for each other and taking care of each other. Maybe they know each other from the trip, maybe they don't, or maybe they're from the same country." Whatever the point of connection, the families gain solidarity with each other and also with the volunteers and advocates they interact with. Migration is the unifying connection to stand alongside one another in solidarity.

The Catholic sister said another gain for her is to see how much they "love and care for the children. It doesn't make any difference whose child. Their love is all-embracing." She said she also gains from observing their survival skills. She exclaimed, "Wow! How do they teach their survival skills?" She explained that by their being at the bus station and knowing all that they would've been through, this sister wonders how anyone from this country could do likewise and "still have all their energy, enthusiasm, and hope." She added she feels certain that they're going to make a difference in their new life in America. Interacting with two hundred to three hundred migrants each time she helps at the bus station, the sister said she's impressed by their faith and also by their energy and enthusiasm for faith and for life.

Gaining a Sense of the Holy

Working alongside the families in various settings on both sides of the border brings a profound sense of the holy into life through the witness of their gratitude amid both suffering and adversity for literally anything and everything that's contributed to helping them in any capacity, large and small. The families experience and express their gain with a gratitude that can't not rub off on the volunteers and advocates around them. There's gratitude for large gains, like the joyous smile a newly released mother gave as she was walking out the front door of GEO Karnes after receiving temporary legal status for custodial care with a family member. In my field journal later that day, I wrote:

> As we left for lunch, a mother and daughter were just being released. They walked out the front door of GEO Karnes with a family member, and I said, "*Vaya con Dios!* [Go with God!]" The mother's face glowed. I was struck in that instant by all of the suffering this young mother would've experienced before her journey, during her journey, and while incarcerated in the ice box and the dog kennel. The next spontaneous thought was the realization that there's so much more struggle before her—even with a supportive family in the United States and even with eventual (hopeful) asylum. It was a humbling moment and a poignant reminder to trust God at all times, through the good and bad, and also to invite God in.[12]

Each interaction in solidarity with the families reiterates the blessedness of encounter, which keeps resurfacing as the Big Gain that shapes and upholds spirituality in the borderlands. A volunteer chaplain who's assisted the families in various contexts on both sides of the Texas-Mexico border said: "Each time I'm with the families, I realize how much this pastoral care presence means to me. The direct connection grounds me to the reason behind my advocacy and action, in whatever form it takes. Without this direct interaction, it would be much more difficult for me to feel such a strong link. Their love, hope, and faith inspire and motivate me to response, much more so than anything that I could feel without their physical and spiritual presence."[13] The interactions are not necessarily profound. Some of the biggest spiritual gains emerge through the most mundane interactions and normal human-to-human conversations. After an afternoon of sitting together with the mothers and making bracelets and earrings with them during Art Inside Karnes, I told the other volunteer chaplain that these simple, normal conversations are my greatest gain; as I noted in my field journal, "We can't solve their asylum claim concerns or make the pain and suffering of their past disappear, but we can engage in simple, yet beautiful conversations which touch on the kinds of conversations which occur women-to-women. These are the small moments of 'normal' amidst the unsettledness of their lives."[14] There are spiritual gains amid the ordinary as well as in the profound.

GAIN REINFORCES A SPIRITUALITY OF DISSENT IN THE BORDERLANDS

Interactions with the families reinforce a spirituality of dissent at the borders because volunteers experience the blessedness of their own humanity as it mingles with the with blessedness of the migrants. For example, my journal reflection following the February 10, 2016, art session during Art Inside Karnes, which fell on Ash Wednesday, the first day of Lent in the Christian liturgical calendar, includes:

> The writing theme today was to name who had been, or is, important in sharing and teaching love to them throughout their lifetime. Nearly every single reflection began with thanks to God, including naming God as their primary source of love. The words of endearment they used for God included *Dios, Padre Celestial, Diosito,* and *Papito Dios*. Most of the mothers consistently described God's works as being "marvelous." One short reflection best sums up the collection: "The love of God inspires me because it is unconditional, transparent, sincere. God teaches me to love and to pardon; for this reason, I love much my family, son and spouse. They give me the strength and the reason to leave quickly for to be able to realize all of my goals." They gave thanks to God for giving breath, life, health, family, and for teaching them to know love. The next phrases of thanks were directed to particular

family members who have shown or given love (mother, father, siblings, children, spouse, aunts and uncles, grandparents). After translating these reflections, I was struck by the depth of love the mothers have for God, but also for their children.

The words they use to describe their love express a deep bond, almost soul to soul. It's not sappy or hokey. Rather there's such a genuine depth to their love, which they compare to the love their Heavenly Father has shown to them. I found myself wondering if I've ever felt that deep sense of love for my own son—whom I definitely love and care for greatly—but still I wonder at the intensity of the love they have expressed for their children. Likewise, they've expressed a similar depth of love toward their parents—a consistent theme was gratitude for having "the best parents in the world" or "the best mother in the world."

Their faith in God always has been evident in my interactions with the families. These reflections show a much deeper essence of the love they have for their children. The mothers always express great confidence in God. They might include a brief mention of one or two points of distress related to their incarceration and anxiety about passing the credible fear interviews, but then they always bring it back to their absolute trust that God will prevail. In the midst of what could be extreme fear and anxiety about possible deportation and also the uncertain future if/when they would be released to their family in the United States.[15]

The families emit a calm sense of trust that God is in control and ultimately all will be well, a spiritual gain that's contagious for those who interact with them and choose to look for, see, and respect the humanitarian connection.

Intangible Gains for Volunteers and Advocates

Volunteers and advocates experience numerous intangible gains, such as when the families affirm *our* selfhood through *their* generous appreciation for the little we're doing at any given moment. Other than the tangible benefits provided by a pro bono attorney in an immigration court; a volunteer searching the desert to save disoriented, injured or disabled migrants from certain death; or a medical professional treating an injured or infirm migrant, the most that many of the volunteers and advocates can do is stand in solidarity with the families. We can't magically get the families through the convoluted, grievously evil US immigration matrix.[16] We can't fix things to ensure the families get the Big Gain of safety in this country. However, we can be present in compassionate solidarity in various settings, contexts, and moments, offering intangible spiritual gains through tender loving care (TLC), with a few helpful tangible gains such as food, clothing, and shelter. There are so many little things we can do, and there's gratitude for even the most miniscule presence. All of this nets mutual spiritual gain.

The gain is mutual as we give and receive love. For example, I wrote in my field journal after facilitating Art Inside Karnes, "So many of the little girls, and even the teens, gave me a hug as they were leaving. The hug lingered, not clinging, but a loving linger, as we let our love, care, and compassion flow back-and-forth. It was incredibly beautiful."[17] This beautiful love overflows to people who choose to notice, acknowledge, and accept it. For example, in another journal reflection I noted, "Today Rec Spec 2 [recreation specialist] walked us out through security. She had tears in her eyes from listening to the women sing in chapel. She said their singing always moves her to tears because, despite all their suffering, they have such strong faith and always give thanks to God."[18] My journal entry for this day also included:

> Compassion is the word that most describes today for me. I see compassion in so many aspects of my view inside Karnes. Specifically, it's very clear how much several of the Rec Specs care about and for the mothers and children. (Not all, but several do care very much.) They take their role very seriously, and I consistently see that they put the cares and concerns of the women and children first. A simple example: A woman from Guatemala spoke zero English and zero Spanish. She became very frustrated with the bracelet project, so she returned the beads and prepared to leave the art room. Instead, Sister Denise [a volunteer chaplain who assisted with the art ministry] asked Rec Spec 2 to help her, and Rec Spec 2 patiently sat beside this woman, using nonverbal communication, for at least thirty minutes as she helped this mother to finish the bracelet. There was no sense of rush or of annoyance; simply compassion, patience, and kindness.[19]

Compassion is a particularly beautiful gain to give and receive, a frequent occurrence in the borderlands.

It's also possible to gain transcendence from insecurity, ineptitude, and uncertainty by leaning into the experience of simply being fully present with the families. For example, after our morning session with the families inside Karnes, a volunteer chaplain who assisted with this ministry reflected during our lunch break before the afternoon session, "When you were praying with a distraught mother, you had your arm around her, and your eyes were closed too. For a moment it was like she was out of the room in the detention center and in a sacred place. It was a beautiful moment." The Catholic sister added, "Even with your struggling Spanish, you were not worried about your limitations. You were completely comfortable in the moment to be in spontaneous prayer."[20] It's just such a transcending moment where limitations are set aside so that the gain of being fully present is mutually experienced. Spirituality in the borderlands also enhances self-identity and self-actualization in the borderlands.

Self-Identity and Spirituality in the Borderlands

Confirmation of call through affirmation of self-identity is one of the intangible gifts of spirituality in the borderlands. It's the gain of knowing who you are and what you're supposed to be doing to fully live into being, doing, and experiencing a meaningful life (chapter 11). Confirmation of call is a big thing in vocational ordained ministry. It has to do with knowing you're supposed to be doing a particular job, task, or service and that God has truly and clearly called you forth to do so, whatever that thing might be. Understanding one's sense of call is a gain that equates to self-identity and knowing, being, and doing what matters most in this moment in time. It includes listening to who you are, what your gifts are, where/how/when you are to use these gifts, and in what context and capacity. A simple example is when I served as a volunteer chaplain during the vacation Bible school that the staff chaplains conducted at GEO Karnes during the family detention era; one mother started calling me "Pastorita Helenita" as a term of endearment.[21] I was just doing my *Pastora Helena* thing and sharing love. I gained affirmation of my spiritual calling through her tender nickname. Because my sense of self-identity has been so markedly influenced by my interactions with countless families, I asked the volunteers I interviewed, "How have the migrants influenced your self-identity of who you are?"

Self-Actualizing

Sometimes it takes a stranger to point out and affirm personal strengths and gifts, leading to self-actualizing that moves from the outside in. A volunteer chaplain explained, "During the simplest of interactions with the families while I'm engaged in ministry presence visits in the borderlands, the observations the families make about me upgrade my sense of self, of who I am, and what my gifts truly are." She offered the example of sitting at a table and visiting with the families while they made bracelets and earrings from the supplies she'd brought. During the afternoon session, a mother opted to make a complicated style of earrings, following the sample of the pair that this volunteer chaplain's daughter-in-law had made when she'd gone with this pastor's church on a mission trip to Mexico three years earlier. The earrings became a springboard for chitchat while the volunteer chaplain and the displaced mothers made earrings together at a shelter:

> **Madre:** When do you see your family?
> **Chaplain:** They are coming to visit us in November. It's been five years since my son and his wife have visited us.
> **Madre:** Why so long?
> **Chaplain:** My daughter-in-law does not like her mother-in-law.
> **Madre:** But listen to how much you laugh. You are clearly a fun, happy, and content person.
> **Chaplain:** Thank you for your kindness. Maybe she just doesn't like having a mother-in-law.[22]

The volunteer chaplain said this simple conversation with virtual strangers "reminded me who I am, the gifts I bring, and the generosity in my spirit that far exceeds the non-flattering image of a particular family member." It's self-actualization in the sense of "I'm okay after all."

Gaining a Voice of Inner Authority

A volunteer and mother of four children who lives in Dallas and who stepped aside from her lifetime religious affiliation because it was insufficient in meeting her spiritual hunger explained that when she visits with migrant mothers in the borderlands, she feels "just like them, and they feel just like me, and we're all of a sudden one. Every time I go into this to help them, they have helped me right back." She added, "I think growing up with my organized religion, I didn't know my sense of inner authority as much as I do now. I don't know if that comes from a place of deciding how it is I'm going to show up instead of how other people want me to show up, or how much, or realizing that I can actually show up as much as I want to with something." She said her spiritual gain is that her decision to volunteer with the families has definitely given her "a different outlook on life in general, and how I feel about myself in a really positive way." It's the witness of the families that overflows, informs, and inspires this volunteer's own sense of spiritual calling.

When I asked her to elaborate with an example, she described a worship service she'd attended in Matamoros two months earlier in response to the pastor's invitation to attend the church he held for asylum seekers in a shelter there. She said at one point in the service the children, and many of the mothers, went forward to put on a little program that included a song. She explained:

> One of the moms was just praising God in her special way, and I just looked at her and I thought of her situation. I had just seen where she slept every night, and she was just in her zone, and she was so at peace in that moment. And it's so beautiful to me, and I often think like, *With all the faith in the world, could I do that? Could I get up and live in these conditions and praise God like that?* I don't know. I don't know if I have the strength. But this mom just kind of like radiated all of this light, and it was like she just pumped some strength into me.

The volunteer said it was a powerful witness to experience the strength of faith amid such harsh circumstances. She added, "It's really beautiful to see their perseverance." Their faith keeps on going. Their religious spirituality is inspiring to volunteers, even if being particularly religious isn't something a volunteer is interested in. Nevertheless, it's inspiring because it's so genuine, steadfast, and real.

Similarly, a pastor who oversees a church-sponsored shelter for migrants in San Antonio explained that before she started working in this capacity, she was an introvert. However, the two years she's spent working closely with the families completely changed her sense of self for the better. She said that before she began working with the families, "I really didn't interact with people, and I really didn't feel comfortable talking to anybody, or doing anything, or being social, or sharing anything about myself, or being really my whole self in front of anyone." She said now she is "completely different. I'm a transformed person. I love to share a meal and talk to people I've never met before. All of my social anxiety and inhibitions are gone." Now she easily interacts with everyone "in a more authentic way, but specifically with the immigrant families and being able to receive love in that way." She said one of the important points she came to understand is that, for the families, "just being present is what's valued. I realized that you don't have to do anything else except show up." She gained her sense of self because the families love and appreciate her for who she is, *as is*. Being willing to be there with the families creates the mutual gain of being present in solidarity together.

Just as the families affirm the spiritual gifts of selfhood that the volunteers share, the families receive similar self-actualization from the volunteers. The families gain each time a volunteer visits, assists, or interacts because, as a volunteer from Chicago said, "people deserve the dignity of being heard. We believe in them. We respond with pastoral care and advocacy and public witness. We listen. We sit with them in the ashes."[23] The families regain or reclaim their dignity, even as they generously offer their affirmation back by recognizing, seeing, appreciating, and affirming the visitors in their midst.

Empathy

Empathy is another important spiritual gain in the borderlands. The volunteer from Dallas, who also brings small groups to the borderlands to work together with the displaced families, said it's important for her to bring young people on these trips because empathy is shaped by personal experiences and interactions with displaced and distressed people, whoever they are and wherever they live. She said she's often asked why she doesn't just help the homeless "here in Dallas. Why are you going to the border and helping asylum seekers that are homeless when there are homeless (Americans) here?" She said she responds that she hopes there are "people who are pulled to working for the homeless in Dallas. We need those people, and if that's where you feel fulfilled, do it. Do something somewhere. It doesn't matter which displaced population; go wherever you feel pulled." She added that more often than not, "helping the homeless in Dallas" is merely a deflection from helping the displaced families in the borderlands. People choose to miss the benefits, the gain, of the personal interaction with the families. It's through going, doing, and being present that it's possible to gain the blessing that the displaced families freely give.

This volunteer said it's wonderful for people to drop off the much-needed supplies various immigrant assistance organizations collect to provide tangible needs of the families in the borderlands, but true gain comes through personal interaction with them. She explained, "I like to take people to the border so they can experience it firsthand. We've had some people go with us on these trips to the borderlands again, and again, and again, and again. They feel pulled." She added, "Sometimes it's just going one time that can change your whole paradigm about something. Experience alone can shape empathy. If you have the opportunity to sit with someone or a situation that is so different from yours, that to me is where we change the world." She emphasized, "That's why we're so encouraging of younger kids to go to the border." The goal is for an emerging generation to keep being engaged with helping throughout their lives.

SPIRITUAL TRANSFORMATION

Experiential presence in the borderlands becomes a lifetime calling to be present in difference-making, even when time and chance change circumstances so that the borderlands are no longer accessible to a volunteer. Nevertheless, the time spent being present instills profound spiritual gains that remain forever in their internal spiritual calling to work for justice and peacemaking wherever their lives take them. Spirituality in the borderlands becomes a way of life beyond the border. Reverend Fife calls it "a spiritual transformation." Reflecting on his motivation and inspiration to continue working for justice in the borderlands long after he retired from vocational ordained ministry, the reverend said he has a whole series of experiences that are "profoundly meaningful," lessons that will stay with him for the rest of his life. He said, "The desert out there is dotted with shrines that have been put up by migrants, all of whom cross the border with either a rosary or a Bible." He added, "The faith that those folks cling to when their lives are on the line every moment in every day there in the desert is just extraordinary. They're my teachers about spirituality. It's their faith that is remarkable. And I've learned over and over and over again." Similarly, another volunteer in the Texas borderlands said, "People have asked me, 'Oh, are you bringing the immigrants the gospel? Are you bringing them Jesus?' I would mentally roll my eyes and think, 'Are you kidding me? They're bringing the gospel to me.' What I would say is that the families have a depth of faithfulness, and trust, and belief that is so genuine that, for me, it's just really humbling." The volunteer added, "Such presumptuous questions speak to the pride, self-centeredness, and arrogance of First-World people who just think we've got it all down. But we don't know anything about true faith. I mean, we just don't." Volunteers gain the living witness and reminder from the families of what spirituality is and also what it *could* be.

Spirituality in the borderlands contributes to what Reverend Fife said: "You just have to say, 'Wow! What an incredible moment that I wish more and more folks experienced."[24] It's this Big Gain that brings volunteers back to the borderlands again and again. Similarly, a GVS Samaritan said, "I couldn't live without doing it. I get tremendous enjoyment from helping people. I've done that almost all my life with farmworkers in California. Then when I first heard about the Samaritans about thirteen years ago, I've been doing this ever since. I gain a lot of pleasure, and feel like I'm giving something back to help people." It's a gain that keeps this volunteer going, who added, "And at eighty-six, I'm ready to go another ten years."

MUTUAL GAINS IN THE BORDERLANDS

A doctor who organizes medical professionals to volunteer in the borderlands said her gain is the implicit example from the families. The doctor explained, "Like a lot of those of us who are involved in this work, we think about what they've endured and their resilience in the face of adversity." She said it's very inspiring, but the doctor quickly added that the families "definitely don't think of it that way," as being inspiring. Nevertheless, their lives definitely are an inspiring gain for the volunteers. The doctor said it's always interesting for her to witness the facial expressions of the families in response to anybody saying anything like "I'm so inspired by what you've done to get to America, how you've been able to navigate this, and you've managed to make it." The families see their life and witness as being a desperate struggle to protect themselves and their children. They rarely understand why or how their faithful, dedicated, and courageous response to grievous evils, as they slog along the long, tedious, and often painful migration trail, contributes to the profound spiritual gains the volunteers receive from them. But it does.

The doctor said that because of all she personally gains from the families, she's reframed her perspective about this volunteer work. She explained, "I was thinking about this work as if it's philanthropic work, where you think you're the one giving while getting nothing in return versus thinking about it in terms of being in community with people." She added, "It's when you realize that there's a mutuality to the gain, not one side doing all the giving and the other side doing all the receiving. There's definitely a mutuality in gain." She said it's healing to realize and accept this mutuality, this gift in the borderlands. She sees her role as helping to facilitate change in the borderlands, but the mutuality draws her back in and makes her time and effort infinitely worthwhile. By focusing on the community connection, she said it brings a sense of humility to her life because "I do really feel like I get so much out of these relationships. Whenever I'm quote, unquote, 'helping someone,' I feel like I also gain a lot of benefit from those relationships."

Personal Presence versus Sending Funds:
What's the Greater Gain?

It's long been a question of whether it's a greater gain for volunteers to raise funds to cover the cost of a trip to travel to an impacted area where they then experience the suffering firsthand or if it's better to send the cost for a service-oriented trip directly to the location where the funds could be used in direct assistance. So raise the funds to travel to the borderlands and help directly or send the same funds to an agency that's already on the ground offering various types of assistance? It's a better-than question that addresses which would net the greater gain. Several core team members of Team Brownsville said the answer is *both/and*. One volunteer specified, "I think we need both. Absolutely, because firsthand knowledge goes a long way in getting the word out." He said as long as Team Brownsville was getting both direct donations and in-person volunteers, the families received a double gain: new volunteers who would share their experiences once they returned home, often generating more direct funds to help back at the border from people who wanted to help but who wouldn't or couldn't come in person. The direct funds make it possible to provide the supplies that the short- and long-term volunteers need to offer ongoing direct assistance to the families.

Another core team member reflected on the time frame when COVID-19 closed the border, which also meant there weren't any volunteers coming from faraway places. She said, "The families still needed assistance, but we didn't have any volunteers to help, and so it had to be us. Everything changed when all this happened. We didn't get the volunteers, so they couldn't spread the word. That meant that then we didn't get the donations." She said it was a struggle and that they were still trying to figure out what to do about it. She explained, "It's been really difficult because how we can keep Team Brownsville running is (the visiting) people who later spread the word. We can only spread it so far. It's the volunteers who come here and have a good experience, and they take the word back to their friends and family at home about what they saw, what they did, how they helped, and the difference that made." She said the coming and going of the volunteers is part of the cycle that keeps Team Brownsville fluid, ready, willing, and able to continue sharing the gain of hospitality and welcome with the families. She emphasized, "Volunteers are very important. *Very, very important.*" Their coming nets tangible, mutual gain in the borderlands.

A volunteer with the GVS Samaritans said he hopes when people make a trip to the borderlands to work with any of the assistance organizations that "they get more than just learning the facts," which he emphasized "are horrible in terms of the hardships of the people who come here to seek asylum." He added, "I hope they also gain a sense of their own capacity to be compassionate and to help." He said he hopes they don't "just see it as some factually based thing but as a call to treat all people in a decent way." He explained that by just looking at the facts about the suffering and mistreatment in the borderlands, it's too easy for people to become discouraged and so overwhelmed that they won't do anything more to help. The advocate emphasized that it requires "real spiritual growth as well." Spiritual growth in the borderlands is a phenomenal mutual gain that leads people to notice, experience, and appreciate a greater sense of joy.

NOTES

1. Seow, *Ecclesiastes*, 103–104.
2. See Michael V. Fox, *A Time to Tear Down and a Time to Build Up: A Rereading of Ecclesiastes* (Grand Rapids, MI: William B. Eerdmans Publishing, 1999), 141–143.
3. de Beauvoir, *Ethics of Ambiguity*, 23.
4. Weil, *Gravity and Grace*, 95.
5. William P. Brown, *Ecclesiastes: Interpretation—A Bible Commentary for Teaching and Preaching* (Louisville, KY: John Knox Press, 2000), 77.
6. Bonhoeffer, "To Eberhard Bethge [Tegel] 5 February 1944," in Bonhoeffer, *Letters and Papers from Prison*, 210.
7. Claribel, Honduras, while in a migrant shelter in Nuevo Laredo, Mexico, during MPP, December 4, 2019.
8. Boursier, Field Notes, vol. 6, August 26, 2018, 138.
9. He concluded his post with "Please donate to Team Brownsville so we can continue to help families like this: https://www.gofundme.com/f/teambrownsville-help-asylum-seekers," Facebook post December 12, 2022, shared by permission.

10 Julia Ainsley and Annie Rose Ramos, "Inside Tornillo: The Expanded Tent City for Migrant Children," NBC News, October 12, 2018, https://www.nbcnews.com/politics/immigration/inside-tornillo-expanded-tent-city-migrant-children-n919431.
11 Jeffrey Bloechl, "Ethics as First Philosophy and Religion," in *The Face of the Other and the Trace of God: Essays on the Philosophy of Emmanuel Levinas*, ed. Jeffrey Bloechl (New York: Fordham University Press, 2000), 130.
12 Boursier, Art Inside Karnes, Field Notes, vol., 3, October 26, 2016, 84.
13 Boursier, Field Notes, vol. 7, August 28, 2018, 55–56.
14 Boursier, Art Inside Karnes, Field Notes, vol. 5, October 5, 2016, 33–34.
15 Boursier, Art Inside Karnes, Field Notes, vol. 2, February 10, 2016, 1–2.
16 See Boursier, "The Immigration Matrix: A Systemic Overview," chapter 4 in Boursier, *Ethics of Hospitality*, 59–79.
17 Boursier, Art Inside Karnes, Field Notes, vol. 4, November 23, 2016, 87.
18 The volunteer chaplains ranked the recreation specialists ("rec specs") based on how kind they were to the families, so Rec Spec 2 was our second favorite as the second nicest to the detained families. Boursier, Art Inside Karnes, vol. 2, November 2, 2015, 31.
19 Art Inside Karnes, Field Notes, vol. 2, November 2, 2015, 31.
20 Boursier, Art Inside Karnes, Field Notes, vol. 5, August 24, 2016.
21 Boursier, Art Inside Karnes, Field Notes, vol. 3, July 18, 2016, 66.
22 Art Inside Karnes, Field Notes, vol. 5, October 5, 2016, 33–34.
23 Cited in Boursier, *Ethics of Hospitality*, 218.
24 Madeline Hilf conducted the interview with Rev. John Fife as part of her academic project with Fordham University; shared by permission.

CHAPTER TEN

Joy

Enjoy life with your [spouse], whom you love, all the days of this meaningless life that God has given you under the sun—all your meaningless days. For this is your lot in life and in your toilsome labor under the sun.
—Ecclesiastes 9:9 (NIV)

Appreciating the benefits, blessings, or gains in life makes it possible to experience joy, not necessarily from being, doing, or achieving the ultimate successes but through appreciating life in the present moment. Ecclesiastes uses five summary statements to wrap up its key insights about what contributes to the benefits or gains that make joy possible (Ecc. 2:24–26, 3:22, 5:18–10, 8:15–17, and 9:7–10). These summary statements tell us, in light of the fact that it's impossible to know or experience true justice, nor is it possible to know the outcome of the future, that it's still possible to choose our attitude while going about living the one and only life we'll have. We can respond to life with a bad attitude, or we can choose joy.

Ecclesiastes maintains a *carpe diem* ("seize the day") type of perspective about making the best of the circumstances, whatever they are, because this is the one and only life anyone is going to get. This is it. Ecclesiastes prioritizes centeredness in appreciation, which leads to gratitude and makes joy possible. Joy is set against the absolute belief in the presence and providence of God, which offers a comforting reassurance that God ultimately is in control. The buck stops with God and not with human beings. Hence, there's a freedom in letting go and trusting God. It's this definitive and absolute confidence in God that drives a *spirituality of joy* in the borderlands, not in a shallow or glib sense. Rather, joy emerges through interactions with justice and peacemaking in the borderlands and cherishing the moments of blessing that intersect there. It includes intentionality to be willing to recognize and experience joy, despite all the seriousness that inevitably swirls around. Engaging the key points in the summary statements with the experiential witness of volunteers and advocates and with narratives by displaced migrants, this chapter reflects on how to recognize and celebrate joy within the muck of life.

JOY IN ECCLESIASTES

Joy is the choice Ecclesiastes wants people to make in light of their circumstances. It's not the giddy, shallow laughter of fools that Ecclesiastes condemns (7:6). Rather, joy is an orientation toward life that recenters the spirit from over-focusing on whatever isn't going right to whatever benefit exists incrementally within this present moment. It's a centeredness that lets go of needing to know or needing to be totally in control of a situation. With so many ephemeral aspects of life, including life itself passing quickly, which makes human beings like shadows (Ecc. 6:12), joy is a beautiful diversion. Ecclesiastes scholar Seow proposes, "God is the one who gives a preoccupation through joy, but God also gives a response to humanity through joy in their hearts. It is the same God who makes possible this positive preoccupation."[1] Joy becomes an antidote of sorts for bad business and grievous evil.

Reiterating an earlier point in Ecclesiastes, as well as with displaced families in the borderlands, the intentional spiritual practice of joy trusts that *God is*. Because God is, this takes the pressure off of humans to be or do anything and everything to master control or micromanage life. Because *God is*, humans are free from being shackled to sorrow or fear. Instead, people can recenter on joy. For anyone who hasn't had a first-person experience of volunteering in the borderlands, it might seem like it's farfetched for the families to experience, show, and share joy amid their harsh circumstances. However, literally, everyone who's ever volunteered in the borderlands has experienced something of this joy. Even within all their trauma, suffering, and sorrow, there's joy. This joy amid adversity is a striking and notable contrast to the lack of joy in the cynical postmodern Western context amid comfort, affluence, and ceaseless striving that's always on overdrive, and enough never seems to be enough. The consuming desire to gain and acquire more and more limits joy because there's no acknowledgment or appreciation for what's already been gained that could be a blessing in the here and now. For those who can't or won't embrace the option of joy, discontent, and the *never-enough syndrome* make the self-absorbed live in darkness (Ecc. 5:17), resonating with the Scrooge effect noted earlier.

For those who are affluent and comfortable, it might seem like it's inconceivable for there to be joy in abject poverty and suffering because, too often, joy in the fancy First World comes through gaining and doing more and more. For spirituality in the borderlands, in agreement with Ecclesiastes, it's better to find gratitude and joy in the present than to strive into eternity without pausing to smell the flowers along the way. As the popular expression affirms, life is about the journey, not the destination. Without joy, what's the point in life? Ecclesiastes goes so far as to say someone could live a thousand years without enjoying the present, then they might as well never have been born (6:6). When the affluent can't or won't be satisfied, and enough is never enough, it's impossible to experience joy in the present. Seow points out that "the insatiability of the rich is not only self-destructive, it poses dangers to others who fall prey to their greed . . . personal greed has social consequences."[2] Given the philosophy of Ecclesiastes that readily acknowledges and accepts that every single human being is going to die, if there's no joy in this life, then what's the point in having life in the first place? If not for joy, then what? Joy makes life worth living. Nouwen compares what he terms "a good death" with joy that comes through "solidarity with others." It's this joyous acceptance of all others that makes it possible for death to unify each person with the full human race. Nouwen proposes that this living in joy in communion and community with others is what allows us to die well. Instead of life ending with death, death becomes the unifying force that "can give rise to joy; instead of simply ending life, [death] can begin something new."[3] The unifying joy that comes through genuine open communion with the entire created world is life-informing and life-giving.

JOY AS A SPIRITUAL PRACTICE

Joy as a spiritual practice is an important lesson from the borderlands. Joy is a permission-giving opportunity to reorient the view from the overachieving striving in the Global North or the suffering and sorrow of the families in the borderlands to a spirituality that shifts the view from inside self-focus to an external gratitude-based joy. It's definitely not easy, nor is it simplistic. Shifting from being an overachiever workaholic in an affluent context for people who can't and or don't appreciate the blessings and gifts they already have to celebrating the joy in the moment is no trite challenge. It requires the intentional spiritual practice that looks for, sees, feels, and cherishes now. The particular blessing in the borderlands is that many of the families already embody this spiritual practice. Even in the midst of their suffering beyond all suffering, the families consistently find moments of joy within their chance hardships, which are imbued with one grievous evil after another. Joy doesn't belittle or diminish suffering. Rather, it mingles together with the sorrows, making them more manageable despite the misery.

SORROW AND JOY

Bonhoeffer wrote about this interconnection between sorrow and joy while he was a prisoner in Nazi Germany. In the fourth stanza of his poem "Sorrow and Joy," he says that these feelings are "indistinguishable from each other" as he explains "joy is rich in fears," whereas "sorry has its sweetness."[4] In the sixth stanza, he summarizes the nuanced differences between these two seemingly opposite emotions, determining that "time alone can decide between them."[5] The interconnection between joy and sorrow is evident even in the midst of great sorrow or great joy. For example, a Team Brownsville volunteer remembered her feelings when the families who had been stuck in Matamoros, Mexico, during MPP were finally allowed to enter the United Sates. She said, "I think back to the joy on the faces of the people getting off the buses." The volunteer said, "It felt unbelievable that they were finally being allowed into this country after the extensive time stuck just south of the border." She added, "You couldn't help but cry, and smile, and laugh, and hug. To this day I still get goosebumps thinking about what it was like to see them come off the buses because they knew that they had made it [to the United States] after all they had gone through. For me that's the best thing in the world, to see their smiles," She added, "Because they always smile." Even during MPP and the horrible conditions that remaining in Mexico forced on them, they always smiled.

There can be joy in the sorrow, as a Samaritan reported in the bi-monthly meeting on team interactions with migrants on both sides of the US-Mexico border. Describing the scene in a soup kitchen for displaced migrants in Nogales, Mexico, a Samaritan volunteer reported that the newly deported families "seemed to be in good shape, even in good spirits. Some of them from the Northern Triangle were sitting together and joking a bit." Even as they were sharing their war stories of the migration and detention experiences, still there was joy. They were, no doubt, laughing about their ridiculous mistreatment while they were detained in US custody.

Similarly, Beauvoir argues that life "will be lived in both heartbreak and joy." The heartbreak enters in because things clearly cannot and will not ever go exactly as planned, but the joy is ever-present because of the possibility for a "new future."[6] It's easier to focus on misery when someone is among those who are oppressed, just as the compulsion for more striving, success, and financial gain seems more normative among those who are affluent. It's a much more difficult task to reorient from sorrow or over-striving to gratitude that fosters joy. Chittister explains, "Adversity, at least, gets our attention. But joy we take for granted. Joy we consider [our] birthright and wait to inherit in outrageous proportions. Yet, joy we too often ignore."[7] She says there are negative consequences, psychological and spiritual, when people don't recognize blessings and count them as joy. On the other hand, she argues, "Joy is the spirit of God in time. It is the only taste of eternity that is freely given. We have, in other words, cultivated our capacity to slight life. Joy is the energy to carry us through dull days knowing that miracles can happen in the future because we have seen them in the past."[8] Noticing, acknowledging, and naming the gains, benefits, or blessings in the present tense, no matter how miniscule these seem to be, reorient the spirit to a place and space of gratitude that beget joy. Joy might not include busting out with laughter, but it does prioritize a contentedness that nurtures a sense of internal peace amid external chaos.

JOY BEGETS GENEROSITY OF SPIRIT

Joy begets a generosity of spirit, not only with each other but with the virtual strangers in our midst. Throughout the two years I facilitated Art Inside Karnes, there were countless examples of when a detained mother or child generously gifted me the art project, earrings, or bracelet that they'd just labored over so carefully. I've kept their gifts of beaded bracelets, artwork, and earrings as cherished reminders of their generosity, love, and joy. They had so little tangible things to give. Yet when the opportunity arose, they gave with abundant generosity. I've heard multiple experiences of similar generosity from the families who've shared as their expression of gratitude, love, and joy.

On a parallel but more intense and larger scale, Frankl notes that this generosity was a similar occurrence in the Nazi concentration camps. He explains, as briefly noted earlier, "We who lived in concentration camps can remember the men who walked through the huts comforting others, giving away their last piece of bread. They may have been few in number, but they offer sufficient proof that everything can be taken from a [person] but one thing: the last of the human freedoms—to choose one's attitude in any given set of circumstances, to choose one's own way."[9] When grievous evils beyond someone's control enact injustice, suffering, and sorrow, the one freedom remains: choosing their attitude about how they live and respond within the grievous evil and bad business. A big part of this choice is allowing for the option to claim joy within the sorrow.

Even when things are out of control, given that we're all going to die, and this is the one life we have to live, Ecclesiastes says it comes down to each person living into this one and only life with appreciation and joy for the now, for this moment in time. For example, Ecclesiastes 9:1–6 says we're all going to die but then follows almost immediately in 9:7–10 to say we should enjoy: "Go, eat your bread with joy and drink your wine with a happy heart because God has already approved of your deeds." The point is that there are few things we can enjoy, so at least enjoy what we can and accept it as our gift from God with God's blessing and approval. If, while living our lives in the present moment we can't or don't get exactly what we hoped or wanted, then at least accept the gifts God already has given, however they appear. Most importantly, accept them with a thankful heart (Ecc. 3:22). It's this pervasive sense of gratitude, even as the families are struggling for the barest level of bare life, that profoundly impacts spirituality in the borderlands. When shit happens, nevertheless there is gratitude to, and centeredness on, the one God, who is The God (Ecc. 5:7). It's this beautiful depth and strength to be able to see, feel, and experience gratitude for the most minuscule gain that nets joy as gain and gain as joy for the volunteers who assist them. Our spirits are forever moved by their depth of gratitude for the slightest gains. Despite all the other things that aren't going well, gratitude expresses that nevertheless *God still is*. Joy becomes an expression and extension of love.

LOVE CONTRIBUTES TO JOY

Though not a specific theme in Ecclesiastes, love is the connectional spiritual point for the families to lean on through the sorrow and loss, making it possible for gratitude that opens the door to joy. They love God, and they love their families, including the family members they're traveling with, the ones they had to leave behind, and the others who await them in the United States. As the earlier examples show, even amid anguished separation, a binding love keeps them spiritually connected in an almost visceral sense. This connection sustains their spirits in the present, and they remain hopeful for the future. Frankl writes about the primacy of love in his reflections on the meaning of life as a survivor of Nazi Germany. He explains it occurred to him during his incarceration that "for the first time in my life I saw the truth as it is set into song by so many poets, proclaimed as the final wisdom by so many thinkers. The truth—that love is the ultimate and the highest goal to which [anyone] can aspire." He adds that he also came to understand that salvation comes to humans "*through love and in love.*" Even when everything is taken away, even the memory of love is empowerment to survive suffering. He summarizes, "In a position of utter desolation" when there's nothing else, no hope, nothing but the possibility to endure and survive present "sufferings in the right way—an honorable way . . . through loving contemplation of the image [someone] carries of [their] beloved," it is possible to "achieve fulfillment."[10] Frankl reflects:

> My mind still clung to the image of my wife. A thought crossed my mind: I didn't even know if she were still alive. I knew only one thing—which I have learned well by now: Love goes very far beyond the physical person of the beloved. It finds its deepest meaning in this spiritual being, his inner self. Whether or not he is actually present, whether or not he is still alive at all, ceases somehow to be of importance.[11]

How is it possible for the displaced families to experience any sense of joy amid their horrific suffering, oppression, sorrow, and loss? Like Frankl, they claim the love that binds their hearts with their beloveds. No matter how many horrible experiences the families share about what forced their departure, during their journey, or the additional suffering meted on them in the borderlands, love that passes all understanding sustains them, inspires them, and brings them joy.

Joy in Sorrow, Sorrow in Joy

Sorrow is present in joy, but joy also must be present in sorrow. Early in my art ministry with the families, an eighteen-year-old shared with me that she literally saw her father's face blown off in her homeland, and then the perpetrators turned and shot her with two bullets in her left leg. She survived but with a noticeable heavy limp. Her mother told her to flee for her life. When I talked with her, I told her it was important to tell everyone her story, including the horrible details of her father's death. It would be important for her safety to explicitly describe her horror. She agreed. We prayed together, hugged, and cried.[12] Two months later, I wrote in my field journal for Art Inside Karnes, "My greatest joy today: the young woman who saw her father's face shot off was released early this morning to continue on her journey. She ran to tell Rec Spec 1 her news, and she asked her to make sure to thank *Pastora Helena* for my prayers." Adding my personal assessment of this experience, I wrote, "It continues to be overwhelming to process the pains mingled together with the joys. I love these women dearly, though I barely know them in the traditional sense. I also couldn't tell you any of their names. What I do know; what I can say, is that their courage is amazing. Their faith is profound."[13] This is the profundity of joy and sorrow, sorrow and joy. Just because there's sorrow, it doesn't mean joy can't also be there, just as there will be some bittersweet sorrow amid joy.

Notice Joy

Noticing and/or appreciating joy seems to be the challenge, oftentimes due to a limited vision with a narrow or unrealistic perspective. In relaying a conversation with a friend who said, "I just want things to be normal," Madeleine L'Engle remembered thinking, "What is normal? Normal is the reality of living with precariousness, of never knowing what is around the corner, when accident or death are going to strike. Normal is cooking dinner for friends in the midst of this precariousness, lighting the candles, laughing, being together. Normal is trusting that God will make meaning out of everything that happens."¹⁴ Or, as American humorist Erma Bombeck used to quip, "Normal is the setting on my dryer." There's some really horrible stuff that happens in the borderlands. It's this trusting God through precariousness that enables joy (Ecc. 5:20). The bits of joy that bubble up don't belittle that very real suffering. Rather, joy is a spiritual survival tool to move through grievous evils while also embracing Beauvoir's point about hoping for and expecting a better future. The families definitely don't want the sorrow and suffering, but acknowledging what they do have, what's gone well, remains steadfast. Again, gratitude opens the door to joy.

MIGRANT JOY

Even after all of the awful grievous evils the families have endured to get to the borderlands, on both sides of the border and in various contexts, they readily share their joy with those around them, making joy a notable gain from the families for the volunteers who witness their joy despite the sorrow and suffering surrounding them. The volunteers experience abundant gain through migrant joy. Again, not to belittle or downplay the suffering, which is absolutely dreadful, but even when life super sucks, still the families manage to radiate some joy. For example, in my field research notes following the Art Inside Karnes session I facilitated two days before Christmas, I wrote:

I cannot photograph the faces of the families, which would show their beautiful love and joy, so words will have to suffice to describe the children today:

- Angelic
- Sweet
- Beautiful
- Boys and girls
- Hesitant smiles
- Tots and teens
- Vivacious smiles
- Bubbles
- Love
- Laughter
- Delight
- Joy

- Anticipation
- Expectation
- Hope[15]

Sometimes I wrote a succinct journal entry to synthesize the day of solidarity with the families: "We talked about a lot of silly nothings. There was a lot of laughter today."[16] Other days I wrote more thorough assessments. Whether short or detailed, the notations always documented their joy. For example, during a session when we made collages from strips of pretty paper, I highlighted there were "a lot of sweet memories of the little ones." In addition, I specified:

1. Rec Spec 2 helped two 3-year-olds glue strips of paper. The children were very opinionated about what colors and patterns that they wanted to glue in exactly which location on their paper.
2. A little boy fell asleep on the floor underneath the table while his mother was making jewelry.
3. Another little boy used a dry paintbrush to pretend he was putting on eye shadow.
4. A rec spec painted faces of the little ones in the afternoon.[17]

Being around all this love and joy contributes to self-actualization and recognizing we can be joyful too. For example, during the afternoon of the art session described above, a mom said to me, "Listen to how much you laugh. You are clearly a fun, happy, and content person." Before I facilitated art with the families, my self-image was that I was a bit of a fuddy-duddy because the rest of the people in my immediate family are the fun ones. I'd only ever been the solid steady who *organized* the fun that other people then had. Through the contagious joy of the families, I've learned that I'm actually fun too. Their joy has become mine![18]

Whenever I've ever spent time with the families, in whatever context on either side of the border, there's always some joy. I observe it, I feel it, and I embrace it. In another journal entry, I wrote about one of the moments I cherished from a day with the families: "A sweet little girl was so precocious, delightful, and also enamored with me. She brought me the rubber zoo animals one-by-one to show me. I'd ask a nearby mother the name in Spanish, say it to the little girl, and then she'd laugh with joy and race off to bring me another animal. She repeated her silly game until she'd brought me all of the zoo animals." This simple moment is typical of the experiences volunteers have with the families, particularly with the children. As I added in my journal, "I wanted to stop everything I was doing with the moms and sit down on the floor and play make-believe with this adorable and precocious child. She was filled with such delightful joy."[19] I made a similar joy-filled entry after the March "spring break" session that was overflowing in the gymnasium with over 250 children and teens during Art Inside Karnes: "Indescribable joy! There were smiles on so many faces, especially when the little ones showed off the bracelets they'd made. Delight beyond anything words can describe: mothers helping daughters, friends helping friends, sisters helping younger siblings. JOY!"[20]

The volunteer chaplains regularly debriefed via telephone as we were driving home in opposite directions from Art Inside Karnes, sharing and celebrating the most poignant, profound, or meaningful moments. These often intersected with joy. For example, Sister Denise shared when there was a particular woman in the afternoon during the jewelry-making time who was very quiet, withdrawn, and sad when she arrived at the project room. She made a bracelet and then came to ask for supplies to make one for her other child. In that conversation time, the sister noticed that she was so much happier. Sister Denise said, "It might seem like a simple thing to make a bracelet, but they get to make choices about how it will be made. There's much freedom in the process. It might seem like a simple project, but it obviously matters very much to the women. They can move from a place of suffering and sadness to a place of joy." The Catholic sister added, "The challenge for me is to find ways to enter into that place of joy with them—to be more playful and to share their delight and their joy amidst the institutional place where they're currently residing. Many of the staff people are very kind to them, but it's an institution so all the kindness matters. The call for action then is to be intentional in entering in with them and being a part of the joy."[21] After the next Art Inside Karnes two weeks later, Sister Denise again reflected on joy. She explained, "The first two women who came in were joyfully working together, and I was touched by their joyfulness. It was almost contagious and brightened up the room." Sister Denise added, "It speaks to me to be more intentionally joyful, to be in the present, and to have a sense of appreciation for the moment without being sidetracked with whatever worries I may have."[22] Joy is a spiritual practice that's contagious, easily overflowing from the families to the volunteers and advocates (illustrations 10.1 and 12.1).

Illustration 10.1 *Hug of Joy* 11" × 15" graphite pencil with watercolor portrait of two little girls hugging a volunteer after she gave them Barbie dolls, April 9, 2022. The children were living with their parents along the riverbank of the Rio Grande River near Piedras Negras, Mexico (see illustration 8.1). This illustration is based on a photograph by Kay Geurin; shared by permission. Art © Helen T. Boursier.

VOLUNTEER JOY

A seventy-five-year-old grandmother who regularly makes day trips down and back to the Texas border said it's easy for her to make these long drives, four hours each way, because being with the families there brings her so much joy. She described a recent trip when she'd brought a load of nonperishable food, clothing, and kitchen supplies to the border. They'd met a migrant family who was camping along the riverbank of the Rio Grande outside of

Piedras Negras, Mexico, while they waited for permission to cross the river and enter the United States, where they planned to reunite with family. They were cooking over an open fire, and they asked this volunteer if she'd brought any pots or pans they could use. The volunteer explained that she returned to the church where she'd left all of the donations she'd taken to the border. She found some heavy pots and pans that would work over an open fire, plus a big pot to boil water. She also brought some plastic plates and silverware. As she was going through the donations to find these functional kitchen items, she noticed two Barbie dolls and remembered two little girls who were living with the family at the riverbank. The volunteer said when they arrived back to the river, the families were already in the remote section where the asylum seekers take shelter under the overhanging bushes (illustration 8.1). She said, "We waved our arms wide and held up the two Barbie dolls." The family brought the little girls back to the central location so they could receive the dolls. She said, "Those two little girls just kept hugging me. They were so happy to get those little dolls. They were so excited. They ran up to me and just grabbed and hugged me." The volunteer said, "We've been doing this for a long, long time. It feels so good to help someone." When I asked what keeps her motivated to continue driving to the border to help the families, what keeps them going, she immediately responded, "Those little girls hugging me. It's just the feeling you get when you help someone." It's a feeling of indescribable joy.

Breaking Bread on Christmas

A GVS Samaritan volunteer shared her favorite joy memory of "breaking bread" on Christmas with newly deported families at the Migrant Resource Center in Nogales, Mexico. For many years, volunteers have been serving Christmas dinner for displaced migrants who are stuck on the Mexico side of the border. As these volunteers were raised on both sides of the border, they would make all kinds of food to share with the migrants who happened to be displaced at Christmas. She reflected on one year when they'd prepared and shared the festive meal and "had a really good time. We finished up all the food. We were cleaning up. People were starting to leave when the Mexican migration people brought in thirty more migrants." She emphasized, "Thirty more people came in on Christmas Day! Oh my goodness! It turned out that the border patrol gave them the choice, and they decided they wanted to go ahead and be deported on Christmas Day." She asked, "So what do we do?

What do we do?" She concluded, "Well, we did what we always do against that, you know, you're just in that rhythm and this is what you did. We made burritos and bologna sandwiches because that's what we always had available. Somebody was able to get some tamales and some other foods, so we fed thirty more people." She asked, "And what's more spiritual than breaking bread together on Christmas Day?"

Joy in the Desert

A retiree who relocated to Arizona from Vermont said the experience volunteering with the GVS Samaritans to help displaced, disoriented, and stranded migrants in the deserts is a striking contrast to her earlier background. She said, "Growing up in the atmosphere in the Northeast was very different." She explained, "Not that the people I grew up with were necessarily racist or bigots, though there were some, but I didn't grow up in a community where people took care of other people. I grew up where good fences make good neighbors. Where 'if you need something, ask me,' but otherwise 'don't bother me, and I won't bother you' kind of attitude." She said when she relocated to southern Arizona, someone in her neighborhood talked about the work the Samaritans were doing and invited her to attend a meeting. She clarified,

> Now, the reason I moved out here was for my health because like a lot of us, you know, we are having a lot of difficulty with aging and living in New England, so I had doubts that I could do anything in my retirement. I can't stand a long time. I can't walk a long time. And I didn't think that there was anything that I could do, but since I now have this free time, I thought there must be something I can do charity-wise, community-wise. So this person invited me to go to one of the Samaritan meetings, and I walked in, and there was a summit of about fifty people. All gray hair, or all white hair, many with canes, a couple with walkers, and I thought, "Well, if they can do it. I can do it; I can do what they do." I immediately became enthralled with this group. And, right away I went out on a ride. And for me what's a thrill, if you can call it a thrill, is searches. I go on searches once a week, a couple times a month, and I absolutely love it. I call it my four-wheel-drive-ride. I love four-wheel driving on dirt roads, combined with the possibility of helping somebody, to keep somebody from dying in the desert. "How can I not like this?" has been my attitude. I get goosebumps just talking about it.

It's a thrill in the desert that brings her spirit great joy. This volunteer added that she learned from her recent trip back to the Northeast to visit with family and friends that not everybody there was as supportive about her adventures in the desert. She said, "I have met the greatest group of people through this organization, from all over the country. I have heard so many different stories of people who have lived in other countries, who have come back here, who have grasped the idea of being grateful for what we have." She moves forth from gratitude to help stranded migrants in the desert.

This transplant from New England added, "I have this nice little house here in the desert. How can I not try to help somebody else to find their little place wherever that might be?" She went on to explain, "I know there's a lot of controversy around what we do, what a lot of humanitarian groups do." She said, "When I run into somebody who has an open enough mind to talk about that, I will talk about it, but otherwise I don't say anything unless I'm with my group of people because a closed mind is a closed mind. There's nothing that I can say to get through to it." Meanwhile, she said, "I have nothing but good words to say for this group of people that I've met here." The people and the volunteer work in the desert bring her spirit joy.

This spirit of joy is contagious throughout this group of Arizona-based volunteers. Another GVS Samaritan said she wanted to highlight Rev. Dr. Randy Mayer, senior minister at Good Shepherd UCC and a key leader for this group of Samaritans: "God bless him. He believes in the joy of the work. He believes in having music, and art as common ground on the border, and also in having fun with what we're doing." This volunteer emphasized that the pastoral leader makes it so it's not always about the suffering. She said he's especially intentional about "celebrating the joy of the border and the joy of the desert." She said, "It might be as simple as going on a search for migrants and also getting an impromptu lesson about the birds in the desert you didn't even know we're there." She added, "You're actually gonna have fun, even though we're doing serious, difficult work." At the conclusion of the Zoom conference call where the GVS Samaritans shared their joy, the session facilitator said, "Everybody's smiling. Everybody's smiling. Isn't that nice?" The computer screen was filled with smiling faces, confirming their individual and collective joy.[23]

JOY HELPS TO BUILD RECONCILIATION

A Catholic sister who serves with IWC in San Antonio, greeting migrants as they travel through the Greyhound bus station, said she sees her role as helping to build peace and reconciliation. She connects peace and reconciliation directly with joy, explaining, "Joy just bubbles up. I see it. I've experienced it again and again." Recounting a recent example of the previous day when she'd spent most of it helping the families in the bus station, she said she sets up the assistance supplies first thing in the morning. She said typically she's alone for about the first forty-five minutes, but the previous day it was already bustling with traveling migrants who immediately began coming to her for assistance. The Catholic sister explained, "I said, 'Just a minute; let me get organized.' And a man from Venezuela immediately stepped up and asked, 'How can I help you?' And another woman came over, a young mother, and asked, 'What can we do?' And so immediately I said, 'Well, why don't you distribute the food?' And so they started putting together the sandwiches, and the juice, and the cookies, and water."

The sister said that when these tasks were done, they helped her sort through the bag of clothing to see if anyone needed something. She explained that at one point after everything was organized, she needed to go back to her car to get more food, and the man who had been helping asked if he could come with her. The sister said of course he could, and then his little boy, about five years old, wanted to follow his dad, who said he needed to wait for him inside the bus station with his mother. The sister said it would be fine for the little boy to come with them, and she explained, "So his son took *my* hand to cross the street, not his father's hand, *my* hand." The sister said it's these simple but precious moments that bring joy to her heart. The moments aren't profound in the Big Picture of Life, but they're deeply moving and very precious in the moment-to-moment action of accompanying these families on their journey to safety. The sister specified that these simpler interactions also generate peace and reconciliation through gracious presence that emits joy between complete strangers who become forever friends through their shared time in the borderlands.

Another IWC volunteer who greets the families as they travel through the Greyhound bus station in downtown San Antonio said, "I can't even begin to put into words what I feel about my experiences with the families. The blessings I receive from the families are indescribable. Whatever you think you're going to do to 'help' is completely not the point of the experience of being there and being present." The volunteer said, "For me, it might be doing art with the children while sitting on the floor at the bus station or asking the mothers if they have any questions about their travel itinerary. Then a child will come up to me and ask, 'Will you come play with me?' Of course, I'm going to stop whatever I'm doing and sit on the floor in the bus station and play with this child." She added, "How do you quantify that? For me, spending time with the families is about meaning-making. My life needs to be meaningful, even if that means slowing down and taking time to play with a little girl in the bus station." Joy in the borderlands is a spiritual gain that contributes to legacy through living a meaningful life in the present that lingers into the future.

NOTES

1. Seow, *Ecclesiastes*, 224.
2. Seow, *Ecclesiastes*, 226–227.
3. Nouwen, *Our Greatest Gift*, 26–27.
4. Bonhoeffer, *Letters and Papers from Prison*, 344.
5. Bonhoeffer, *Letters and Papers from Prison*, 345.
6. de Beauvoir, *Ethics of Ambiguity*, 30.
7. Chittister, *There Is a Season*, 2.
8. Chittister, *There Is a Season*, 2.
9. Frankl, *Man's Search for Meaning*, 65–66.
10. Frankl, *Man's Search for Meaning*, 37–38; emphasis his.
11. Frankl, *Man's Search for Meaning*, 38; emphasis his.
12. Boursier, Art Inside Karnes, Field Notes, vol. 1, October 14, 2015, 31.
13. Boursier, Art Inside Karnes, Field Notes, vol. 1, December 15, 2015, 36.
14. L'Engle, *Sold into Egypt*, Book Three, 163.
15. Boursier, Art Inside Karnes, Field Notes, vol. 1, December, 23, 2015, 51.
16. Boursier, Art Inside Karnes, Field Notes, vol. 2, September 21, 2016.
17. Boursier, Art Inside Karnes, Field Notes, vol. 4, October 5, 2016, 80.
18. Art Inside Karnes, Field Notes, vol. 4, October 5, 2016, 82.
19. Boursier, Art Inside Karnes, Field Notes, vol. 3, May 11, 2016.
20. Boursier, Art Inside Karnes, Field Notes, vol. 2, March 17, 2016, 51.
21. Boursier, Art Inside Karnes, Field Notes, vol. 2, May 25, 2016. See also Boursier, *Arts as Witness*, 87–103.
22. Boursier, Art Inside Karnes, Field Notes, vol. 2, June 22, 2016.
23. Group interview with the author via Zoom, July 11, 2022; shared by permission.

CHAPTER ELEVEN

Legacy

Whatever your hand finds to do, do with all your might, for there is no work or thought or knowledge or wisdom in Sheol, to which you are going.
Ecclesiastes 9:10 (NASB)

What's the antidote to finding or making meaning amid this seemingly meaningless life? Given that we're all going to die, what's a worthwhile legacy to live during this one and only short life, and how does that intersect with spirituality? Religion offers various nirvana-type pathways to a yellow brick road that ends with happily ever after in a place with pearly gates where the streets are paved with gold. Unfortunately, no one actually knows what this really looks like until after they're dead. While it's true that religious belief or faith drives the plane, train, or automobile that gets the faithful followers safely to those pearly gates in the hereafter, there really isn't absolute certainty until each person actually arrives at this mystical nirvana. Meanwhile, Ecclesiastes asks, "What about now?" Given that we can't and don't get to know the unknown future, either in this lifetime or in the possible hereafter, what's a worthwhile legacy to work toward while we're still alive? As William Brown explains in his commentary on Ecclesiastes, "The ultimate desire that even wisdom and pleasure cannot satisfy is the desire for remembrance," for someone's life to still be important long after they're no longer among the living. Brown suggests that to have "an enduring memory" of who and what they are is "the next best thing to immortality."[1] Against a review of the key points in Ecclesiastes about what gives meaning to life, this chapter offers a hopeful antidote to cynicism, striving, and grievous evil with a spirituality that embodies legacy through justice and peacemaking in the borderlands.

THE MEANING OF LIFE

As explained briefly in the previous chapter, Ecclesiastes uses five summary statements to synthesize the good stuff, the most worthwhile or beneficial gains that make this life worthwhile (Ecc. 2:24–26, 3:22, 5:18–10, 8:15–17, and 9:7–10). These five statements point to where to focus time, energy, passion, love, and financial investment, not in the sense of making money off of the stock market or capping off an individual retirement account. Rather, Ecclesiastes specifies the core components for what adds genuine blessing and value to this short life. Religious and biblical scholars sometimes criticize Ecclesiastes for being too shallow, selfish, and overly *carpe diem* as its wisdom seems to primarily apply to the affluent world without offering anything helpful for those who are struggling and marginalized. Despite this scholarly criticism against Ecclesiastes, the summary statements do highlight gains or benefits that directly contribute to meaning-making and legacy-leaving for regular people.

This legacy isn't meant to be about gaining fame and fortune or leaving a big chunk of assets for heirs. In fact, Ecclesiastes warns that it's futile to place faith in such legacy because just as everyone dies, everyone also is quickly forgotten (Ecc. 2:17). Consider your own genealogy. How many family members do you personally recall, including who they were and what they did? How many generations ago do you personally remember a family member? What memories do you still have of your grandparents, great-grandparents, or great-great-anyone? Even those who are rich and famous, who may be memorialized with a portrait that gathers dust in a museum, or a granite statue in a public park where pigeons roost, or a building named in their honor at a college, university, or church, are rarely or barely remembered by the general public that casually strolls past. All of the endless striving to stash funds away for a happily-ever-after life that also attempts to ensure lasting legacy is meaningless and becomes nothing more than "chasing after the wind" (Ecc. 2:21–23). This foolish futility fosters discontent, inspiring a spiritual calling to engage in difference-making for justice and peace. It's exactly this sense of legacy that empowers the moral ethical call in the borderlands.

Legacy begins with permission-giving to live life fully now, in this present moment. For example, the fifth summary statement in Ecclesiastes emphasizes:

> Go, eat your bread with enjoyment and drink your wine with a merry heart, for God has long ago approved what you do. Let your garments always be white; do not let oil be lacking on your head. Enjoy life with the [spouse] whom you love all the days of your vain life that are given you under the sun, because that is your portion in life and in your toil at which you toil under the sun. Whatever your hand finds to do, do with all your might, for there is no work or thought or knowledge or wisdom in Sheol, to which you are going. (Ecc. 9:7–10)

In the ancient-world context of Ecclesiastes and its affirmation that everyone dies and ends up going to Sheol beneath the earth, legacy includes being intentional about living life now. Enjoy this time, this moment, this situation now. It will never come back.

This ever-changing time that is continually moving from one moment to the next is also why I've always diligently documented each of my experiences with the families. This here-and-now moment exists only in this here-and-now present time. The moments we're living through have this singular distinction: now is only now *now*. The clock continues to tick as time marches on (chapter 6). Otherwise, what future time brings remains uncertain. Legacy embraces and celebrates the present without holding out for whatever may or may not come with tomorrow. Ecclesiastes resonates with Psalm 118:24 regarding the primacy of now: "This is the day that the LORD has made; let us rejoice and be glad in it." Today is the one guarantee we have. We are alive now.

Meaning-Making in Ecclesiastes

After examining a myriad of options about what conventionally makes life meaningful and worthwhile, Ecclesiastes comes to the conclusion that the present time is what matters the most in life. It isn't an eat-drink-and-be-merry, party-hardy, yeehaw life. Nor is it working obsessively to leave a building, an endowment fund, or a pile of money for children or grandchildren. Ecclesiastes advises that everything about stockpiling for a physical future, whether for oneself or for one's heirs, ultimately is foolishness and "chasing after wind" (Ecc. 2:26). Ecclesiastes says to enjoy where you are, who you're with, and what you have the option to do now, in this moment. Now could be as good as it gets. Instead of worrying about whatever else you can do or achieve, consider what it looks like to simply be present in this moment with the ones around you. Legacy means appreciating what you have, whatever that is, and counting whatever you do have as joy. Legacy also considers each person's particular gifts and skills, and naming them as gifts and skills that can be used for the greater good through helping others. It's by occupying our minds and hearts with joy in the present tense that life gains meaning (Ecc. 5:18–20). Instead of hoarding funds for an uncertain, distant future, live with abundant generosity while also enjoying whatever wealth, possessions, or opportunities you may have. Legacy is about life now, which is the primary motivation for the families who are seeking new life in America. Life itself is their legacy for themselves and for their children. The families walk the migrant trail so their children might have life. Everything about the journey is about living each today with life in view for themselves and their children (illustration 11.1).

Illustration 11.1 *Biding Our Time* 11" × 14" cut paper collage portrait of a father holding his baby daughter on his lap in a hammock, December 15, 2019, while his family languished at a migrant encampment in Matamoros, Mexico, during MPP. Art © Helen T. Boursier.

LEGACY LIVES WITH DEATH IN VIEW

The reality of death offsets the shallow and frivolous time-wasters that ultimately have little or no value. Death nets perspective about what really matters because life is precious, precarious, and short. L'Engle suggests that instead of bemoaning "the precariousness of all life, we are taught to look for a security that does not exist. No one can promise that we will end a day in safety, that we, or someone dear to us, will not be hurt."[2] Given the choice between continuing to run on the treadmill of more, more, more, including status, achievement, and wealth, compared with spending time doing something to help make the world better, legacy opts to work for justice and peacemaking to unify the broken human family and Planet Earth. Chittister proposes, "Death asks us what we want to have become of our lives before we die." She asks, "What, death says, will be the alleluia of your own life?"[3] Being confronted with death pushes the families to make their radical decision to migrate. Immanent death also influences why many aging volunteers and activists choose to engage in meaning-making in the borderlands during their retirement years, working to make the world better through their labor of love for justice and peacemaking. Facing the reality of death inspires the families to seek a new life elsewhere while simultaneously inspiring volunteers and advocates to live into the fullness of their lives by tangibly helping these traveling brothers and sisters in the borderlands and working to protect the environment.

Chittister points out that such actions of compassion beyond oneself create growth, what she calls "death's final gift." The Catholic sister explains, "We find ourselves different than we were before death confronted us with our limits, prodded us toward new possibilities, gave us a new look at life and all its little pieces, made us choose again for the lasting beyond the ephemeral."[4] Similarly, in *Speaking the Truth about Oneself*, philosopher Michel Foucault argues that the importance of reflecting on death is that it provides a groundedness to the present. It also takes the evil sense away from what ultimately happens to everyone.[5] Legacy looks death in the face and considers, "What is mine to do while there's still time? What matters most for the remaining time during this short life?"

The Void

The unknown and not yet determined future, what some philosophers term the *void*, offers nothing but uncertainty. For example, theologian James

Loder argues, "The void is more vast than death, but death is the definitive metaphor; 'nothing' in itself is ultimately unthinkable, but death, shrouding all our lived 'worlds,' gives us our clearest picture of nothing."[6] Living for legacy in the present provides meaning-making while pushing through into that future unknown void. Living into the present through justice and peacemaking, of course not only in the borderlands but wherever the spirit for justice muse calls, shifts the focus from the egocentric self to love as justice in solidarity with those who are oppressed and marginalized. Loder proposes, "We continue to live precisely because in the center of the self, for all its potential perversity, we experience again and again the reversal of those influences that invite despair and drive toward void."[7] Loder points to Danish theologian-philosopher Søren Kierkegaard, who's well known for insisting that "the faces of the void become the faces of God."[8] It's a *void* that, for Kierkegaard, motivates a *leap of faith* to see God in this empty place and space where life seems futile, pointless, meaningless, or a "vanity of vanities" (Ecc. 1:2).

Instead of fear and trembling, dreading that unknown future void of uncertainty, philosopher Michael Polanyi suggests an "indwelling," what Loder describes Polanyi using "to indicate the phase of knowing in which the knower moves into deep personal interaction with the known. To indwell a situation, object, or person is to allow its features and essential nature to impress themselves upon the knower, and to establish therefore in terms of its own intelligibility the conditions under which it may be known."[9] Being known in the borderlands includes interconnection through compassionate action as volunteers and advocates work together to care for displaced families and Mother Earth.

Embracing a Lifelong Journey toward Death

Michel de Montaigne, a well-known philosopher during the French Renaissance, said, "The continuous work of our life is to build death."[10] Legacy moves forth from this reality of each person's inevitable impending death. With the inevitability of death, the question becomes what legacy can anyone leave from their short stint on Planet Earth? Death is inevitably coming, which makes life now matter. Living life in the present, with that ultimate end in view, shapes choices in the present moment that hopefully and ideally will contribute to a better world long after each person is gone.

Legacy typically comes from something someone accomplishes, a *thing* that marks their life forever after. In her analysis of the *Human Condition*, Hannah Arendt synthesizes:

> The task and potential greatness of mortals lie in their ability to produce things—works and deeds and words—which would deserve to be and, at least to a degree, are at home in everlastingness, so that through them mortals could find their place in a cosmos where everything is immortal except themselves. By their capacity for their mortal deed, by their ability to leave non-perishable traces behind, [humans], their individual mortality notwithstanding, attain an immortality of their own and prove themselves to be of a "divine" nature.[11]

Of course, there's the One Big Death, the end of physical life, but Roman Catholic priest Ronald Rolheiser points out there are actually several "little deaths" along the journey to the Big Death:

1. The death of our youth.
2. The death of our wholeness.
3. The death of our dreams.
4. The death of our honeymoons.
5. The death of a certain idea of God and Church.[12]

Each one of these little deaths contributes to meaning-making and legacy. Each little death we die is one less opportunity to achieve a profound *thing* that we will be remembered for because we didn't do it after all. Whatever someone didn't do, couldn't do, or won't be able to do leaves the lesser-than options of what provides meaning in life, not in light of all that can't or won't be done but in view of what can and will.

Ecclesiastes doesn't actually consider that people need to become prepared for the reality of death through what Chittister calls "little dyings," though there is an ongoing active sense to each one of these.[13] She explains, "The fact is that we cannot rise until we are willing to die a little. We can be alive but we cannot be human until we confront the inhuman in ourselves. We cannot bring life until we admit that we are part of the death around us." She adds, "Dying a little, in fact, is what life is all about."[14] Taking the chance and embracing risk with dying to self creates a pathway for legacy because it shifts the focus from me, myself, and I to the cares and concerns of the world around us. Dying to self also begins to disentangle the ego from any unhealthy beliefs, practices, attitudes, and ideas inherited from a racist, anti-immigration, misogynistic, and/or self-absorbed past, making a way for compassion, kindness, openness, hospitality, and solidarity in the borderlands. Legacy-making looks for ways to embrace otherness with generosity, kindness, compassion, love, and peace.

Our Greatest Gift

Ecclesiastes says to make the most of life now, which creates a legacy moment by-moment, building what Henri Nouwen beautifully expresses in his context that addresses the significance of caring for people who are dying, such as palliative care, hospice, or care for people who have long-term disabilities and need special ongoing care throughout their lives. Nouwen asks, "How can I live so that I can continue to be fruitful when I am no longer here among my family and friends? That question shifts our attention from doing to being. Our doing brings success, but our being bears fruit." Nouwen adds, "The great paradox of our lives is that we are often concerned about what we do or still can do, but we are most likely remembered for who we were."[15] His wise insights parallel the ministry of presence that's so integral to spirituality in the borderlands through being fully present with the families and not rushing through life, attempting to do more and more and more. Instead, this ministry of being present creates future legacy in the moment-to-moment care and compassion in the borderlands. As one volunteer said, "The only epitaph I want said at my funeral, or written on my gravestone, is 'She showed up; she cared'" (illustration 12.1). It's a legacy that builds toward *dying well*.

Dying Well

Caring enough to be fully present with compassion in the borderlands exemplifies what Nouwen calls "befriending death" and "dying well." Instead of being overly interested in personal "success, our productivity, our fame, or our importance among people," dying well means living in the present, carefully attuned to the needs of others instead of to the desires of self.[16] Nouwen eloquently explains, "To befriend death, we must claim that we are children of God, sisters and brothers of all people, and parents of generations to come. In so doing, we liberate our death from its absurdity and make it the gateway to a new life."[17] Legacy enters in when we live our lives in the present so that who we are/were matters even more so after we've died as our *fruitfulness* continues to prosper through the ministry of compassion and presence that we engaged in while we were still living. Our life goes on through the lives we've blessed by choosing to be love and grace and mercy and compassion present in the here and now.

Reflecting in the *Cancer Journals* about her own anxieties about dying, Lorde writes, "If I can look directly at my life and my death without flinching, I know there is nothing they can ever do to me again."[18] For Lorde, looking directly at death includes "living a self-conscious life, under the pressure of time, I work with the consciousness of death at my shoulder, not constantly, but often enough to leave a mark upon all of my life's decisions and actions."[19] She explains the issue isn't *when* she dies but that she will die; whether it's sooner or later is irrelevant. It's the intentionality in living into the options in the present that enhances legacy and makes life meaningful.

Lorde makes an important point that resonates with spirituality in the borderlands: "It does not matter whether this death comes next week or thirty years from now; this consciousness gives my life another breadth. It helps shape the words I speak, the ways I love, my politic of action, the strength of my vision and purpose, the depth of my appreciation of living."[20] It's also true, as Chittister points out, that "death may, of course, be the trigger of despair. But death is also the answer to despair. Once we have known death, up close and personal, despair can barely touch us again. Death teaches us that my life only ends when it ends."[21] Moving toward death is the unalterable reality. The question to consider, as German theologian Jürgen Moltmann poses, is "What wisdom about life do we gain when we remember that we must die, and what foolishness when we forget that we are mortal?"[22] Now is the only time anyone has to choose to die well, in the present moment, by also deciding and acting on what their legacy will be, literally one moment at a time.

In *Living Life Backward*, David Gibson explains, "To die well means that you realize death is the limit God has placed on creatures who want to be gods."[23] His insight is, of course, all-inclusive because who doesn't want to be the center of the universe with everything revolving around their wishes, desires, and needs? Our future hope of eternal life, not in the Christian sense but in the broader interreligious view of whatever life looks like beyond the grave, begins today with the choices we make to live compassionate lives in the present. In Ecclesiastes, as in spirituality in the borderlands, life holds the advantage over death only when people live their lives with death in view.

Living with the ultimacy of death shapes present choices for the greater good rather than for selfish gain. Brown explains that the key point in

Ecclesiastes "lies in recognizing that one works not for self-gain but for the thrill of applying one's gifts and talents for the sake of another without any self-driven expectations of the results."[24] In other words, living life with death in view becomes a *spirituality of finitude* that affirms the finiteness of life while also shaping choices for the greater good over against personal selfish gain. Embracing finitude reshapes spirituality, like it does in the borderlands, as Chittister explains, with "a spirituality of death that brings light into the shadowland, life into the world, pulse into the flat lines of sickly systems. Without it, the world will never rise again out of its tombs of dry clay into the light of new life."[25] The choice to die well also is the choice to live life with intentionality that brings meaning to others, making their lives better in whatever possible ways. What Chittister calls "the spirituality of death" is an invitation to live new life in the present for the betterment and benefit of others.[26] Her spirituality of death resonates with Bonhoeffer's insight that death brings freedom, but it's a freedom that begins before death when each person chooses to die well. Paraphrasing his fourth and closing section in his poem "Stations on the Road to Freedom," Bonhoeffer believes this freedom includes (self-) discipline and action for others.[27] There's freedom in death when it begins by living life in the present *for* and *with* others.

EMBRACING FINITUDE PRIORITIZES LIVING LIFE FOR TRUE LEGACY

Embracing finitude, the finiteness of life that affirms we're all going to die, means letting go of certitudes about virtually anything and everything we think we know. Instead, embracing finitude generates humility. We don't and can't know it all. We won't and can't accomplish all of the fancy things we set out to be and do. Finitude cherishes this moment in time with these people around us, shaping legacy through choosing to be about embracing ethical actions for the betterment of all. In James Baldwin's letter to his nephew on the one-hundredth anniversary of the Emancipation Proclamation, he wrote, "Perhaps the whole root of our trouble, the human trouble, is that we will sacrifice all of the beauty of our lives, will imprison ourselves in totems, taboos, crosses, blood sacrifices, steeples, mosques, races, armies, flags, nations, in order to deny the fact of death, which is the only fact we have. It seems to me that one ought to rejoice in the *fact* of death—ought to decide, indeed, to *earn* one's death."[28] To do so, Baldwin argues, "One is responsible to life: it is the small beacon in that terrifying darkness from which we come and to which we shall return. One must negotiate this passage as notably as possible, for the sake of those who are coming after us."[29] The choices each person makes about living for difference in this life leave a lingering legacy for future generations to benefit from. It's the choices each person makes to nurture justice and peacemaking in the present that clear the way, bit by bit, for a better future.[30] It's a legacy that requires the full human community.

Embracing finitude is more than merely acknowledging the reality of the existence of death. Rather, it means to live each moment of each day as if this is the only possible moment to leave any legacy. Tomorrow may be too late because there's the ever-present possibility that the Grim Reaper might arrive during the wee hours of this night. Today is the day to live. Today is the day to build the legacy that may be all that's left of anyone's life this time tomorrow. Embracing finitude means death is about life now. Death is not something that's in the distant future. Rather, it's almost here now.

Finitude Reorganizes Priorities

Being fully cognizant of one's mortality, one's finiteness in life, opens up what matters in the day-to-day moments, not only for what you want to do and be but also what you want others to remember you for. It's this sense that contributes to spirituality in the borderlands, particularly for those who advocate for ecojustice and human justice. It's a spiritual strength that shapes and makes decisions to live intentionally in the present, not for selfish gains and desires but for the betterment of all creation. It's a spirituality shaped by justice and peacemaking.

Legacy intersects with time, chance, choice, risk, gain, and joy in the borderlands because human temporality forces what Heidegger terms a "time-reckoning" that's formed, informed, and shaped by human temporality.[31] However, this temporality is not a standalone, disconnected from anyone or anything. Rather, temporality is situated in cosmic time and the ongoing flow of the interconnected continuum of all life in all times and in all places. Each life in this moment intersects and interrelates with what's gone before, what else is happening in the now, and what will be becoming as time continues into the future. Legacy embraces these past, present, and future contexts. The spiritual legacy includes who we were, who we are, and who we are becoming, including the legacy that continues after mortal life ends.

A Legacy of Love after Death

Poets, songwriters, novelists, and screenwriters are enamored with love, probably because life without love has much less meaning. Moltmann proposes that "as far as the personal structuring of life is concerned, the problem is not simply *life* and death; it is *love* and death."[32] Life is bound together with death, and the binding agent is love. Moltmann elaborates, "Through love we come alive, and make other people alive, but love also makes us vulnerable for disappointments and hurts, and ultimately for death. Love doesn't give us joy in life without the pain of death. If we want to avoid the pain, we reduce our capacity for happiness too."[33] If love makes life meaningful, then it follows that it also must contribute to a *legacy of love after death*. It isn't just about loving in the present moment. Love endures beyond the grave through a legacy of a life well lived.

In his funeral sermon for esteemed German theologian Dorothee Soelle, Bishop Baerbel von Wartenberg-Potter described hosting a group at his home two weeks prior to her death when Soelle remarked, "Everything carries on; that's what death is about." The bishop went on to explain what he saw as her words to the congregation during her funeral service: "Everything carries on. Love carries on, praying and doing justice carry on. Bread is still baked. Children are conceived and born. The grain of wheat will fall into the soil and grow in the field, and the heart of humans. We shall carry on reading Dorothee's books and she will carry on speaking to us. She has passed the torch to us: We must love and work for the reign of God and its justice. We shall find our own ways of keeping that word."[34] Legacy continues beyond the grave through justice and peacemaking, which leave behind a lingering legacy of love.

For instance, I was devastated after ICE rescinded my security clearance and closed the art as spiritual care ministry with detained families shortly before we were to host *las posadas* celebration of Christmas inside Karnes. It felt like I was fired from my church on Christmas Eve. When I later lamented this sudden death to a Catholic sister who assists with IWC, she consoled me with the important reminder that all the benefits, blessings, and joys that had occurred during the two years of the art ministry would remain forever in the hearts of the several thousand mothers and children this ministry of presence had touched. The legacy will linger in their hearts long after the death of Art Inside Karnes. It's a legacy of love that continues in their hearts and also in mine. It's also a legacy that continues far beyond the detention center walls, through the families who received temporary legal status to pursue their asylum claims and also through the various books, articles, and public presentations where I've shared their witness.[35] The ministry died in its particular form and shape, but the legacy of its witness lives on.

Love Lives On

Spirituality in the borderlands carries on this same sense of legacy to make love beyond the grave into perpetuity because of solidarity, compassion, and presence now. It's the legacy of love that Mother Teresa lived in her commitment to the untouchables in India, Desmond Tutu's love that motivated his commitment to see the end of Apartheid in South Africa, Martin Luther King Jr.'s love that marched him to racial justice, and all the other prominent names for justice. But it's not just the headliners who are called to live for love and justice. It's also all the regular people who slog along in the dailiness of life as they seek to live their lives for love through justice and peacemaking. As MLK Jr. insists, "Love is the most durable power in the world."[36] Love is the strongest and most effective tool available to transform grievous evils in all their hideous manifestations.

It's this sort of difference-making, with love at the center, that drives spirituality in the borderlands. It's a passionate, compassionate love that will continue long after death as people seek to leave a spiritual footprint in the sand through the physical presence they offer in solidarity with displaced migrants in the borderlands. As one volunteer expressed, "I keep thinking about how much it's an incredible privilege to spend this time with these families. Really, all my ministry is about simply being present. No more. I simply feel called to be present with these families in the borderlands. It's a gift of grace." Love reflects back and forth in the borderlands: from the families to the volunteers and then right back from the volunteers to the families. This same love permeates activists to protect endangered animals in the borderlands. For some, love originates from earlier experiences in their personal lives, secular and/or sacred. For others, their volunteering with the families is a singular first for the depth, breadth, and intensity of love, making it viscerally alive and vibrant in a way they'd never before experienced.

The coordinator for a church-sponsored shelter for traveling migrants located in San Antonio said her greatest joy is sharing this experience with her two eight-year-old children. She said she "feels incredibly blessed" that she's able to bring her children to the migrant shelter and also to the church where they can interact and play with people who speak six different languages, and who are from so many different countries. She said, "I think that it's an incredible gift to be able to offer to my children. It's a gift for me every day." She explained that she hasn't been able to do a lot of traveling, but she loves that she can give her children a sense of it through all the displaced families who travel through San Antonio. She said, "I just love that they hear people speaking Spanish, and it's not just something that we practice. It's something that people speak for their whole lives. I love it." She said her children also "taste the different foods that they cook here. I really love that they play with kids who look completely different from them and who they've never met before. All of this is really, really an incredible thing to be able to offer to my children." The shelter supervisor said these experiences her children have also "spur other conversations" when they ask questions like "Why don't they have shoes?" she and explained, "They just don't. Maybe they lost them, or there's a million reasons why they don't have shoes that fit, like maybe they just got a donated pair that was way too big." This mother of two said that for her children "to be able to understand that there are people who don't have, not just a fancy house, but the basic necessities of life, and to start to engage and wrestle with why that is, I think it's so powerful." Such experiences and conversations contribute to meaning-making, to legacy, and to what really matters in life.

A volunteer chaplain at a facility in Arizona for unaccompanied migrant children who are detained in government custody said she led the children in singing and then invited them to pray: "We lifted the roof with our singing." Then, as the children did what is termed a *strong prayer*, they would put a piece of paper over their face to create their own confessional or private sacred space, and then each child would say their own prayers out loud. The volunteer chaplain said, "They'd start out soft and then get louder and louder, then softer at the end with all of the children sobbing." She said the only way that she was allowed to touch them was to bless each one of them individually: "I could hold them briefly for a moment through the blessing."

These interactions with the families while witnessing their injustice in the borderlands reinforce a layer of spiritual motivation to keep on keeping on through participation in solidarity *with* the families. Love flows back and forth in the borderlands.

Living for Legacy Isn't Easy

One of the reasons for the depth of legacy-building through solidarity in the borderlands is because none of it's easy. The volunteers can't make any of the difficulty magically disappear. For instance, I wrote about this frustrating sense of helplessness after a day of being present with the families inside Karnes, when I held, cried, and prayed with three different women who were in deep emotional pain:

1. Today this young mother just received the news that she was being deported with her young daughter. She has no living family in her homeland. All of her relatives now live in the United States.
2. A middle-aged woman asked to speak with a pastor. Her husband was killed. She brought one child with her, and an older son and older daughter are already living in the United States. She hasn't seen them in eight years.
3. A young mother was making a birthday card for her brother who turns 15 the next day in Los Angeles. She said she hopes to go there—to see him. We cried together, and I prayed for her.

The journal entry specified I was feeling an emotional overload to hear the suffering and to feel their pain and anguish and that I felt helpless because I couldn't change their circumstances. Similarly, advocates and environmentalists can't instantaneously change the policies in Washington that are harming the environment in the borderlands. Building a legacy of justice and peacemaking is a team effort that resembles a relay race, with one person completing their segment and then passing the baton along to the next. Solidarity through presence in the borderlands requires consistency and tenacity in being present. It's not about fixing things or solving all the problems in the short term. It's about making the time and commitment to be present for life now, all life, with the hope and vision for a better future life for all.

A regular volunteer in the borderlands who later relocated elsewhere, reflecting on her experiences with the families, said they will always be a part of her heart and her spirit. The volunteer said, first and foremost, she was struck by the profound faith that the women and children have. She said even among the teenage boys, their faith is evident and clearly important to them, something that, all things being equal, she wouldn't expect in a gathering with American teenage boys. She said their faith and spirituality continue to inspire and encourage her own. This volunteer's second significant takeaway insight from her time with the families is the overall meaningfulness of the experience itself. She explained that all of the time and energy she'd put into her many trips to volunteer with the families were very meaningful, which is what made it so worthwhile and kept her coming back again and again. She said there'd been times when she'd been distracted, and even a little depressed on the morning of the day she was to volunteer, but she said she would quickly become energized through her experience of ministry with the women and children. She said it's made her consider how other things she does in life drain her, including some things that require much less time, energy, and commitment. She added, "There's clearly a message there." Legacy is about fostering life as we walk together in solidarity, living into a holistic spirituality in the borderlands that's both holy and whole.

NOTES

1. Brown, *Ecclesiastes*, 35.
2. L'Engle, *Rock That Is Higher*, 272.
3. Chittister and Williams, *Uncommon Gratitude*, 172.
4. Chittister and Williams, *Uncommon Gratitude*, 172–173.
5. Michel Foucault, *Speaking the Truth about Oneself: Lectures at Victoria University, Toronto, 1982*, ed. Henri-Paul Fruchaud and Daniele Lorenzini. [English version established by Daniel Louis Wyche.] (Chicago: The University of Chicago Press, 2021), 68.
6. Loder, *Transforming Moment*, 84.
7. Loder, *Transforming Moment*, 85.
8. Loder, *Transforming Moment*, 85.
9. Loder, *Transforming Moment*, 225.
10. Michael de Montaigne, cited in de Beauvoir, *Ethics of Ambiguity*, 5; no source given.
11. Arendt, *Human Condition*, 19.
12. Ronald Rolheiser, *The Holy Longing: The Search for a Christian Spirituality*, 15th anniversary ed. (New York: Random House, 1998, 2019), 148–162.
13. Chittister, *There Is a Season*, 61.
14. Chittister, *There Is a Season*, 61.
15. Nouwen, *Our Greatest Gift*, 41.

16 Nouwen, *Our Greatest Gift*, 38–39.
17 Nouwen, *Our Greatest Gift*, 47.
18 Lorde, "April 4, 1979," in Lorde, *Cancer Journals*, 4.
19 Lorde, *Cancer Journals*, 9.
20 Lorde, *Cancer Journals*, 9.
21 Chittister and Williams, *Uncommon Gratitude*, 169.
22 Jürgen Moltmann, *In the End—The Beginning: The Life of Hope*, trans. Margaret Kohl (Minneapolis: Fortress Press, 2004), 118.
23 David Gibson, *Living Life Backward: How Ecclesiastes Teaches Us to Live in Light of the End* (Wheaton, IL: Crossway, 2017), 109.
24 Brown, *Ecclesiastes*, 130.
25 Chittister, *There Is a Season*, 63.
26 Chittister, *There Is a Season*, 63.
27 Bonhoeffer, "Stations on the Road to Freedom," in Bonhoeffer, *Letters and Papers from Prison*, 371.
28 James Baldwin, "The Dungeon Shook: Letter to My Nephew on the One Hundredth Anniversary of the Emancipation," in *The Fire Next Time* (New York: Random House, Vintage Books, 1962, 1993), 91–92.
29 Baldwin, "The Dungeon Shook," 91–92.
30 See Olive Schreiner, *A Track to the Water's Edge: The Olive Schreiner Reader*, ed. Howard Thurman (New York: Harper and Row, 1973), 55–56.
31 Heidegger, *Being and Time*, 464–465.
32 Moltmann, *In the End—The Beginning*, 120.
33 Moltmann, *In the End—The Beginning*, 120.
34 Bishop Baerbel von Wartenberg-Potter, "Funeral Sermon," in *The Theology of Dorothee Soelle*, ed. Sarah K. Pinnock (Harrisburg, PA: Trinity Press International; Continuum, 2003), x–xi.
35 See Boursier, *Ethics of Hospitality*; *Desperately Seeking Asylum*; *Art as Witness*; and *Willful Ignorance*.
36 King Jr., *Strength to Love*, 56.

Conclusion: Holy and Whole

Even those who live many years should rejoice in them all, yet let them remember that the days of darkness will be many. All that comes is vanity.
—Ecclesiastes 11:8 (NRSVUE)

"Holy and Whole" integrates the lessons from the borderlands into a spirituality for sacredness amid secularity that fosters justice and peacemaking as antidotes to futility, despair, or meaninglessness. It's a spirituality that engenders value, blessing, and meaning in the present that continue into the future. Navigating through the ups and downs, making prudent decisions between the better-thans, acknowledging present times or seasons as they are, and experiencing joy all culminate with creating a place and space for holy ground, which becomes a spirituality for a precarious *precious* life that embraces the spiritual moral call for justice and peacemaking.

Ecclesiastes offers a challenging yet vibrant philosophy of life for the postmodern cynical West. Reality is complex. Ecclesiastes doesn't believe in conventional wisdom with its standard retribution ideology. Ecclesiastes also doesn't trivialize theology with the belief that good people get good things, or bad people get bad things. God is present; God is in control, but it's simply not possible from the mere mortal perspective to know, see, or even experience exactly what that looks like. Despite the limited and often skewed human view, Ecclesiastes offers a reassuring *nevertheless, God is.*

In the first summary statement, Ecclesiastes 2:34–26 says to consecrate the place where each person happens to be at any given place and time, to let this be what's meaningful and beneficial in life, rejoicing in the present time, place, and space. This practical view on life isn't a glib or passive response to bad stuff happening to good people. Rather, Ecclesiastes exemplifies what Hebrew Bible professor R. Mark Shipp once termed "a theology of the pit" (Ps. 40:2, 69:2). Whenever shit happens, when someone takes an inevitable hard fall (chance) into a grievous evil pit in life, one that isn't easy to climb back out of but where there will be languishing in suffering and distress, this theology of the pit prioritizes the option that it's still possible to invite the sacred into this pit so it becomes holy ground. The pain and suffering don't magically disappear, but the place and space become sacred as this pit is transformed into consecrated ground. By inviting the sacred into the pit, it becomes holy, and we become whole. It also widens the pathway to engage in justice and peacemaking.

SOWING AND REBUILDING

Life is about being sowers, not reapers, and rebuilders, not builders, which Chittister suggests is "both the struggle and the gift." She explains, "The function of each succeeding generation is not to demand change; it is to prepare for it. The function of one generation is to make change possible for the next. The real function of each generation is to sow the seeds that will make a better world possible in the future."[1] Whereas Chittister sees this as requiring "the spirituality of urgent patience,"[2] there also must be perennial resolve to work for justice and peacemaking in the present tense. Justice and peacemaking require tenacity. No single systemic injustice will ever be solved or resolved within one lifetime. There will forever be an urgency to repair, correct, mediate, mitigate, and so forth the damage already done while also forging ahead to make the future better. Hence, this continually forging ahead requires patience, in Chittister's perspective, but it also demands fortitude, tenacity, and solidarity in community to keep pressing on.

Of course, in working for justice and peace, people first have to identify, verify, and name *in*justice, particularly the larger forms that hide within and are perpetuated on a grand scale through structural evil and whopper-size grievous evils like systemic racism; environmental genocide; generational poverty; gender oppression; and anti-immigration rhetoric, policies, and practices that foster exclusion from asylum. In *Resisting Structural Evil: Love as Ecological-Economic Vocation*, ecofeminist Cynthia D. Moe-Lobeda argues,

"Love that seeks justice is the counterpoint of structural evil. The magnificent call to love is heard in many tongues through many faith traditions and other schools of wisdom." She argues that love is stronger, more forceful, and more productive than any other possible human emotion, feeling, or response. Even though humans are mired within the muck of grievous evils, "humans are nevertheless charged with seeking the widespread good, abundant life for all, through ways of justice-making love." She adds, "For fulfilling this calling, we are bearers of that divine and indomitable love."[3] This isn't someone else's calling or charge. It's yours, mine, and ours.

There's something for everyone to do along this journey to becoming holy and whole, beginning with choosing to listen to and hear the spiritual call for justice and peace. Instead, Chittister argues, "People listen but do not believe or people do not listen at all. People listen and scoff. People listen and argue. People listen and yawn. People listen and reason the unreasonable."[4] Changing the world doesn't happen overnight. Nevertheless, the urgent call for tenacious presence marches on. It's the torch that brings hope in the present while preparing the way for the next generation's better, safer, and more peaceful future. It's the journey toward a world that's becom*ing* holy and whole.

CALLINGS TO JUSTICE AND PEACEMAKING IN THE BORDERLANDS

Justice in the borderlands is a deeply spiritual concern that lets go of self-centered selfishness and *us-ness* and embraces the global perspective to love life on Planet Earth, including the sacred earth and our brothers and sisters on both sides of an international border. It means working for ecojustice, gender justice, racial justice, and immigration justice in the borderlands and beyond. It also means welcoming people like Wendy with her husband and their four children from Honduras who made the risky journey to America; as she described, "We didn't know anyone. We were strangers in a strange land. We called on the Lord." After they'd turned themselves in at US Immigration, they were "locked up for four days" and then sent back to Nuevo Laredo, Mexico, during MPP. This mother of four said, "We have nothing in Honduras, but the good thing is we are a respectful and honorable family. Glory to God."[5]

A volunteer who assists displaced families in San Antonio said, "I'm compelled and propelled by the witness of the families and their profound spirituality. It has overflowed from the families and is embedded in my spirit." Another volunteer who'd shifted from reading a book a day in her retirement to participating with the GVS Samaritans elaborated, "Why wasn't the book a day good enough? Well, you can read a book a day, but then you're not living a life. You're living the life in the book." The volunteer added, "And I don't want to live a life that somebody else wrote. I want to live the life side that's in front of me and around me, the life that I see and that I hear about. I want to live life face to face." Another GVS Samaritan said it's easy to stay motivated in her assistance in the borderlands because "we always see gratitude. The families are always grateful to God, grateful to the people who have helped them. They are grateful for whatever and in whatever their situation is. We see so much gratitude." She added that for anyone considering helping the families, the single most important aspect of being present with the families in the borderlands is to "treat people decently and to acknowledge that we're all God's children." It's the same sort of respect the environmentalists have for the endangered species in the borderlands.

EXPERIENCING THE SACRED

A pastor who supervises a church-sponsored shelter for displaced migrants in San Antonio said, "I don't want to lump them together [the families] and say they're all super faithful, but there is a culture of faith that 'God is in control. God has a plan for me. God is always with me.'" She emphasized, "And that's kind of an amazing thing to hear people say who have just lost their children, don't have anything, or don't have anywhere to go." Consistently observing the faith of the families despite their desperate circumstances contributes to what this pastor terms "spiritual resilience." After her time of working with the families, she said, now when bad stuff chances to happen, she doesn't think, "Oh, God must hate me." Learning from the witness of the families, she said now she accepts that chance happens. The faith of the families helps her to refocus and remember that "God is good. And there's goodness everywhere. I just need to *see* it." She said she didn't want to "over-glorify" suffering, but "it's just very clear to me that God is present in suffering." She added, "Again, I don't want to glorify suffering, but I feel God's presence very strongly when I'm with people who are suffering." It's an experience of the sacred that she finds nourishing for her own spirit so that she has the energy to continue being present with the families.

Another minister who works closely with the families interjected in this conversation, noting their similar experiences in feeling the presence of the sacred, the divine, the holy of holies. This volunteer chaplain explained, "When I've been with the families, I've wept with mothers who learned they were going to be deported the next day, or whose children were taken from them at the border during family separation, or whose child or spouse died before or during the journey. It's a holy bond and connection that surpasses all bounds, including languages, ages, ethnicities, or any of the other boundaries that we put upon it." It's a multicultural, interreligious, global, human connection with the sacred (illustration 12.1).

Illustration 12.1 *Holy and Whole* 11" × 9" graphite pencil sketch against a poured watercolor background of *Pastora Helena* and a migrant child at the Greyhound bus station in San Antonio, April 4, 2017. The child was traveling with her mother after they were released from family detention. Art © Helen T. Boursier.

The shelter coordinator immediately responded, "It's like there's always this spiritual bond between us right, but I think it's revealed in those moments of suffering in a way that feels stronger." She added, "When we're not engaging with suffering or thinking about it, like when we're distracted or worried about something else, then we don't have that spiritual bond. It's not revealed to us in that same way, or we ignore it, or maybe we're thinking about something else and not paying attention." It's in the focused moments of being intentionally present during times of suffering, when we're not distracted by anything else, that it's easier to fully sense, witness, and experience the presence of God. These sacred moments contribute to a sense of being that's holy and whole.

HOLY AND WHOLE: LIVING A CONSCIOUS LIFE

Spirituality in the borderlands comes down to *living a conscious life*, which means living with an intentionality that responds to the ethical moral call. It's a choice that prioritizes the greater good for Planet Earth and all humanity. Heidegger argues that what he terms "the *potentiality*-for-Being" is only possible when individuals live into their particular living and being in and for the world and doing so intentionally and with a conscience.[6] Rabbi Heschel recognizes this inner sense of a conscious moral call: "In spite of our pride, in spite of our acquisitiveness, we are driven by an awareness that something is asked of us." He proposes that it's through "this inner awareness that we are asked to wonder, to revere, to think and to live in a way that is compatible with the grandeur and mystery of living."[7] Of course, there's always the option to refuse to answer this sacred call to see, hear, feel, and fully experience being holy and whole. It's that freedom of choice that every human being has to respond to the grievous evils around them. As Heschel observes, "God is hiding in the world. Our task is to let the divine emerge from our deeds."[8] Spirituality in the borderlands values the precious precarity of life by valuing *all* life. Each person's experiences in the borderlands mark their life with a sense of the sacred forever after.

Blessedness and Love Divine

Whether named, claimed, or attributed to any particular religious tradition or god/God, these precious times in the borderlands are spiritually charged with a blessedness and love divine. The observations and experiences forever after make their mark on the spirits of those who come and go, bringing all who willingly walk together with the displaced families an experience of the sacred. It's this sacred time and place that make a forever mark on the inner consciousness and sense of being. It also shapes each person toward becoming their better than best self. As Rabbi Sally Priesand expresses in the *Women's Torah Commentary*, "Life is not measured by wealth or power, material possessions or fame. Life is counted in terms of goodness and growth."[9] Leaning into the holy makes life whole, but this always requires prioritizing others over self. Instead of competing against anyone else, measuring personal success against others, holy living means continually growing in the spiritual moral calling to care more and more for others and less and less for self.

Rabbi Priesand insists success means "to get ahead of ourselves, always to play a better game of life." She adds that the questions to consider include "Have we done our best? Are we continuing to grow? Are we affected more deeply today by love and beauty and joy than we were yesterday? Are we more sensitive and compassionate toward others? Have we learned to overcome our fears and accept our failures? Have we triumphed over selfishness and bitterness, cruelty and hatred? Do we count our blessings in such a way that we make our blessings count?"[10] The answers to these questions are helpful in discerning to understand what it means to embrace justice and peacemaking as spiritual practices where individuals, the community at large, and the environment are able to experience being holy and whole.

Rabbi Heschel argues that it's only when we're able to stand in awe about the unknown—trusting that what we can't know, God does—that it's possible to live into the mystery of the sacred, even when we don't really understand it. One of the keys to spirituality in the borderlands is paying attention to the holy—noticing and celebrating these sacred moments, people, places, and spaces and counting these as blessings with gratitude and joy. Spirituality in the borderlands isn't about *feeling spiritual*, as a pro bono attorney remarked earlier. Rather, the point is to choose the intentionality to be present in this broken world and to do so in such a way that your sacred presence in solidarity and accompaniment shares abundant blessing and joy with those around you so that their lives can experience what it means to be holy and whole. Spirituality in the borderlands embodies love through solidarity by being there fully and wholly, not for self but for the betterment of humanity and Planet Earth. As my Introduction to Spirituality students consistently define in their self-introduction during the first week of class, spirituality means that you have a sense and connection to something "bigger than you." That *bigger-than-you* is the sacred sense of the ultimate better-than or greater-than-us that calls each person to become their best selves.

The pastor who facilitates a shelter for displaced migrants in San Antonio said the work she does for justice and peacemaking through hospitality causes her to experience "a sense of completeness." She explained, "It's not about being perfect but about being whole, being your whole authentic self." This young pastor and mother of two added, "It's only when you're in the flow with the sacred and the divine that you can be your whole complete self with God." She emphasized, "There's no such thing as a wholeness without God," which resonates with Saint Augustine, who wrote in his *Confessions*, "Thou has made us for thyself, O Lord, and our heart is restless until it finds its rest in thee."[11] Whether named *god/God* or simply *humanity*, *Planet Earth*, and the *greater good*, working in solidarity in the borderlands nets this profound sense of peace that reinforces and reinspires the will to serve and be and do more for justice and peacemaking in the borderlands.

Staying the Course

Life in the borderlands is imperfect, but it's also a place where imperfect people are trying to live into being their best selves to make a transformative difference for justice. As Daniel Lombroso, the producer of *American Scar*, said, "As a storyteller, that's all I can try to do is to try to correct that broken narrative and help people see it in a very different way."[12] He said his hope in the borderlands and all that massive amount of work for justice that must be done rests in the "relentlessness" of the people who work for justice in the borderlands. Myles Traphagen, coordinator for Wildlands Networks' borderland program, said his encouragement amid what's otherwise "very disheartening" in the borderlands is that he's had people from all around the world reaching out to him. He explained, "There's a commonality of feeling, of sentiment, how people feel towards these things and that we know that there has to be a better way."[13] Stephania Taladrid, a contributing writer and reporter for the *New Yorker*, said, "My hope and my intention is to generate these more truthful and hopefully humane conversations around the border." She added, "And I think that what we can do, as storytellers, is amplify the voices of the people who live along the border who suffer and live through these issues day after day."[14] Again, regardless of the particular gifts or sense of calling to the borderlands, the spiritual moral call is always to be present, standing in solidarity alongside those who are working for compassion and justice. It's a spirituality that, as Kurtz and Ketchum argue, "must touch *all* of one's life or it touches *none* of one's life."[15] This call is to a spirituality of being holy and whole. It's a philosophical-spiritual-emotional-physical leaning toward holistic justice that embraces peace, liberty, and justice for all.

Reverend Fife said this orientation toward holistic well-being in the borderlands begins with setting aside fear. He said so much about the borderlands has been about fear. He emphasized, "We have been taught to be afraid." He believes the way to move beyond the fear is to become personally acquainted with people in the borderlands, to truly get to know them one on one. Once we eliminate fear and move into relationships, then it becomes possible to make the changes necessary for holistic well-being in the borderlands.

Ultimately, Life Is Short

A week before his seventy-fifth birthday, a Team Brownsville volunteer said the main point he wants people to realize "is that our lifespans are very short. And none of us are guaranteed another day on this earth. So why not spend the day that you have today and do kind things for people? Why are we spending that short little window of time that we have being angry at others, being angry with ourselves?" After all, life is short.

REORIENTATION FOR JUSTICE AND PEACE

Living, feeling, and being holy and whole is a lifestyle *reorientation* toward wholeness for all. As a GVS Samaritan expressed regarding inviting the group to be supportive of a Journey for Justice caravan that would be traveling through the area, "My hope is that members of the journey will remember their Nogales stop as one where they were met with generosity, interest, and kindness." It's a perversive sense of compassion that sees all people as being children of The God. For example, Pastor Randy Mayer of the Good Shepherd UCC in Sahuarita, Arizona, the host church for the GVS Samaritans, shared his experience when he was hiking in the desert with his wife when another hiker told them about a seriously injured and stranded migrant on October 31, 2022. Pastor Randy explained, "We rushed down and eventually found two hikers with a Guatemala man in very bad shape. The male hiker was on the ground holding the man, trying to warm him up. The woman had gone down to call the EMTs and was back with them. We helped to get him comfortable and warm. He was wet, delirious, and hypothermic. I really thought he was going to die." When they heard sirens, Pastor Randy explained they "ran down the trail to help guide them to where he was because it was significantly off the trail." He described the difficulty the paramedics had to get their rescue equipment to the injured migrant from Guatemala and then to get him safely down the mountain. Pastor Randy concluded, "It was amazingly powerful and a beautiful sight coming into the creek bed and seeing this male hiker literally on the ground comforting and holding [the injured migrant], doing everything he could to keep him alive. They were extremely compassionate." He added, "I want to live in a community with Good Samaritans who do the right thing and treat people with dignity and love—period. That is what I witnessed on Monday morning."

Shifting from *I* to *We*

Spirituality in the borderlands embraces this precarious life through compassionate action where there are no borders or boundaries or right or wrong sides. Generosity of spirit that prioritizes generosity with justice and peacemaking opens a pathway for what John Steinbeck describes in *The Grapes of Wrath* as "the beginning—from 'I' to 'we.'"[16] Becoming holy and whole is all about the universal inclusive humanity, together with Planet Earth, where we're called to live equitably and peacefully during this short, precarious life. Together, we become holy and whole: "The end of the matter; all has been heard. Fear God, and keep God's commandments, for that is the whole duty of everyone. For God will bring every deed into judgment, including every secret thing, whether good or evil" (Ecc. 12:13–14 NRSVUE). Alleluia. Amen.

NOTES

1 Chittister, *There Is a Season*, 54.
2 Chittister, *There Is a Season*, 55.
3 Cynthia D. Moe-Lobeda, *Resisting Structural Evil: Love as Ecological-Economic Vocation* (Minneapolis: Fortress Press, 2013), xviii.
4 Chittister, *There Is a Season*, 55.

5 Wendy from Honduras while at a migrant shelter in Nuevo Laredo, Mexico, during MPP, November 5, 2019.
6 Heidegger, *Being and Time*, 242.
7 Heschel, *God in Search of Man*, 112.
8 Heschel, *I Asked for Wonder*, 87.
9 Rabbi Sally J. Priesand, "Epilogue: Looking Backward and Ahead," in *The Women's Torah Commentary: New Insights from Women Rabbis on the 54 Weekly Torah Portions*, ed. Elyse Goldstein (Nashville: Jewish Lights Publishing, 2000), 408–409.
10 Priesand, "Epilogue," 408–409.
11 See Saint Augustine, *Confessions*, trans. Henry Chadwick (Oxford, UK: Oxford University Press, 1991).
12 Daniel Lombroso, "*American Scar* Post-Film Q&A," 1:10:20.
13 Myles Traphagen, "*American Scar* Post-Film Q&A," 1:18:23.
14 Stephania Taladrid, "*American Scar* Post-Film Q&A," 1:21:49.
15 Kurtz and Ketcham, *Spirituality of Imperfection*, 145.
16 Steinbeck, *Grapes of Wrath*, 152.

Bibliography

Ainsley, Julia, and Annie Rose Ramos. "Inside Tornillo: The Expanded Tent City for Migrant Children." NBC News, October 12, 2018. https://www.nbcnews.com/politics/immigration/inside-tornillo-expanded-tent-city-migrant-children-n919431.

Arendt, Hannah. *The Human Condition*. 2nd ed. Introduction by Margaret Canovan. Chicago: University of Chicago Press, 1958, 1998.

Augustine, Saint. *Confessions*. Translated by Henry Chadwick. Oxford, UK: Oxford University Press, 1991.

Baldwin, James. *The Fire Next Time*. New York: Random House, Vintage Books, 1962, 1993.

Barnes, Robert, and Ann E. Marimow. "Supreme Court Leaves in Place Title 42 Border Policy for Now." *Washington Post*, December 27, 2022. https://www.washingtonpost.com/politics/2022/12/27/title-42-supreme-court-decision/.

Beauvoir, Simone de. *The Ethics of Ambiguity*. New York: Open Road Integrated Media, 1947, 2018.

―――. *The Second Sex*. Introduction by Judith Thurman. Translated by Constance Borde and Sheila Malovany-Chevallier. New York: Vintage Books, Random House, 1949, 2009.

Ben Sira. "Alphabet of Ben Sira 78: Lilith." Jewish Women's Archive, 2022. https://jwa.org/node/23210.

Bloechl, Jeffrey, ed. *The Face of the Other and the Trace of God: Essays on the Philosophy of Emmanuel Levinas*. New York: Fordham University Press, 2000.

Bonhoeffer, Dietrich. *Ethics*. Vol. 6 of *Dietrich Bonhoeffer Works*. Edited by Clifford J. Green. Translated by Reinhard Krauss, Charles C. West, and Douglas W. Stott. Minneapolis: Fortress Press, 1941, 2005.

―――. *Letters and Papers from Prison*. Enlarged ed. Edited by Eberhard Bethge. New York: Simon and Schuster, 1953, 1997.

Bosque, Melissa del. @MelissaLaLinea. Twitter, 11:41 a.m. November 30, 2022. https://twitter.com/MelissaLaLinea/status/1598009218417983490.

―――. "Arizona Governor Builds Border Wall of Shipping Crates in Final Days of Office." *Guardian*, December 11, 2022. https://www.theguardian.com/us-news/2022/dec/11/arizona-governor-border-wall-shipping-containers.

Boursier, Helen T. *Arts as Witness: A Practical Theology of Arts-Based Research*. Lanham, MD: Lexington Books, 2021.

―――. *Desperately Seeking Asylum: Testimonies of Trauma, Courage, and Love*. Lanham, MD: Rowman and Littlefield, 2019.

———. *The Ethics of Hospitality: An Interfaith Response to US Immigration Policies.* Lanham, MD: Lexington Books, 2019.

———. "Faithful Doxology: The Church's Allyship with Immigrants Seeking Asylum." *International Bulletin of Mission Journal* 41, no. 2 (April 2017): 170–177.

———. "The Necessity of Social Just-Ness as Ecclesial Praxis in a Postmodern Context." *Theology Today* 72, no. 1 (April 2015): 84–99.

———. "The Power of Hope: Art inside an Immigrant Family Detention Center." *The Arts in Religious and Theological Studies Journal* 29, no. 2 (May 2018): 50–67.

———. *Willful Ignorance: Overcoming the Limitations of (Christian) Love for Refugees Seeking Asylum.* Lanham, MD: Lexington Books, 2022.

Boursier, Helen T., ed. *The Rowman and Littlefield Handbook of Women's Studies in Religion.* Lanham, MD: Rowman and Littlefield, 2021.

Brockell, Gillian, and Jodie Tillman. "'Reverse Freedom Rides': An Echo of Martha's Vineyard Migrant Flights 60 Years Ago." *Washington Post*, September 16, 2022. https://www.washingtonpost.com/history/2022/09/16/reverse-freedom-rides-marthas-vineyard-desantis/.

Brown, William P. *Ecclesiastes: Interpretation A Bible Commentary for Teaching and Preaching.* Louisville, KY: John Knox Press, 2000.

Burge, Ryan P. *The Nones: Where They Came From, Who They Are, and Where They Are Going.* Minneapolis: Fortress Press, 2021.

Butler, Judith. *Undoing Gender.* New York: Routledge, 2004.

Capps, Donald. *The Poet's Gift: Toward the Renewal of Pastoral Care.* Louisville, KY: Westminster John Knox Press, 1993.

Chittister, Joan. *There Is a Season.* Art by John August Swanson. Maryknoll, NY: Orbis Books, 1989.

Chittister, Joan, and Rowan Williams. *Uncommon Gratitude: Alleluia for All That Is.* Collegeville, MN: Liturgical Press, 2010.

Chiu, Allyson. "Climate Solutions: People Don't Really Talk about Climate Change: Here's How to Start." *Washington Post*, September 16, 2022. https://wwww.washingtonpost.com/climate-solutions/2022/09/16/climate-change-conversation-action/?utm_campaign=wp_post_most&utm_medium=email&utm_source=newsletter&wpisrc=nl_most&carta-url=https%3A%2F%2Fs2.washingtonpost.com%2Fcar-ln-tr%2F37f07f7%2F632497aef3d9003c58db65b2%2F601b21b3ae7e8a31ba652c5f%2F31%2F72%2F632497aef3d9003c58db65b2&wp_cu=c69473bc37b1c5a5d5387d9454883ddd%7CBA76FEAA9C964D77E0530100007F5803.

Christiansen, Andrew. "Santa Cruz County Sheriff Threatening Action against People Working on Shipping Container Border Wall." *KGUN 9 News*, December 5, 2022. https://www.kgun9.com/news/local-news/santa-cruz-county-sheriff-threatening-action-against-people-working-on-shipping-container-border-wall.

Cone, James H. *The Spirituals and the Blues.* Maryknoll, NY: Orbis Books, 1972, 1991.

Copan, Paul, and Chad Meister, eds. *Philosophy of Religion: Classic and Contemporary Issues.* Malden, MA: Blackwell Publishing Ltd., 2008.

Crenshaw, James L. *Old Testament Wisdom: An Introduction.* Atlanta: John Knox Press, 1981.

De La Torre, Miguel A. *Trails of Hope and Terror: Testimonies of Migration.* Maryknoll, NY: Orbis Books, 2009.

De La Torre, Vincent. *Trails of Hope and Terror: The Movie.* Centennial, CO: V1 Educational Media, Inc., 2018. https://www.trailsofhopeandterrorthemovie.com/about.html.

Diamant, Anita. Foreword to *New Jewish Feminism: Probing the Past, Forging the Future*. Edited by Rabbi Elyse Goldstein. Nashville: Jewish Lights Publishing, 2009.
The Ed Sullivan Show. "The Byrds' 'Turn! Turn! Turn! On the Ed Sullivan Show.'" December 12, 1965. YouTube, August 16, 2021. https://www.youtube.com/watch?v=W3xgcmIS3YU.
Encyclopedia Britannica. "Howard Hughes." Accessed December 27, 2022. https://www.britannica.com/biography/Howard-Hughes.
Foucault, Michel. *Speaking the Truth about Oneself: Lectures at Victoria University, Toronto, 1982*. Edited by Henri-Paul Fruchaud and Daniele Lorenzini. [English version established by Daniel Louis Wyche.] Chicago: The University of Chicago Press, 2021.
Fox, Michael V. *A Time to Tear Down and a Time to Build Up: A Rereading of Ecclesiastes*. Grand Rapids, MI: William B. Eerdmans Publishing, 1999.
Frankl, Viktor, E. *Man's Search for Meaning*. Foreword by Harold S. Kushner. Boston: Beacon Press, 1959, 2006.
Fricker, Miranda. *Epistemic Injustice: Power and the Ethics of Knowing*. Oxford, UK: Oxford University Press, 2007.
Gadamer, Hans-Georg. *Truth and Method*. 2nd ed. Translation revised by Joel Weinsheimer and Donald G. Marshall. New York: Continuum, 1975, 1989.
Gibson, David. *Living Life Backward: How Ecclesiastes Teaches Us to Live in Light of the End*. Wheaton, IL: Crossway, 2017.
Goldstein, Elyse, ed. *New Jewish Feminism: Probing the Past, Forging the Future*. Foreword by Anita Diamant. Nashville: Jewish Lights Publishing, 2009.
———. *The Women's Torah Commentary: New Insights from Women Rabbis on the 54 Weekly Torah Portions*. Nashville: Jewish Lights Publishing, 2000.
Gottlieb, Roger S. *A Spirituality of Resistance: Finding a Peaceful Heart and Protecting the Earth*. Lanham, MD: Rowman and Littlefield, 2003.
Gray, Noah. "More Migrants Dropped Off Outside Vice President's Home in Freezing Weather on Christmas Eve." CNN, December 26, 2022. https://www.cnn.com/2022/12/24/politics/migrants-dropped-off-vice-president-christmas-eve/index.html.
Green Valley-Sahuarita Samaritans. https://www.gvs-samaritans.org/.
Guthrie, Shirley C. *Christian Doctrine*. Rev. ed. Louisville, KY: Westminster John Knox Press, 1994.
Haight, Roger. *Spiritual and Religious: Explorations for Seekers*. Maryknoll, NY: Orbis Books, 2016.
Harris, Maria. *Dance of the Spirit: The Seven Steps of Women's Spirituality*. New York: Bantam Books, 1989, 1991.
Haslanger, Sally. *Resisting Reality: Social Construction and Social Critique*. Oxford, UK: Oxford University Press, 2012.
Hayes, Diana L. *No Crystal Stair: Womanist Spirituality*. Maryknoll, NY: Orbis Books, 2016.
Healy, Jack. "Arizona Agrees to Dismantle Border Wall Made from Cargo Containers." *New York Times*, December 21, 2022. https://www.nytimes.com/2022/12/21/us/arizona-border-shipping-containers.html#:~:text=Dec.%2021%2C%202022%20PHOENIX%20%E2%80%94%20Gov.%20Doug%20Ducey,the%20Biden%20administration%20against%20Mr.%20Ducey%2C%20a%20Republican.
Hector, Wayne Anthony, and Stephen Paul Robson, songwriters. "Feels Like Today." Sung by Rascal Flatts. Lyric Street Records, 2004.

BIBLIOGRAPHY

Heidegger, Martin. *Being and Time*. Translated by John Macquarrie and Edward Robinson. Foreword by Taylor Carman. New York: Harper and Row, 1962, 2008.

Hemmings, Clare. *Why Stories Matter: The Political Grammar of Feminist Theory*. Durham, NC: Duke University Press, 2011.

Heschel, Abraham Joshua. *God in Search of Man: A Philosophy of Judaism*. New York: Farrar, Straus and Giroux, 1955.

———. *I Asked for Wonder: A Spiritual Anthology*. Edited by Samuel H. Dresner. New York: Crossroads, 1983, 2002.

Herman, Judith. *Trauma and Recovery: The Aftermath of Violence from Domestic Abuse to Political Terror*. New York: Perseus Books, 1992, 2015.

Irshai, Ronit. "'And I Find a Wife More Bitter Than Death' (Eccl. 7:26): Feminist Hermeneutics, Women Midrashim, and the Boundaries of Acceptance in Modern Orthodox Judaism." *Journal of Feminist Studies in Religion* 33, no. 1 (Spring 2017): 69–86.

It's Going Down. "Protests Along Arizona Border Halts Construction of Governor's Wall of Shipping Containers." December 6, 2022. https://itsgoingdown.org/protests-halt-contruction-shipping-container-wall/.

Kaur, Valarie. *See No Stranger: A Memoir and Manifesto of Revolutionary Love*. New York: Random House, 2020.

Kierkegaard, Søren. *Purity of Heart Is to Will One Thing: Spiritual Preparation for the Office of Confession*. Translated by Douglas V. Steere. New York: Harper and Row Publishers, 1956.

King, Martin Luther, Jr. *Strength to Love*. Philadelphia: Fortress Press, 1963.

Knight, Amy. "The Borderlands Forum: Humanitarian Aid in the Borderlands." Border Community Alliance, June 22, 2022. https://vimeo.com/726106679.

Kurtz, Ernest, and Katherine Ketcham. *The Spirituality of Imperfection: Storytelling and the Search for Meaning*. New York: Bantam Books, 1992.

L'Engle, Madeleine. *And It Was Good: Reflections on Beginnings*. Book One in the Genesis Trilogy. Foreword by Rachel Held Evans. New York: Convergent, 1983, 2017.

———. *The Rock That Is Higher: Story as Truth*. Wheaton, IL: Harold Shaw Publishers, 1993.

———. *A Stone for a Pillow: Journeys with Jacob*. Book Two in the Genesis Trilogy. Foreword by Rachel Held Evans. New York: Convergent, 1986, 2017.

———. *Sold into Egypt: Journeys into Human Being*. Book Three in the Genesis Trilogy. Foreword by Rachel Held Evans. New York: Convergent, 1989, 2017.

Loader, J. A. *Ecclesiastes: A Practical Commentary*. Translated by John Vriend. Grand Rapids, MI: William B. Eerdmans Publishing Company, 1986.

Loder, James E. *The Transforming Moment*. 2nd ed. Colorado Springs, CO: Helmers and Howard, 1989.

Lombrosco, Daniel. "American Scar: The Environmental Tragedy of the Border Wall." *New Yorker* Documentary. YouTube, April 30, 2022. https://www.youtube.com/watch?v=Cx71C4iguuk&t=13s.

Lorde, Audre. *The Cancer Journals*. Foreword by Tracy K. Smith. New York: Penguin Books, Random House, 1980, 2020.

———. *Sister Outsider: Essays and Speeches by Audre Lorde*. Berkley: Crossing Press, 1984, 2007.

Mann, William E. "The Epistemology of Religious Experience." In *Philosophy of Religion: Classic and Contemporary Issues*. Edited by Paul Copan and Chad Meister, 9–22. Malden, MA: Blackwell Publishing, 2008.

Manne, Kate. *Down Girl: The Logic of Misogyny*. Oxford, UK: Oxford University Press, 2018.
Marshall, Garry, dir. *Pretty Woman*. Burbank, CA: Buena Vista Home Video, 1990.
Miller, Douglas B. *Symbol and Rhetoric in Ecclesiastes: The Place of* Hebel *in Qohelet's Work*. Atlanta: Society of Biblical Literature, 2002.
Moe-Lobeda, Cynthia D. *Resisting Structural Evil: Love as Ecological-Economic Vocation*. Minneapolis: Fortress Press, 2013.
Moltmann, Jürgen. *In the End—The Beginning: The Life of Hope*. Translated by Margaret Kohl. Minneapolis: Fortress Press, 2004.
Montoya-Galvez, Camilo. "The Facts about the Legal Battle over Title 42 and What Its End Could Mean for US Border Policy." CBS News, January 2, 2023. https://www.cbsnews.com/news/title-42-what-its-end-could-mean-us-immigration-border-policy/.
Newton, Caleb. "Protesters Shut Down Illegal Border Wall Construction by GOP Governor." Bipartisan Report, December 11, 2022. https://bipartisanreport.com/2022/12/11/protesters-shut-down-illegal-border-wall-construction-by-gop-governor/.
Niebuhr, Reinhold. *Moral Man and Immoral Society: A Study in Ethics and Politics*. Introduction by Langdon B. Gilkey. Louisville, KY: Westminster John Knox Press, 1932, 2001.
Nouwen, Henri J. M. *Our Greatest Gift: A Meditation on Dying and Caring*. San Francisco: HarperCollins, 1995.
Olinga, Luc. "FTX Collapse: Sam Bankman-Fried Will Stand Trial in October." MSN, January 4, 2023. https://www.msn.com/en-us/money/markets/ftx-collapse-sam-bankman-fried-will-stand-trial-in-october/ar-AA15Xrm8.
Peck, Scott M. *People of the Lie: The Hope for Healing Human Evil*. New York: Simon and Schuster, 1983.
Plaskow, Judith. *The Coming of Lilith: Essays on Feminism, Judaism, and Sexual Ethics, 1972–2003*, edited with Donna Berman. Boston: Beacon Press, 2005.
―――. *Standing Again at Sinai: Judaism from a Feminist Perspective*. San Francisco: Harper Collins, 1990.
Poling, James Newton. *Deliver Us from Evil: Resisting Racial and Gender Oppression*. Minneapolis: Fortress Press, 1996.
Putnam, Rober T. *Bowling Alone: The Collapse and Revival of American Community*. New York: Simon & Schuster, 2009.
Putt, B. Keith, ed. *Gazing through a Prism Darkly: Reflections on Merold Westphal's Hermeneutical Epistemology*. Perspectives in Continental Philosophy. New York: Fordham University Press, 2009.
Relph, Edward. *Place and Placelessness*. London: Pion Limited, 1976.
Ricœur, Paul. *Figuring the Sacred: Religion, Narrative, and Imagination*. Minneapolis: Augsburg Fortress Press, 1995.
Rio Valley Relief Project. "The Resilience of the Human Spirit." (Blog). January 4, 2020. https://www.riovalleyreliefproject.org/post/the-resilience-of-the-human-spirit.
Rolheiser, Ronald. *The Holy Longing: The Search for a Christian Spirituality*. 15th anniv. ed. New York: Random House, 1998, 2019.
Rosenzweig-Ziff, Dan, Maria Sacchetti, Molly Hennessy-Fiske, Joanna Slater, Hannah Knowles, and Ellen Francis. "DeSantis Move to Fly Migrants to Mass. Stokes Confusion, Outrage from Critics." *Washington Post*, September 15, 2022. https://www.washingtonpost.com/nation/2022/09/15/marthas-vineyard-desantis-migrants-venezuela/.

Ruether, Rosemary Radford. *Sexism and God-Talk: Toward a Feminist Theology*. Boston: Beacon Press, 1983, 1993.

Schmidt, Frederick W., Jr. *When Suffering Persists*. Harrisburg, PA: Morehouse Publishing, 2001.

Schreiner, Olive. *A Track to the Water's Edge: The Olive Schreiner Reader*. Edited by Howard Thurman. New York: Harper and Row, 1973.

Seow, Choon-Leong. *Ecclesiastes: A New Translation with Introduction and Commentary*. Vol. 18C of The Anchor Bible. New York: Doubleday, 1977.

Sky Island Alliance. "American Scar Post-Film Q&A." YouTube, May 5, 2022. https://www.youtube.com/watch?v=p9xcrXMbd4M&t=1s.

Sobrino, Jon. *Jesus the Liberator: A Historical-Theological Reading of Jesus of Nazareth*. Maryknoll, NY: Orbis Books, 1993.

⸻. *The Principle of Mercy: Taking the Crucified People from the Cross*. Maryknoll, NY: Orbis Books, 1994.

Soelle, Dorothee. *Death by Bread Alone: Texts and Reflections on Religious Experience*. Translated by David L. Scheidt. Philadelphia: Fortress Press, 1978.

⸻. *The Mystery of Death*. Minneapolis: Fortress Press, 2007.

Spretnak, Charlene, ed. *The Politics of Women's Spirituality: Essays on the Rise of Spiritual Power within the Feminist Movement*. Garden City, NY: Anchor Books, 1982.

Steinbeck, John. *The Grapes of Wrath*. New York: Penguin Books, 1939.

Tillich, Paul. *The Courage to Be*. New Haven, CT: Yale University Press, 1952.

⸻. *Dynamics of Faith*. New York: Harper, 1957; First Perennial Classics 2001.

Tirosh-Samuelson, Hava, and Aaron W. Hughes, eds. *Judith Plaskow: Feminism, Theology, and Justice*. Leiden, the Netherlands: Brill, 2014.

Tracey, Caroline. "'The Numbers Kept Going': The Forensic Office Identifying Human Remains at the Border." *Guardian*, September 19, 2022. https://www.theguardian.com/world/2022/sep/19/arizona-migrants-remains-border-forensics?CMP=Share_iOSApp_Other.

Tweed, Thomas A. *Crossing and Dwelling: A Theory of Religion*. Cambridge, MA: Harvard University Press, 2006.

US Citizenship and Immigration Services. "Questions and Answers: Credible Fear Screening." May 31, 2022. https://www.uscis.gov/humanitarian/refugees-and-asylum/asylum/questions-and-answers-credible-fear-screening.

Van Ham, Lane. *A Common Humanity: Ritual, Religion, and Immigrant Advocacy in Tucson, Arizona*. Tucson, AZ: University of Arizona Press, 2011.

von Wartenberg-Potter, Bishop Baerbel. "Funeral Sermon." In *The Theology of Dorothee Soelle*, edited by Sarah K. Pinnock, x–xi. Harrisburg, PA: Trinity Press International; Continuum, 2003.

Walker, Alice. *In Search of Our Mothers' Gardens*. New York: Houghton Mifflin Harcourt Publishing Company, 1967, 1983.

Weber, Peter. "439 Texas Churches Split from United Methodist Church as Slow-motion Schism Continues." MSN News, December 5, 2022. https://www.msn.com/en-us/news/us/439-texas-churches-split-from-united-methodist-church-as-slow-motion-schism-continues/ar-AA14Vqws.

Weil, Simone. *Gravity and Grace*. London: Routledge, 1947, 1999.

⸻. *Love in the Void: Where God Finds Us*. Edited by Laurie Gagne. Walden, NY: Plough Publishing, 2018.

Westphal, Merold. *Overcoming Onto-Theology: Toward a Postmodern Christian Faith*. New York: Fordham University Press, 2001.

———. *Whose Community? Which Interpretation?: Philosophical Hermeneutics for the Church*. Grand Rapids, MI: Baker Academic, 2009.

Wiesel, Elie. "Longing for Home." In *The Longing for Home*. Edited by Leroy S. Rounder, 17–29. Notre Dame, IN: University of Notre Dame Press, 1996.

———. "The Perils of Indifference." YouTube, April 12, 1999. https://www.youtube.com/watch?v=JpXmRiGst4k.

Wolfe, Lisa Michele. *Qoheleth (Ecclesiastes)*, Wisdom Commentary. Collegeville, MN: Order of Saint Benedict, 2020.

Wright, N. T. *Evil and the Justice of God*. Downers Grove, IL: InterVarsity Press, 2006.

Wyschogrod, Edith. "Remaining Faithful: Postmodern Claims, Christian Messages." In *Gazing through a Prism Darkly: Reflections on Merold Westphal's Hermeneutical Epistemology*, Perspectives in Continental Philosophy. Edited by B. Keith Putt, 74–85. New York: Fordham University Press, 2009.

Zamora, Javier. *Solito: A Memoir*. London: Hogarth, 2022.

Zemeckis, Robert, dir. *Back to the Future*. Universal City, CA: MCA Home Video, 1985.

Index

Page references for illustrations are italicized.

acceptance: blessings, 194; boundaries of, 31; chance, 228; death, 191; displaced migrants, 15, 178, 184; fear, 150, 231; gain, 167; imperfection, 75; passive, 133–34; pessimism, 9; pursuit of justice, 121; time/timing, 104, 112, 121
accompany/accompaniment, 136–37, 147, 152, 163, 204, 231
accountability: Christian church, 36–37; individuals, 36, 129; state, 4, 39, 147
American dream, 66, 67, 80, 82, 94
American drive, 76
American Scar: The Environmental Tragedy of the Border Wall (Lombroso), 70, 232
And It Was Good: Reflections on Beginnings (L'Engle), 73
anger/angry: against church, 12; against volunteers, 162, 233; politics, 14; righteous, 76; value for advocacy, 78; value in resistance, 78. *See also* Kaur, Valerie
anxiety: and dying/death, 153; exile, 54; fear, 149, 150–51, 170, 177; of migrants, 54, 113, 156; Paul Tillich, 157; property ownership, 66; striving, 67; of volunteers, 181
apathy, 10, 69, 79. *See also* indifference
Arendt, Hannah, 86, 164, 138, 213
Arizona, 70–71, *72*, *88*, 89, 118, 137. *See also* Samaritans, Green Valley-Sahuarita (GVS); Sonoran Desert
Art Inside Karnes, *52*, *58*, 63, 113, 126, 176–78, 193–94, 196–99

asylum seekers/migrants (the families): children, *125*; families, *28*, 32, *52*, 94; injustice against, 11, 87, 96, 97, 132, 135, 139, *210*, 226; racism, 37, 121; suffering, 126, 157, *154*; testimony, 109. *See also* choice; credible fear; Migrant Protection Protocols (MPP)
Augustine, Saint, 232
Auschwitz, 128, 149
awareness, 7, 105, 230

bad business: challenging, 62, 147–48; Ecclesiastes, 45–46, 48, 137; environmental, 69; hiddenness, 47–48; indifference, 50; of migrants, 129; paradox, 81; suffering, 126; time, 120–21; US complicity, 74. *See also* grievous evil; heavy burden; indifference
"bad parents," 130–31, 134
Beauty, 41, 113, 216, 231
Beauvoir, Simone de, 31, 45, 75, 94, 131, 168, 193, 197
belief(s): Ecclesiastes, 190; future, 115; God's care/plan, 37, 59, 93, 99, 113, 172; Hebraic, 169; religious, 97, 138–39, 207; volunteers' awe of, 183. *See also* disbelief
Being and Time (Heidegger), 38, 106
better life. *See* safe life (better life as)
better than: accompaniment, 124; Ecclesiastes, 123–24, 135; gender concerns, 124; migrants, 124, 126–27, 135; volunteers, 147, 281. *See also* choice; risk
Biding Our Time, *210*

INDEX

Big Picture of Life, 105, 115, 204
blessed, 142, 175, 176, 215, 220, 230–31
blessing, 75, 120, 182, 189–90, 192–93, 194, 204, 208, 218–19, 231. *See also* joy
Bloechl, Jeffrey, 174
Bonhoeffer, Dietrich: adversaries, 126; freedom, 216; homesickness, 57; kindness, 170; "religionless time," 7; "responsible response," 116; sorrow and joy, 192; time, 114–15
Bosque, Melissa del, 71, *72*
Boursier, Helen T., as *Pastora Helena*, 179, 196, *229*
Bowling Alone: The Collapse and Revival of American Community (Putnam), 5
Brownsville, Texas, 117–18. *See also* Team Brownsville
Burge, Ryan P., 5–6
Butler, Judith, 32

Camping Alongside the Rio Grande, 154
Cape Cod, Massachusetts, 4, 56
carpe diem (seize the day), 190, 208
cartel (Mexico), 90, 92, 95, 98, 111, 118, 124, 130, 135, 163
"cast your bread," 146
Chance/chance: big C (death), 67, 88, 90, 99; little c, 90–91, 99. *See also* death/dying; risk; time
"chasing after wind," 209
children, unaccompanied, 14, 116, 119, 139–40, 141, 152, 155, 220
Chittister, Joan, 7, 79, 115, 120, 121, 127, 193, 211, 213, 215–16, 226–27
choice: "bad choices," 50, 139; better than, 123–24; death, 153, 212, 215; faith, 133; freedom, 127–29; gain, 170; joy, 190, 194, 199; legacy, 217, 230; migration, 17, 59, 82, 125–26, 130–31; moral choice, 128–29; *non*choice, 127–27, 139–40, 141; personal agency, 17, 47, 55, 201, 211; *Sophie's Choice* (Streep), 128; spirituality, 40, 146, 216; trauma, 131–32; US Immigration, 135; volunteers, 135–39, 147–48, 164; women and girls, 133–34. *See also* better than; death/dying

Christian church, 7–8
clergy/religious leaders, 14, 36, 56, 121
Clinging to Life, xvii
Clinton, President Bill, 51–52
cognitive dissonance, 32
commonality, 35, 81, 107, 232
community: beloved, 16; benefit, 184–85, 202, 234; declining role, 5; global, 4, 7, 10, 75, 217; Henri Nouwen, 191; Joan Chittister, 226; Jon Sobrino, 81; Robert Putnam, 5; role, 37; spirituality, 4
compassion: benefit, 6; of God, 35; lack of, 152; lesson, 186; love, 178, 219; response, 4, 117, 154, 161, 171, 212; spirituality, 47, 79–81, 128, 234; volunteers, 11, 14–16, 35–37, 39, 76, 214–15
confirmation of call, 179, 208. *See also* gain
context: affluence, 21–22, 192; borderlands, 141; differentials, 37; of displaced families, 32, 65, 109–10, 132; Ecclesiastes, 209; ecojustice, 77; grievous evils, 48; justice, 47; oppressed, 25, 27; patristic, 21; religious, 38; suffering, 97; women, 131. *See also* postmodern/postmodernity
contradiction, 74. *See also* Weil, Simone
coronavirus. *See* COVID-19 pandemic
courage: chance, 157; confidence, 148; Diana L. Hayes, 93; faith, 163; fear, 153; migrants, 146, 157–59, 196; Paul Tillich, 150, 157–58; risk-taking, 147; spirituality, 159–60; volunteers, 162–63. *See also* risk
COVID-19 pandemic, 134, 185
credible fear, 62, 98, 111, 156–59, 177
Crenshaw, James, 9–10
culture/cultural, 17, 54, 80, 131n 228
cynicism: antidote, 14–16, 76, 98; Ecclesiastes, 1–2, 8; political, 14; postmodernity, 4–5; Rabbi Abraham Heschel, 9–10; religious disaffiliation,

INDEX

5, 7; spirituality, 10, 16–17; volunteers, 10–11, 17. *See also* postmodern/postmodernity

death/dying: Audre Lorde, 215; Big C, 213; Big Death, 213; David Gibson, 215; Dietrich Bonhoeffer, 216; Dorothee Soelle, 10, 218; early, 126, 128, 131, 133; Ecclesiastes, 107; fear, 149; femicide, 156; final gift, 211; finitude, 217; Great Equalizer, 107; Henri Nouwen, 191; James Baldwin, 216–17; James Loder, 211–12; Joan Chittister, 211, 213, 215, 216; Jürgen Moltmann, 218; legacy, 211, 218, 219; "little deaths/dyings" (Chittister), 213; Martin Heidegger, 107; Michel de Montaigne, 212; Michel Foucault, 211; Paul Ricœur, 155; Paul Tillich, 150; perspective, 136; Psalm 23:4, 114, 150; reality, 153; Ronald Rolheiser, 213; spirituality, 2, 86, 106–9, 216; threats, 110, 125; time, 106; Viktor Frankl, 115; violence, 133; void, 211. *See also* Chance/chance; legacy; risk; time

"death by bread alone" (Soelle), 76–77

"*desconocido*" ("unknown"), 49

dehumanization, 39. *See also* racism

deport/deportation: Central Americans, 62; consequences, 97; faith despite, 99; fear, 112, 127; hope after, 155, 193; time, 113

detachment, 136

determinism, divine, 106

Diamant, Anita, xxi

dichotomy, xxv

difference, fear of, 3, 37, 78, 123, 138. *See also* indifference

dignity, human: Alice Walker, 73; dying/death, 49, 171; migrants, 140, 182, 234; women and girls, 26–27, 128–29

disaffiliated (with religion), 5, 14, 139, 140. *See also* nones (Burge)

disbelief, 80, 114

discontent: bad business, 82; environmental abuse, 69–70, 74–75; immigration injustice, 40, 52; moral rage, 79; spiritual, 69, 80; striving, 65, 66, 68, 75, 78, 81, 191, 208

Disengaged, 108

(dis)order, 22

displaced persons, 54

dissent: definition, 24, 25, 120; Ecclesiastes, 25, 86; environmentalists, 76; examples, 38–39, 139; to gender injustice, 25–26, 27, 30, 33; James Loder, 25; midrash, 31–32; motivation for, 66; patriarchy, 30; physical, 32, 33; racism, 24, 25; religion, 7; religious silence, 36–37; spirituality of, 22–23, 32, 34, 40–41, 131, 139, 141, 176; suffering, 17, 32; wisdom of, 86, 120; against violence, 34; voice of conscience, 37; volunteers, 35–36. *See also* spirituality; wisdom

"divine rage" (Kaur), 78–79

domestic violence. *See* femicide; rape and sexual assault

Down Girl: The Logic of Misogyny (Manne), 27

drugs, 33, 70, 94, 135

Ducey, Doug, 72, 118

ecojustice, 68, 73–74, 77, 118, 121, 148, 217, 227

economic injustice, 69–70

economic migrant, 139

El Salvador: migrant testimonies, 33, 58, 60, 61, 88, 126, 133, 134, 152, 158; violence in, 33, 49, 58, 88, 133, 136

"enduring memory" (Brown), 207

environmentalists, 65, 68, 72, 75–76, 79, 80, 120, 124, 221, 228

Epistemic Injustice: Power and the Ethics of Knowing (Fricker), 46

ethics, 109, 129

Ethics of Ambiguity (de Beauvoir), 45, 94, 168

"Everything is vanity," 45

INDEX

evil: bad business, 46, 48, 49; catalyst for migration, 130, 132; denial, 48, 50; Ecclesiastes, 48–49, 68; Elie Wiesel, 51; Global North complicity, 48; grievous, 46–47, 74, 75, 80, 81–82; hiddenness, 47; human factor, 47–48; Jon Sobrino, 48; midrash, 111–12; migrants experience, 49–50, 56, 81–82; moral, 46–47; natural, 46–47; N. T. Wright, 50; paradox, 46; Paul Ricœur, 46; placelessness, 54; Shirley Guthrie, 48; spirituality refutes, 66; state inflicted, 117; time, 112–13. *See also* Chance/chance; choice; indifference; spirituality; time/timing

exodus, 6, 7, 92, 109

faith: action, 138–39; hope, 115; leaning into, 133; migration, 152, 158; migrant, 113–14, 127, 128, 173, 175, 178; Paul Tillich, 157–58; Reverend John Fife, 160–61, 183; risk-taking, 159; Søren Kierkegaard, 212; spiritual resilience, 228; Viktor Frankl, 115; volunteers, 160–61, 175–76, 181, 196, 222

family (migrant): commitment, 111, 159, 170, 176–77; gangs extort, 124; *The Grapes of Wrath* (Steinbeck), 53; Martin Luther King Jr., 40; migration, 93, *108*; sponsors, 56; suffering, 58–59, *125*, 126, *210*; traveling separately, 148–49, 195; traveling together, 113, 130, 195, *200*; volunteers host, 171. *See also* "bad parents;" family detention (for profit)

family detention (for-profit): asylum seekers, 110, 112, 113–14, 116; children, *13*, 97, 172, 179, *229*; for-profit, 116; GEO Karnes, 116, 140, 158, 179; grievous evil, 113, 152; suffering, 158; women and children, 61, 110, 112–13

family separation, 36, 49, 113, 119, 126, 229. *See also* family detention (for profit)

fancy first (nations), 21, 62, 66, 68, 191

fear(s): antidote, 212, 233; versus anxiety, 150–51; Audre Lorde, 150; courage, 157–58; credible fear, 156–57, 177; death, 77, 94, 97, 150, 153; Dorothee Soelle, 10, 77; failing asylum interview, 98, 112; future, 115; migrants, 94, 110, 149; Paul Tillich, 150; Psalm 23, 150; Rabbi Joshua Heschel, 105; Reverend John Fife, 233; risk, 149–50, 155; State-of-Mind (Heidegger), 151–52; women and girls, 32, 133–32, 152–53. *See also* risk

femicide, 46, 133–34, 156

Flores Settlement Agreement, 119, 140, 149

Fife, Reverend John, 161, 183–84, 187n24, 233

Figuring the Sacred: Religion, Narrative, and Imagination (Ricœur), 154

finitude: borderlands, 86; courage, 157; death, 90; embracing, 90; humans, 10, 148; humility, 216; James Baldwin, 216; of life, 217; Martin Heidegger, 107–8, 217; priorities, 216–17; spirituality of, 2, 85, 106, 216; temporality, 217; time, 106–8. *See also* time/timing

Flores Settlement Agreement, 119, 140, 147

Foucault, Michel, 211

Frankl, Viktor, 96, 115, 149, 194, 195–96

freedom: choice, 47, 55, 164, 199, 230; Dietrich Bonhoeffer, 216; Donald Capps, 127; future, 115; from grievous evils, 121; life, 94; Madeline L'Engle, 73; personal agency, 127; trusting God, 190; Viktor Frankl, 149, 194; of volunteers, 135. *See also* choice

Fricker, Miranda, 46

futility, 1, 60, 62, 66, 81, 208, 225

futility factor, xxvii

Gadamer, Hans-George, 3

gain: Big Gain, 170, 175, 178, 184; borderlands, 168–69; compassion, 178; dignity, 171, 182; Ecclesiastes, 167; empathy, 182; entrance to United States, 113, 132; faith, 114; financial,

66; freedom, 127; gift, 169; gratitude, 169–70; "greater gain," 185–86; holy, 175; inner voice, 180; intangible, 174, 177–78; legal status, 61; meaningfulness, 80, 147, 157; mutual, 178, 184–85; safety, 82; self-actualization, 179; selfhood, 181–82; spirituality of dissent, 176–77; transcendence, 178; wisdom, 23; *yitron*, 167; volunteers, 138, 171–73, 174–75, 183–84. *See also* joy; legacy; spirituality; striving

Gateway International Bridge (Brownsville, Texas), 117

generous/generosity: legacy, 210, 214; migrants, 177, 182; spirit, 148, 180, 193–94, 234; volunteers, 55, 76, 146–47, 233

Gibson, David, 215

Global North, 2, 21, 47–49, 54, 70, 127, 191–92

Global South, 47–49, 54, 69

God: as Compass, 16–17, 34; confidence in, 17, 23, 61, 62, 93, 128, 130, 134, 179, 228; in control, 225, 228; and creation, 37, 73; Diana L. Hayes, 37, 93; Dietrich Bonhoeffer, 115; Ecclesiastes, 8, 21, 105, 148, 189, 194, 197, 209, 234; fear of, 234; glory to, 227; gratitude to, 17, 94, 97, 98, 152, 169–70, 177, 228; human dignity and, 233; Joan Chittister, 7; Judith Plaskow, 95; justice of, 23–24, 46; justness of, 23; is love, 98, 152, 176; migrant testimony about, 33, 34, 55–56, 58–59, 60, 61, 110–11, 127, 127, 152–55, 159–60; moral order, 22; as mystery, 9; Paul Tillich, 157–58; present in suffering, 228; Psalm 23, 150; Rabbi Joshua Heschel, 2, 9, 38, 99, 230, 231; Simone Weil, 15; Søren Kierkegaard, 75, 212; The God, 7; timing, 24, 103, 106; volunteers' view of, 117, 140. *See also* death; finitude; joy; spirituality; time

God in Search of Man: A Philosophy of Judaism (Heschel), 99

God is, xxiii, xxiv, 8–9, 17, 190, 225

God still is, 8, 17, 195

God Is Our Compass, 17

good: action, 86; children, 129; Ecclesiastes, 148, 208; God, 228; greater [good], xix, 75, 78, 215–16, 223, 232; life, 174, 227; migrant remembers, 58–59; people, 25, 45; respectful, 129; versus evil, 51; wisdom affirms, 23. *See also* better than; Chance/chance

"good life," xxv, 62, 65, 174

goodness, 17, 170, 228

Good Shepherd UCC, 137, 203, 233

The Grapes of Wrath (Steinbeck), xx, xxiv, 53, 234

gratitude: Ecclesiastes, 168, 194; holy, 175; migrants, 97, 159, 169, 170, 175, 177; Roger Gottlieb, 76; volunteers notice, 228. *See also* gain; God; joy

Gravity and Grace (Weil), 74

grievous evil: Ecclesiastes, 45–46, 48–50; examples, 56–57, 80, 109–12, 121, 152; placelessness, 54. *See also* Chance/chance; choice; time

Guatemala, 49, 130, 136, 160, 178, 233

Haight, Roger, xx

hate, 78–79, 104, 162

Hayes, Diana L., 37, 93

heavy burden, 45

Heidegger, Martin: *Being and Time*, 106–7 109; fear, 151; "potentiality-for-Being," 230; "State-of-Mind," 151; "time-reckoning," 217; "voice of conscience," 38

Heschel, Rabbi Abraham Joshua, 2, 105, 164, 230, 231; "*leap of action*," 154–55; mystery, 9, 99; on religion, 5, 38

hielera (cooler or refrigerator), 110, 152

holiness, 38, 40,

holy: borderlands, 175, 222, 229; God, 9; Paul Tillich, 5; people, 227; scripture, 21; spirituality, 231; time, 103. See also Holy and Whole; gratitude; joy

Holy and Whole: defined, 225; Ecclesiastes, 234; experiencing the sacred, 229; as justice and peacemaking, 233; living a conscious life, 230

INDEX

Honduras: migrant testimonies, 32, 33, 55–56, 94–95, 128, 148–49, 158, 170, 227; violence in, 34, 49, 92, 97, 126, 130

hope: Christian, 68; Elie Wiesel, 51–52, 54; Hebrews 11:1, 68; Jon Sobrino, 81; life, 90, 94; Martin Luther King Jr., 24; of migrants, 58, 60–61, 81–82, 91, 94–95, 96, 125–27, 133, 172, 221; Paul Ricœur, 154–55; Viktor Frankl, 195; volunteers, 39, 73, 171, 186, 232–33

hospitality, 164, 186, 214, 232

Howard Hughes syndrome, 67

Hug of Joy, 200

Human Condition (Arendt), 86, 165, 213

humanitarian crisis (US-Mexico border), 4, 77

ICE. *See* Immigration and Customs Enforcement, US

identity (self), 179

immigrant. *See* asylum seekers/migrants (the families)

Immigration and Customs Enforcement, US (ICE), xxi

indifference: Elie Wiesel, 51; immigration, 68; James Crenshaw, 9; Roger Gottlieb, 50–51; spirituality in decline, 79; volunteers refute, 53, 74

"indwelling" (Polanyi), 212

"infinite passion" (Tillich), 15

injustice: accountability, 39; borderlands, 17, 78; complicity, 62; Ecclesiastes, 46, 49, 111; eco-injustice, 70–73, *72*, 75, 118; gender, 25–26, *28*, 27–29, 32, 47; Martin Luther King Jr., 23–24, 40; Miranda Fricker, 46; naming, 226; racial, 4, 25–27; rule of law, 38; spirituality, 79–81, 221; Valarie Kaur, 78; volunteers challenge, 140–41, 147. *See also* choice; dissent; indifference; justice; paradox; striving; time/timing

Interfaith Welcome Coalition of San Antonio (IWC), 56, 136, 174, 203, 204, 218

Irshai, Ronit, 31–32

"I" to "we" (Steinbeck), 234

Jew/Jewish, 74, 154. *See also* midrash

Journal of Feminist Studies in Religion (Irshai), 31

joy: begets generosity, 193–94; Choon-Leong Seow, 191; Dietrich Bonhoeffer, 192; Ecclesiastes, 189–91, 194, 197, 209; examples, 192–93, 197–99, *200–201*; gain, 175, 204; Henri Nouwen, 191; Joan Chittister, 193; legacy, 210; love, 195–96; migrants, 58, 192–93, 197–99; reconciliation, 203–4; Roger Gottlieb, 76; Simone de Beauvoir, 193; sorrow, 192–93, 196; spirituality of, 186, 189–90; spiritual practice, 191, 204, 231; Viktor Frankl, 195; volunteers, 194–95, 198–99, *200*–204, 218, 220. *See also* gain

justice: through action, 7, 47, 140–41, 147; advocacy, 36, 79–80, 116; Cynthia D. Moe-Lobeda, 226–27; Daniel Lombroso, 232; divine rage, 78; Dorothee Soelle, 218; Ecclesiastes, 45; ecojustice, 68, 73–74, 77, 118, 227; gender, 139, 227; God, 23, 25, 45; Joan Chittister, 226; love, 38, 226–27; Martin Luther King Jr., 79, 219; Miranda Fricker, 46; racial, 27, 140, 227; Reverend John Fife, 183; solidarity, 219; spirituality, 15, 75, 231, 233. *See also* injustice; indifference; paradox; postmodern/ postmodernity; time/timing

justness of God, 23

Kaur, Valarie, 26–27, 163–64. *See also* "divine rage"; "revolutionary love"

Kierkegaard, Søren, 212, 75, 76

King, Martin Luther, Jr. (MLK Jr.): hate, 79; interconnection, 40; love, 219; prejudice, 24; "softmindedness," 23–24; spiritual character, 163; Valarie Kaur, 26–27

Kurc, John, 70–71, 118

legacy: as accomplishments, 212; challenges, 221; death, 211–12; as "dying well," 214–15; Ecclesiastes, 208–9, 210; finitude, 216–17; fruitfulness, 214;

Hannah Arendt, 213; Henri Nouwen, 214–15; Joan Chittister, 211, 213; justice, 221; of/as life, *210*; "little deaths/dyings," 213; love, 218–19; meaning of life, 210, 212, 215; peacemaking, 221; racism, 27; spirituality, 222; William Brown, 170, 207. *See also* joy

L'Engle, Madeleine, 73, 77, 133, 157, 196, 211

less-horrible-than (*non*choice), 126–28, 130–34, 151. *See also* choice, *non*choice

"Let go and let God" (Hayes), 93

Leviticus 19:18, 117

life: precarious, 45, 85, 107, 149, 153, 226, 234; precious, 85, 226; short, 107, 211, 233. *See also* Chance/chance; cynicism; finitude; death/dying; risk; spirituality

LGBTQ/ LGBTQIA, xxiv

Living Life Backward (Gibson), 215

Lombroso, Daniel, 70, 232. See also *American Scar: The Environmental Tragedy of the Border Wall*

longing for belonging, 60, 62

"Longing for Home" (Wiesel), 54–55

Lorde, Audre: advocacy, 39; considered life, 133; death, 215; fear, 150, 153; ignoring the past, 37; love, 215; oppressors, 73–74; women, 33, 133–34, 153

love: as act/action, 138; Audre Lorde, 215; Christian, 138; compassion, 80; Cynthia D. Moe-Lobeda, 226–27; death (after), 218–21; Ecclesiastes, 104, 111–12, 190, 209; familial, 128, 130, 174; gain, 178; of/for God, 98, 114, 152; joy, 195–96; Jürgen Moltmann, 218; justice, 227; labor of, 211; legacy, 218–21; life, 227; Martin Luther King Jr., 219; midrash, 111–12; migrants, 129, 158, 174, 176–77, 195; *Pastora Helena*, 179; Rabbi Sally Priesand, 231; Viktor Frankl, 195; volunteers' experience, 181–82, 196, 197–98, 202. *See also* gain; joy; legacy

Love in the Void: Where God Finds Us (Weil), 40

MAGA (Make America Great Again), 162
Manne, Kate, 27
Mann, William, 95
Man's Search for Meaning (Frankl), 96, 149
Martha's Vineyard, Massachusetts, 4, 56
Mary and Martha House, San Antonio, 220
Mayer, Pastor Randy, 67, 90, 203, 233–34
McAllen, Texas, 16, 119
#MeToo, 67
midrash: Ecclesiastes, 31; example, 20, 31, 42n17, 111–12; feminist methodology, 29–30; Jewish origin, 29–30; Judith Plaskow, 29–30; migrant mothers, 31–32; Rabbi Sandy Eisenberg Sasso, 30; Ronit Irshai, 31; on time, 111–12
migrants. *See* asylum seekers/migrants (the families)
Migrant Protection Protocols (MPP), 11, 96–98, *108*, 114, 117, *125*, 134–35, 170, *173*, 192, *210*, 227
Moltmann, Jürgen, 215, 218
Montaigne, Michel de, 212
more-horrible-than, 131. See also C/chance; choice; *non*choice
Mother Earth, 69, 78, 212
My Case for Asylum, 52
mystery, 8, 9, 99, 231
myth/mythology (American), 27, 57, 82, 94

national security rhetoric, 70
Nazi Germany (comparison to), 96, 128, 149, 160, 192, 194. *See also* Frankl, Viktor; Wiesel, Elie
neighbor: 33, 36–38, 41, 117, 140, 202
never-enough syndrome, 191
nevertheless God is, 225
New Jewish Feminism: Probing the Past, Forging the Future, xxi
#NIUNAMENOS, 28
No Crystal Stair: Womanist Spirituality (Hayes), 37, 93

INDEX

nonchoice: 126–27, 130–32, 139–41. *See also* choice
nones (Burge), 5, 35, 96, 98, 174
The Nones: Where They Came From, Who They Are, and Where They Are Going (Burge), 5
nonlife, 157. *See also* death/dying
nonresponse, 36, 141
Northern Triangle, 193
Nouwen, Henri J. M., 68, 191, 214–15
Nuevo Laredo, Mexico, 17, 33, 55, 61, 97, 111, 156, 163, 170, 227

Old Testament Wisdom: An Introduction (Crenshaw), 9
openness, 24, 76, 214–15
Our Greatest Gift: Meditations on Dying and Caring (Nouwen), 67

paradox: complicity, 62, 74–75, 80–81; evil, 48–50; gender, 25–29; justice/injustice, 46–47; racial, 25–27; spirituality, 75; wealth, 28–29. *See also* Chance/chance; choice; indifference; injustice; justice
peacemaking, 75, 77, 190, 208, 211–12, 217–19, 225–28, 234. *See also* injustice; justice; legacy; spirituality
perrera (dog kennel), 110, 119
Philosophy of Religion: Classic and Contemporary Issues (Mann), 95
Piedras Negras, Mexico, 138–39, *154, 200,* 201
Pima County Office of the Medical Examiner, 89
placelessness, 53–55, 59–62. *See also* void
Planet Earth, 2, 4, 69, 211–12, 227, 230–32, 234
Plaskow, Judith, 29–30, 17n42, 95, 139
poetic reflections, 16, 58, 129, 159–60
political, 3–6, 11, 14–15, 24, 55–57, *72,* 78, 118, 131
Polanyi, Michael, 212
postmodern/postmodernity, 2–6, 8–10
poverty, 26, 70, 191, 226
power/ful: America, 66; Ecclesiastes, 26, 35, 79, 85; gender abuse, 67, 97; harming migrants, 39; Judith Plaskow, 95; patriarchal, 27–28; Rosemary Radford Ruether, 27–28; wealth, 21, 26. *See also* eco-injustice; rape
powerless/ness, 10, 75
pray/prayer: action, 138; migrants, 16, 33–34, 61, 112–13, 158, 220–21; spiritual renewal, 98–99; strong, 220; volunteers, 178–79, 196
precariousness, 85, 107, 196–97, 211
pride, 69–70, 124, 183, 230
Priesand, Rabbi Sally, 231
priorities, 22, 217–18
promised land (America as), 32, 66
Psalm 118:24, 209
Putnam, Robert, 5

racism, 14, 24, 26–27, 37, 42, 121, 226. *See also* King, Martin Luther, Jr.
rape: migrant women, 96, 97, 124, 133–34; Rabbi Lia Bass, 97; Rosemary Radford Ruether, 69–70. *See also* femicide; power; Weinstein, Harvey
religion, 208. *See also* spirituality
remembrance, 207
resilience, 132, 184
resistance. *See under* spirituality
responsibility, 31, 33, 37, 73, 120–21, 140–41, 154, 161
reorientation, 233–34
Ricœur, Paul, 46–48, 154–56
risk: Big-C Chance (death), 93–94, 153–54; Big-R, 155, 163–64; calculated, 148; Choon-Leong Seow, 147; consequences, 164–65; discernment, 162–63; Ecclesiastes, 67, 145–46; fear, 149–50; generosity, 146–47; little-r, 160, 163, 164; migrants, 33–34, 61, 89, 112, 124, 152–53, 159; mitigating, 148–49; Paul Ricœur on, 155–56; retirement, 147–48; volunteers, 160–62. *See also* better than; Chance/chance; choice courage; credible fear; death; fear; grievous evils
Robb Elementary School (Uvalde, Texas), 4

252

INDEX

Rock That Is Higher: Story as Truth (L'Engle), 77
Rolheiser, Ronald, 213
Row v. Wade, 4, 14, 27, 86
Rugged Terrain, 88
Ruether, Rosemary Radford, 27–29, 32, 69–70

sacred: borderlands, 230; creation, 73; earth, 227; experience, 228, 231; God, 37; humanity, 40; scripture, 29–31; time, 104, 113, 231. *See also* God
safe life (better life as), 17, 27, 32, 34, 36, 94
Samaritans, Green Valley-Sahuarita (GVS), 74, 89–90, 95–96, 99–100, 116, 137, 162, 164, 171, 184, 186, 201–3, 228, 233
Sasabe, Arizona, 90
Sanctuary Church/Sanctuary Movement, 36, 160
Schmidt, Frederick, Jr., 97
Scrooge effect, 67, 191
See No Stranger: A Memoir and Manifesto of Revolutionary Love (Kaur), 26
self-centeredness, 40, 183
self-deception, 126
Seow, Choon-Leong, 87, 146–47, 190–91
Sexism and God-Talk (Ruether), 69
Shipp, E. Mark, xv, 226
Shipping Container Border Blockade, 72
"shit happens," xxiii, 194, 226
Shoah, 47. *See also* Frankl, Viktor; Gottlieb, Roger; Weisel, Elie
silence/silent, 6, 28–31, 104
Sister Outsider (Lorde), 39, 73
Socrates, 54
Sobrino, Jon, 48, 81
social justice. *See* justice
Soelle, Dorothee, 10, 76–77, 218. *See also* justice; love
"softmindedness" (Martin Luther King Jr.), 23–23
solidarity: Henri Nouwen, 191; as justice, 212; migrants, 26, 163–64, 198, 221; mutuality, 26, 36, 174–75, 177, 182, 226, 233; spirituality, 14, 36–37, 134–36, 150, 219, 222, 231–32; volunteers, 136–37, 139, 141–42, 164. *See also* risk
Sonoran Desert, 37, 39, 49, *88*, 89–90, 117, 137, 161, 171. *See also* Samaritans, Green Valley-Sahuarita (GVS)
soul, 40–41, 55, 121, 128, 177
southwest border. *See* US-Mexico border
Speaking the Truth About Oneself (Foucault), 211
spirit. *See* spirituality
spiritual growth, 39, 79, 80, 163, 174, 186
spirituality: ambiguity of, 5; bigger-than-you, 232; borderlands, 3, 8, 26, 62, 81, 121, 141–42, 231–32; of compassion, 47, 234; counters cynicism, 10–14; courage, 159–60; of death, 216; in decline, 79; defining, xix–xxi, 48–49, 53; of discontent, 74–75; of dissent, 22–24, 33–36, 41, 65, 131, 139; enacted, 38–39, 234; of finitude, 2, 86, 106–9, 215; gratitude, 169; joy, 179, 189–94; justice-informed, 21–22; Kurtz and Ketcham, 75, 233; as living a conscious life, 230; longing for home, 58–59; love, 219, 231; maturity, 3–4, 75–77, 91; migrants, 32, 58–59, 113; political (influences), 14–16; of resistance, 76–78, 89; of response, 95–99, 128; Reverend John Fife, 183–84; in reverse, 75; sacredness, 40, 226; selfless, 40–41; self-identity, 179–80; Viktor Frankl, 115; volunteers, 16–17; 173, 228. *See also* eco-injustice; ecojustice; God; Gottlieb, Roger; injustice; joy; justice; peacemaking; risk; Soelle, Dorothee; *Spirituality of Resistance*; time/timing
Spirituality of Imperfection: Storytelling and the Search for Meaning (Kurtz and Ketcham), 40
Spirituality of Resistance: Finding a Peaceful Heart and Protecting the Earth (Gottlieb), 50, 76, 78, 80, 89
spiritual schizophrenia, 51
spiritual tenacity, 98
Steinbeck, John, xx, xxiii, 53–54, 234

INDEX

striving: Ecclesiastes, 65–67, 208; ecojustice, 73–74; examples, 66–67; Global North, 62, 76–78, 80, 190–91, 193; Global South, 81–82, 94, 96; Joan Chittister, 127; self-absorption, 68. *See also* futility; ecojustice; Soelle, Dorothee; spirituality; maturity under spirituality

Stuck in Mexico, 125

suffering. *See* testimonies of migrants under El Salvador and under Honduras

Team Brownsville, 11, 39, *108*, 117, 162, 171, 185–86, 192, 233

testimony. *See* suffering

"That's not fair!" 45

Tillich, Paul, 5, 15, 150, 157

time/timing: change, 119–21; *chronos*, 106; death, 85; Dietrich Bonhoeffer, 57; Ecclesiastes, 85–86, 87, 103–5, 111–12; finitude of, 106–7; grievous evils, 112–13; *kairos*, 106; legacy, 217; Martin Heidegger, 38; midrash, 111–12; migration, 109–12, 118–20, *210*; now, 114–15, 156, 173, 209; Rabbi Joshua Heschel, 105; reckoning, 106; retirement, 33; suffering, 55; uncontrollable, 105; volunteers, 116–18; *Turn! Turn! Turn!* 103–4. *See also* Chance/chance; death/dying

"time reckoning" (Heidegger), 106, 217

Title 42 (Trump), 4, 132, 134, 170

Trump administration, anti-immigrant policies: 117, 119, 134. *See also* Migrant Protection Protocols (MPP); Title 42 (Trump)

truth: 47, 51, 78, 141, 195. *See also* postmodern/postmodernity

Truth and Method (Gadamer), xxi

Ukraine, 4

unaccompanied migrant minors, 14, 116, 119, 140, 152, 155, 220

Uncommon Gratitude: Alleluia for All That Is (Chittister), 79

Underground Railroad, 94

"under the sun," 35, 46, 65, 79, 86, 104, 112, 167, 189, 209. *See also* finitude; time

United Church of Christ (UCC). *See* Good Shepherd United Church of Christ

US Immigration, 97, 135, 152, 156, 178, 227

US-Mexico border, 17, 26, 30, 34, 51, 71, 89, 99, 109, 115, 117, 121, 130, 160, 168, 170, 193

US Supreme Court, 4, 14

US White House, 51

"voice of conscience," (Heidegger), 37–38

void: feminism, 30; James Loder, 40, 211–12; placelessness, 59; Simone Weil, 40–41

Vulnerability, 173

vulnerable/vulnerability, 38, 158, 163

Weil, Simone, 15, 40–41, 74, 169

Westphal, Merald, 3, 8

When Suffering Persists (Schmidt), 97

Whose Community? Which Interpretation?: Philosophical Hermeneutics for the Church, 3

wisdom (conventional), 8, 22–23, 35, 45–46, 87, 208–9, 215

wisdom of dissent, 22–27, 86, 120

wisdom literature, 1–2, 24–26, 104, 135, 148, 225

Wolfe, Lisa Michele, 35

Women's Torah Commentary (Priesand), 231

World War II (1939–1945), 7, 10, 54, 55, 114, 128

worship, 181

Wyschogrod, Edith, 8

"vanity of vanities," 4, 212

yitron (benefit or gain), 168